MEDIAEVAL SOURCES
IN TRANSLATION

26

ALAN OF LILLE
THE PLAINT OF NATURE

Translation and Commentary

by

James J. Sheridan

PONTIFICAL INSTITUTE OF MEDIAEVAL STUDIES
TORONTO, 1980

Acknowledgment

This book has been published with the help of a grant from the Canadian Federation for the Humanities, using funds provided by the Social Sciences and Humanities Research Council of Canada.

Canadian Cataloguing in Publication Data

Alain de Lille, d. 1202.
    The plaint of nature

(Mediaeval sources in translation; 26 ISSN 0316-0874)

Translation of De planctu naturae.
Bibliography: p.
Includes index.

ISBN 0-88844-275-0
ISBN 978-0-88844-275-8

I. Sheridan, James J., 1914-1987.   II. Pontifical Institute of Mediaeval Studies.   III. Title.   IV. Series.

PA8240.A5A68 1980   871'.03   C79-094861-3

Contents

Foreword

With the possible exception of Martianus Capella, the Latin of the *De planctu Naturae* is the most difficult I have ever encountered. Throughout most of the work there are two layers of meaning and in a number of places there are three. In addition, puns are an ever recurring feature; most of these cannot be expressed in English. The result is that parts of it defy an accurate and idiomatic translation.

This work was completed with the aid of a Canada Council Senior Fellowship.

I owe a deep debt of gratitude to many friends who were generous with their time and talent. Professor N. M. Häring has produced the first text of the *De planctu* that makes any translation possible. We were in constant contact while he worked on the text and I on the translation. I benefited greatly from our discussions. Professors Laurence K. Shook and Brian Stock were ever ready with scholarly and valuable help. Sister Irene MacDonald read the entire work in manuscript and made numerous corrections and valuable suggestions. I would like to record my gratitude to Dr. James V. McNulty and his wife, Linda, and to my nephew Patrick Sheridan, and his wife, Helen. These contributed more than they realise to the completion of the work.

James J. Sheridan

St. Michael's College
Toronto

Abbreviations

Archives	*Archives d'histoire doctrinale et littéraire du moyen âge*
Beiträge	*Beiträge zur Geschichte der Philosophie und Theologie des Mittelalters*
CSEL	*Corpus Scriptorum Ecclesiasticorum Latinorum*
MGH	*Monumenta Germaniae Historica*
PL	Migne, *Patrologiae Cursus Completus, Series Latina*

All references to the *De planctu Naturae* are to the edition by N. M. Häring in *Studi Medievali*, terza serie, 19.2 (1978) 797-879.

Introduction

LIFE

External Evidence

1. Ralph of Longchamp[1] dedicated his commentary on the *Anticlaudianus* to Arnaud Amalric, archbishop of Narbonne from 1212 to 1225. He states: "I began this work for various reasons — to give a deeper understanding of the *Anticlaudianus* of Alan, the memory of whose love and friendship often forces me to tears . . . to help those who have made comparatively little progress and to show my joy in your₁ knowledge and patronage."[2]

2. Otho of Sankt-Blasien (before 1223): "At this time Masters Peter Cantor and Alan and Prepositinus flourished. . . . One in his writings dealt with many subjects: among other things he wrote the work, entitled *Anticlaudianus*, and *The Rules of Heavenly Law*, *Against Heretics*, *On Virtues and Vices*,

---

[1] Much of the material in this Introduction comes from the Introduction to my *Anticlaudianus: Anticlaudianus or The Good and Perfect Man* (Toronto 1973) 7-23.

[2] *In Anticlaudianum Alani commentum*, ed. J. Sulowski (Cracow 1972) 4. Cf. B. Hauréau, *Notices et extraits de quelques manuscrits latins de la Bibliothèque nationale* (Paris 1890) 1.325ff.

On the Art of Preaching, Book of Sermons and many other sound and catholic works."[3]

3. Alberic of Trois-Fontaines (before 1241): "This year Master Alan of Lille died at the house of the Cistercians. He was a teacher of renown and the author of the *Anticlaudianus*" (Chronicle for 1202).[4]

4. John of Garland (1252): "The inspired bard, Alan, son of Flanders, herded the heretics together and was the first to tame them. Greater than Virgil, more reliable than Homer, he enhanced the wealth of learning at Paris."[5]

5. A monk of Affligem (1270-4): "Alan, a native of Lille, an expert in the Liberal Arts, was head of an ecclesiastical school in Paris. He left monuments to his genius. He wrote a compendium of great value in fulfilling the obligation of preaching. As he was a man of outstanding ability in versification, he wrote a composition in verse, based on a thorough examination of the subject of the completely good man, perfect in all things. He entitled this work *Anticlaudianus*."[6]

6. The epitaph of Alan at Citeaux reads: "Short life brought Alan to a little tomb. He knew the two, he knew the seven, he

---

[3] MGH ss. 20.326. Chronicle is for 1194. Peter Cantor died in 1197 and Prepositinus in 1206.

[4] MGH ss. 23.881.

[5] Joannis de Garlandia, *De triumphis ecclesiae libri octo*, ed. T. Wright (London 1856) 74.

[6] *Catalogus virorum illustrium* 21, ed. N. M. Häring, "Der Literaturkatalog von Affligem," *Revue bénédictine* 80 (1970) 82. The author was probably Henry of Brussels. The work was for long attributed to Henry of Ghent. See Hauréau, *Notices et extraits* 6.162-173; F. Pelster, "Der Heinrich von Gent zugeschriebene Catalogus virorum illustrium und sein wirklicher Verfasser," *Historisches Jahrbuch* 39 (1918/1919) 253-265.

knew all that could be known.''[7] Later, probably in the sixteenth century, four lines were added: ''Despising the goods of a world that was going to ruin, he became poor. Turning his heart to other things, he devoted himself to feeding the flock. Faithful to Christ, he laid aside his mortal frame in 1294.'' The acceptance of these lines as genuine by some scholars led to serious confusion in accounts of his life. Some even postulated two Alans as the only way out of the difficulty.[8]

Internal Evidence

1. The *Contra haereticos* is dedicated to William vIII of Montpellier (1152-1202).[9] The same work contains two references to the *Aphorismi de essentia summae bonitatis*.[10] This is the *Liber*

---

[7] The ''Two'' refers to Philosophy and Theology; the ''Seven'' to the Liberal Arts. In ''Découverte du tombeau du bienheureux Alain de Lille,'' *Collectanea ordinis Cisterciensium reformatorum* 23 (1961) 259-260, M. Lebeau states that the original epitaph contained only the first sentence and that the second was added by Jean de Cirey when he had the tomb constructed in 1482. R. Bossuat has found the second sentence in a manuscript of the *De planctu Naturae* which dates back to the thirteenth century and also in a thirteenth-century manuscript of the *Anticlaudianus*: *Alain de Lille Anticlaudianus, Texte critique avec une introduction et des tables* (Paris 1955) 15, 18. ''He knew all that could be known'' is frequently found in epitaphs. It is found twice in one of the epitaphs of Aberlard, PL 178.103D. Alan's reputation for learning was such that it was inevitable that someone should apply these words to him soon after his death, even if they were not part of his actual epitaph.

[8] C. de Visch discusses this addition and other epitaphs in PL 210.10ff.

[9] PL 210.305-308.

[10] PL 210.332C and 334B.

de causis, a translation from the Arabic made by Gerard of Cremona at Toledo between 1167 and 1187.

2. The *Liber in distinctionibus dictionum theologicalium* is dedicated to Hermengald, Abbot of St. Giles (1179-1195).[11] The *Liber poenitentialis* is dedicated to Henry of Sully, Archbishop of Bourges (1183-1200).[12]

3. One of his sermons is entitled: "For the Annunciation of the Blessed Virgin when it falls on Palm Sunday."[13] This concurrence of feasts took place in 1179 and 1184[14] when Alan was still a layman. The fact that such a sermon was acceptable from him shows that he was by then revered both for learning and piety.

4. Arguments of varying cogency have been used to establish the date of some of Alan's works. The *Regulae* is assigned to 1160, the *Summa Quoniam homines* to 1160-1165, *Anticlaudianus* to 1181-1184, *Contra haereticos* to 1184-1195, *Distinctiones* to 1195, *Liber poenitentialis* to 1199-1202.[15]

What is set down here is, by and large, the material available for a life of Alan until 1960. Scholars did what they could with it. The main dates in Alan's life were reconstructed as follows: Alberic of Trois-Fontaines gives 1202 as the date of his death.

---

[11] PL 210.685A-688A.

[12] Ed. J. Longère, *Alain de Lille Liber poenitentialis*, Analecta Mediaevalia Namurcensia 17, 18 (Louvain 1961) 2:17-18.

[13] PL 210.199B-203B.

[14] J.-P. Escoffier, *Calendrier perpetuel* (Paris 1880) 137, 140. Cf. A. Cappelli, *Cronologia, cronografia e calendario perpetuo* (Milan 1930) 259.

[15] G. Raynaud de Lage, *Alain de Lille poète du XIIe siècle* (Montreal-Paris 1951) 29, 32; C. Vasoli, "Studi recenti su Alano di Lilla," *Bulletino dell' Instituto storico Italiano per il medio evo e Archivio Muratoriano* 72 (1960) 53; *Alani de Lille Liber poenitentialis*, ed. Longère, 1.213-216.

Alberic was using the Paschal method of reckoning years.[16] We know, then, that Alan died between 14 April 1202 and 5 April 1203.[17] He studied in Paris but must have come there in 1148 or later as John of Salisbury, who left Paris that year, does not mention him.[18] It was assumed that he came to Paris in 1148 or very soon after and that he was about twenty, the usual age, when he arrived there. This placed his birth around 1128.

On 22 June 1960, Marcel Lebeau, a monk of Citeaux, completed the uncovering of Alan's grave.[19] His body was exhumed. There can be no doubt about the identity of the grave or the body. The opinion of an expert in forensic medicine was that

[16] In this method Easter Sunday is the first day of the new year.

[17] Cappelli, *Cronologia* 260. There is some reason for thinking that Alan was buried on 16 July 1202. In 1666 C. Charlemont brought out at Paris a work entitled *Series sanctorum et beatorum virorum sacri ordinis Cisterciensium*. He has an entry for Alan (240-241). He gives the date of his *depositio* in both the old Roman and Gregorian style but the dates do not correspond. He states that Alan was buried "on the seventeenth day before the Calends of August, July 15," The seventeenth day before the Calends of August is July 16. July 15 is the Ides of July. He very probably had the old Roman date and miscalculated. His account of Alan in general is inaccurate and replete with legends. Perhaps the date too should be suspect. Hauréau, *Notices et extraits* (Paris 1890) 1.327 states that Alan died in July 1202 but quotes no source for this date.

[18] The argument from silence was never a very strong one. John of Salisbury does not claim that he is giving an exhaustive list.

[19] "Découverte du Tombeau du bienheureux Alain de Lille," 254-260. The exhumation verified the tradition that he was of small stature. His height was 1.64 m. He had suffered a fracture of the right humerus at some time in his life. The broken parts had not been set too expertly; there was a slight overlap, but they knitted well. He must have been rather young at the time of the fracture.

Alan had died at the age of eighty-six.[20] This would put the date of his birth in 1116 or 1117, much earlier than many had thought.

We must try to reconstruct his life in view of this new evidence. He was born at Lille in Flanders ca. 1116.[21] He, no doubt, went to the well-known school of St. Peter in his native city.[22] He came to Paris ca. 1136. John of Salisbury's failure to mention him may be due to Alan's anti-English attitude or even

---

[20] Ph. Delhaye, "Pour la 'Fiche' Alain de Lille," *Mélanges de science religieuse* 20 (1963) 39-51. The expert's opinion would allow a leeway of three to five years in either direction. In view of the number of works attributed to Alan in the last decade of the twelfth century, I would feel inclined to decrease the eighty-six figure. Strangely enough, those who have not kept to the eighty-six figure have increased it. P. Glorieux states that the skeleton indicated a man of eighty-eight to ninety-two years: *New Catholic Encyclopedia* (1967) 1.239, s.v. Alan. S. R. Packard states that "Alan of Lille . . . apparently lived to be ninety": *Twelfth-Century Europe, An Interpretive Essay* (Amherst 1973) 324. J. M. Trout repeats Glorieux's figure of eighty-eight to ninety-two: "The Monastic Vocation of Alan of Lille," *Analecta Cisterciensia* 30.1 (1974) 46.

[21] Other countries have claimed Alan as one of their sons — Germany, Spain, Sicily, Scotland, England. None of these claims can now be taken seriously. An account of claims and their grounds can be found in A. Dupuis, *Alain de Lille, études de philosophie scolastique* (Lille 1859), B. Hauréau, *Histoire de la philosophie scolastique* (Paris 1872) 1.521-532 and "Mémoire sur la vie et quelques oeuvres d'Alain de Lille," *Mémoires de l'Académie des inscriptions et belles lettres* 32 (1886) 1-27.

[22] E. Lesne, *Les Écoles de la fin du VIIIe siècle à la fin du XIIe sicle, histoire de la propriété ecclésiastique en France* 5 (Lille 1940) 338-340.

to jealousy.[23] After studies at Paris, and possibly at Chartres,[24] he taught in Paris and almost certainly at Montpellier.[25] He spent some years in Bas-Languedoc but it is impossible to determine the years with any accuracy.[26] It is quite possible that a close contact was established with the Cistercians during these years as they had gone into that area to combat heresy. He entered Citeaux some time before his death. It is impossible to determine how long he was in this monastery. There was in the twelfth century a marked disposition on the part of bishops, abbots, priests, rulers and noted laymen to spend their last years with the Cistercians. In many cases where dates are available, it

[23] For Alan's anti-English attitude, see *Anticlaudianus* 1.171 (Sheridan 52) and notes. John, who would have liked to be a philosopher and theologian but did not quite succeed in his ambition, may have been jealous of Alan's well-deserved reputation.

[24] He was certainly influenced by the school of Chartres. He could have heard the lectures of Thierry of Chartres at Paris or he may have gone for a time to the famous school. For Chartres and its Masters, see N. M. Häring, "Chartres and Paris Revisited," in *Studies in Honour of Anton Charles Pegis*, ed. R. O'Donnell (Toronto 1974) 268-329.

[25] Ralph of Longchamp states that he was personally acquainted with Alan: *In Anticlaudianum Alani commentum* 4, ed. Sulowski. He does not say that they met at Montpellier but it is very likely that it was there that they came in contact.

[26] Alan's dedication of the *Contra haereticos* to William vⅢ of Montpellier and the familiar terms used in the dedication (PL 210.305Aff.) show that Alan spent time at Montpellier in some capacity. Stephen of Bourbon (died ca. 1261) gives two versions of a legend referring to Alan as a teacher at Montpellier: *Tractatus de diversis materiis predicabilibus* 293, 426, ed. A. Lecoy de la Marche, *Anecdotes historiques, légendes et apologues tirés du recueil inédit d'Etienne de Bourbon, dominicain du XIII siècle* (Paris 1877) 246, 370-371. In both versions Alan takes soldiers to task for robbery in terms akin to those used in his sermon, *Ad milites*, PL 210.186B-C.

seems that the stay in the monastery was quite short.[27] However, even if Alan went to Cîteaux only to prepare for death, any estimate of the years he spent there leaves a wide margin for error in either direction.

We can see from all this that our knowledge of Alan's life is woefully lacking in details. In fact there are only three events in his life to which we can assign a definite date. He was in Paris in 1194.[28] In July 1200, he was in Maguelone to witness an agreement between the provost of Maguelone and the Knights Templar.[29] He died between 14 April 1202, and 5 April 1203.

When he began to write he was already a man with a phenomenal knowledge of literature, both classical and Christian: his knowledge of the latter extended from the Scriptures to contemporary writers. He was proficient in all the Liberal Arts. He was an accomplished philosopher and theologian. He was a competent versifier. When and where had he developed his talents in these disciplines?

An idea has been offered for consideration. In 1891, B. Hauréau described a section of MS Paris, BN lat. 13575.[30] One part contains six sermons on the Lord's Prayer and a very short paraphrase of the Apostles' Creed. Another part consists of seventeen letters. The manuscript originated in the Benedictine monastery of Bec. Both the sermons and letters were written by

[27] M. A. Dimier, "Mourir à Clairvaux!" *Collectanea ordinis Cisterciensium reformatorum* 17 (1955) 272-285; Trout, "The Monastic Vocation of Alan de Lille," pp. 46-53.

[28] See note 3 supra.

[29] J. Rouquette and A. Villemagne, *Cartulaire de Maguelone* 1 (Montpellier 1912) 453-462. I do not think that we can draw any conclusions from this as to whether he had or had not entered Cîteaux by 1200.

[30] *Notices et extraits* 2 (Paris 1891) 226-241.

a Benedictine of Bec for Benedictines. Hauréau is persuaded that the same Benedictine wrote the sermons and letters. References are made in the letters to Raoul, a monk of Bec who had become abbot of Lire. This shows that the letters were written after 1130.[31] There is a reference to Peter of Poitiers, who was secretary to Peter the Venerable of Cluny. Hauréau thinks that this shows that the letters were written before 1150.[32] He makes no attempt to determine the authorship of the sermons and letters, beyond asking if they might be the work of Stephen of Rouen, who was at Bec between 1130 and 1150.

Eighty-one years later, P. Glorieux, an expert on Alan, studied this section in Hauréau. He found enough resemblances to Alan there to lead him to examine the possibility of Alan's having written these sermons and letters.[33] His comparison is based on style and vocabulary. Considering the restricted material he has to work on, he makes an impressive case. He has other arguments. Bec had a marvellous library, details of which he supplies. It could account for much of Alan's learning. The monastery had a reputation for its interest in scholars and scholarship.[34] Its close association with England and the amount

[31] J. Mabillon, *Annales ordinis s. Benedicti* 5 (Lucca 1740) 305. The chronicle is really for the year 1094 and is dealing with the white and black habit of the Benedictines. Reference to Radulfus is to his introducing the white habit "around 1130 when he had been raised to the prefecture of that monastery."

[32] Hauréau, *Notices et extraits*, 2.240. PL 218.507 gives 1160 as the date of Peter's death. Hauréau may have confused him with Petrus Divensis who wrote a poem on the first seven abbots of Bec: PL 181.1709A-1718D. He died in 1150.

[33] "Alain de Lille, le moine et l'abbaye du Bec," *Recherches de théologie ancienne et médiévale* 39 (1972) 51-62.

[34] See Lesne, *Les Écoles*, 148.

of material dealing with England in its library could account for Alan's unusual knowledge of that country. Bernard Itier referred to Alan as a "Cluniac Monk."[35] There is no reason to think that Alan could not have travelled from Bec to the famous schools of his day. We might add that since Glorieux's article, hitherto unpublished Commentaries by Alan on the Pseudo-Athanasian Creed, the Apostles' Creed, the Creed of the Mass and the Lord's Prayer have been brought out.[36] This at least shows Alan's interest in these things.

I do not think that Alan could have been a Benedictine in good standing when he wrote the *De planctu*. The overt anti-clericalism that appears in part of it, the main topic, the risqué treatment of it and the coarseness of some sections hardly seem consonant with a monk, even of the twelfth century. Such, however, would be intelligible, even typical, in one who had left, or more likely, been dismissed from, a monastery. Glorieux points out that the writer of the sermons and letters had his difficulties in the monastery. If Alan was once at Bec and was asked to leave, he followed the usual and oft-trodden path — reaction against monks, stories of excesses, treatment of subjects that would be taboo in the monastery, gradual mellowing and final return. In his case the return would have taken the form of joining a more strict Order, the Cistercians, whose mockery of the Benedictines the monk of Bec had once deplored.[37]

The whole question calls for further investigation. It may hold the key to many puzzling questions about Alan.

---

[35] See M.-T. d'Alverny, *Alain de Lille, textes inédits* (Paris 1965) 25.

[36] See infra, works of Alan.

[37] Hauréau, *Notices et extraits* 2.228.

WORKS

Non-Literary Works

Summa Quoniam homines (Since Men)

This work is named from its opening words.[38] Its purpose seems to be to give a more rigid structure to the science of Theology.[39] It is an incomplete and poorly organised work on God, the Trinity, Angelology and Man. The Prologue envisages a treatment of the subject under three heads: Creator, Creature (angels and men), Recreation (Redemption). Part III is missing and may never have been written. Part II is incomplete.

Tractatus Magistri Alani De virtutibus et vitiis (The Treatise of Master Alan on Virtues and Vices): *De virtutibus et de vitiis et de donis Spiritus Sancti* (On Virtues, on Vices and on the Gifts of the Holy Ghost)

MS Paris, BN lat. 323F preserves a short work, *On Virtues and Vices*, attributed in the manuscript to Alan of Lille. This has

---

[38] Ed. P. Glorieux, "La Somme Quoniam homines d'Alain de Lille," *Archives* 20 (1953) 113-359. The text of this edition is defective. Among other things *ullus* appears for *nullus* in more than fifty instances. See N. Häring, "The Liberal Arts in the Sermons of Garnerius," *Mediaeval Studies* 30 (1968) 71, n. 3.

[39] C. Vasoli, *La Filosofia medioevale* (Milan 1961) 159ff.; J. M. Parent, "Un nouveau témoin de la théologie dionysienne au XIIᵉ siècle," *Beiträge*, Suppl. 3.1 (1935) 289-309.

been edited by J. Huizinga and by O. Lottin.[40] MS London, Royal
9 E XII has a much longer work, *On Virtues and Vices and on the
Gifts of the Holy Ghost*. This work is not specifically attributed
to Alan but is followed immediately in the manuscript by the
Quoniam homines, which P. Glorieux has established as a work
of Alan.[41] It has been edited twice by O. Lottin.[42] Since the sections on Virtues and Vices are practically identical in both the
shorter and the longer versions, there is no reason to question
Alan's authorship of the latter. There are some difficulties.
Which came first? Is the shorter work an extract from the
longer? Is the longer work an amplification of the shorter? If so,
is the amplification due, in whole or in part, to Alan? It is difficult to find an entirely satisfactory answer to these questions.
It would seem that the longer work antedates the shorter. The
abrupt beginning and the end of the shorter work are not in
keeping with Alan's usual method. Some things in the shorter
work would be unintelligible if we did not have the longer version.[43] The shorter work may well be an extract made for, or by,

[40] J. Huizinga, "Über die Verknüpfung des Poetischen mit dem
Theologischen bei Alanus de Insulis," *Mededeelingen der Koninkl.
Akademie van Wetenchappen, Afdeeling Letterkunde* 34B (Amsterdam
1932) 95-110; O. Lottin, "Le Traité d'Alain de Lille sur les vertus, les
vices et les dons de Saint-Esprit," in his *Psychologie et morale aux xiie et
xiiie siècles* (Gembloux: Duculot, 1960) 6.28-36.

[41] "L'Auteur de la somme Quoniam homines," *Recherches de
théologie ancienne et médiévale* 17 (1950) 29-45.

[42] "Le Traité d'Alain de Lille sur les vertus, les vices et les dons de
Saint-Esprit," *Mediaeval Studies* 12 (1950) 20-56; "Le Traité,"
Psychologie et morale aux xiie et xiiie siècles (Gembloux: Duculot, 1960)
6.45-92. The edition in *Mediaeval Studies* is based on MS London Royal
9 E.XII; the edition in *Psychologie* uses in addition MS Laon 146.

[43] We are told that there are eight species of lies. The author then
continues "the first species is mortal and is to be given a very wide

students, interested in a maximum of factual information with a minimum of speculation. There is another difficulty. The style of some parts of the longer work is widely different from the style of the rest of it and is so laboriously like the style of parts of the *Quoniam homines* that it gives the impression of having been written by someone trying to imitate Alan, even trying to out-Alan Alan. One might mention the buildup of short arguments introduced by *item*, the continual use of *ad hoc dicimus* or some variant of it, the strange use of *instantia*, the casting of the arguments in a dry logical form, the dialectical gymnastics of some parts of the work, the marked tendency to omit *est, probatur, ait*, the jerkiness of the style in general. Could it be a parody on some lecturer or on a Disputation in the Schools? It can hardly be a serious imitation of Alan. An efficient imitator would have produced a more convincing piece of work.

Theologicae regulae (Maxims of Theology)

This is a remarkable work,[44] characterised by a novel approach to Theology as a science. When Alan dealt with the

---

berth." No further information is given about it. It is only from the longer version that we learn that the reference is to spreading false religious doctrine. Huizinga, "Über die Verknüpfung" 108; Lottin, "Le Traité," *Mediaeval Studies* 12 (1950) 40.

[44] PL 210.622A-684C. C. Vasoli thinks that Alan's purpose here too is to give a more rigid structure to the science of theology (*La Filosofia medioevale* 159). Cf. V. Cilento, *Alano di Lilla, poeta e teologo del seculo xii* (Naples 1958) 10ff. M.-D. Chenu, "Un Essai de méthode théologique au xiie siècle," *Revue des sciences philosophiques et théologiques* 24 (1935) 258-267.

Seven Liberal Arts in the *Anticlaudianus*, Geometry was given the most superficial treatment of all. Nevertheless, in the *Regulae* the approach to Theology is based on the method used in Geometry. A theorem is established and from this deductions are made. From these, further deductions are drawn. For example, *Regula* 3 begins: "This *Regula* arises from the previous one." *Regula* 4: "This *Regula* is derived from the third one." *Regula* 5: "This *Regula* arises from the first one." He could well apply to this work what he said of Euclid: "[He] joins the parts, so to speak, with a rope of reason and one would think that the subsequent parts followed from just one original." The edited text is very defective. Moreover, the part dealing with Theology ends at *Regula* 115[45] and the text, with no indication of a change, goes on to deal with natural philosophy. It is regrettable that so little has been done on this work.

Liber in distinctionibus dictionum theologicalium (A Work on Various Meanings of Theological Terms)

This is a dictionary of the Bible,[46] giving the literal, allegorical and moral connotation of various words. The work shows a thorough knowledge of the Bible and a fertile imagination but some of the explanations are bizarre. Statements are often made that Alan in this work confused *ibis* (a bird, sacred to the Egyptians, akin to the stork and heron) and *ibex* (a mountain goat). Alan was too good a Latinist to think that *ibices* could be the plural of *ibis*. Copyists, confused no doubt by the irregularities in the declension of *ibis*, compressed two entries into one. There is an addendum to *ibex*, which in Migne reads: "called stempock

---

[45] PL 210.681C.
[46] PL 210.686A-1012C.

in the vernacular." Alan wrote "capestang," the Provençal equivalent for *ibex*. A German editor changed it to "Steinbock," the German equivalent. Successive corruptions have brought it to "stempock."

Elucidatio in Cantica canticorum (Elucidation of the Canticle of Canticles)

A note at the end of the oldest manuscript states that this work[47] was written at the request of the Prior of Cluny. Throughout this interpretation the Spouse of the Canticle is the Blessed Virgin Mary. Raynaud de Lage points out that several of the verses here applied to the Blessed Virgin are referred to the Church in the *Distinctiones*.[48] For this reason he questions its authenticity. However, there is no reason that a term may not be referred allegorically to more than one object, especially if there is a kinship between the objects. A number of terms in the *Distinctiones* have several references. In the Prologue to the *Elucidatio*, we find: "Thus although the Canticle of love . . . is referred to the Church in a special and spiritual way, yet it applies to the glorious Virgin in a very spiritual and very special way." In view of the close relationship in mediaeval thought between the Blessed Virgin and the Church, there is nothing anomalous in Alan's referring certain terms now to one, now to the other. It is a question of emphasis. No doubt the Prior of Cluny had asked for an *elucidatio* associating the Canticle with the Blessed Virgin.[49]

---

[47] PL 210.51A-110B.
[48] *Alain de Lille, poète* 15.
[49] See d'Alverny, *Textes inédits* 73-74.

Tractatus magistri Alani (The Treatise of Master Alan)

This is a strange and oddly-arranged piece of work.[50] The opening passage states that the work will deal with a number of questions: What is faith? What is an article [of faith]? Why is the name *article* used? What is the connotation of an article? What is its denotation? How many articles are there [in the Apostles' Creed]? What is a co-article? He follows the plan fairly closely. When he has finished with his stated project, however, he goes on to deal with other matters: the salvation of those who lived before Christ, explicit and implicit belief for adult Christians, the salvation of children and the mentally retarded, the various uses of *credere*, the nature of heresy. When three quarters of the treatise has been written, he begins to treat some of the topics again on a more elementary level and in an il-logical order in some cases: How many kinds of faith are there? What is faith? Why is it called faith? Why is it said that "the just man lives by faith?"

The matter is definitely Alan's. However, there are problems. One section begins: "Alan's opinion: Master Alan says . . . ." Aristotle is misquoted and mistranslated, even where the correct rendering could be found in Boethius. There is a quote from Horace's *Ars poetica* that seems to indicate that the quoter did not know what Horace meant. The second article of the Apostles' Creed is attributed to Andrew. Elsewhere it is assigned to Paul or Bartholomew and the third is assigned to Andrew.[51]

---

[50] Raynaud de Lage, "Deux questions sur la foi, inspirées d'Alain de Lille," *Archives* 14 (1943) 323-336.

[51] Ed. N. M. Häring, "A Commentary on the Apostles' Creed by Alan of Lille (O. Cist.)," *Analecta Cisterciensia* 30.1 (1974) 28, 44.

The strange repetition towards the end of the article has been
mentioned.

Who put the treatise in writing? If Alan did, he was un-
characteristically careless. It seems more likely that the rendition
we have represents the notes of a student, or students, taken
down at the lectures that preceded Alan's treatment of the
Apostles' Creed, the subject mentioned in the final sentence of
the present treatise.

Super symbolum apostolorum (Commentary on the Apostles'
Creed)

After a discussion of various kinds of knowledge and a statement that the Apostles' Creed is the basis of all Creeds, this
work[52] sets forth its objectives. It will examine five points — the
different meanings of the word *symbolum* (Creed),[53] its meaning
in the present context, how it got this meaning, what are its articles and what is the meaning of each, which article comes from
which apostle, its doctrinal identity with the Nicene Creed.

The work is done carefully and systematically. Every article is
explained. Its dogmatic import is developed. The heresies that it
counteracts are mentioned. Paul is found among the apostles
and the second article (*I believe . . . in Jesus Christ, His only
Son, our Lord*) is attributed to him. Later when there is no place
for Bartholomew, Alan suggests that he gave his place to Paul:
he even concedes that, perhaps Paul should be dropped and Bartholomew given his place. Throughout the Commentary it is

---

[52] Ibid. 7-45.
[53] His explanation of *symbolum* is more detailed, but no more correct, than that given in *Distinctiones* 964c-d.

made clear that the Nicene Creed adds no new doctrine. It expands and clarifies what is in the Apostles' Creed.

Expositio super symbolum (Commentary on the Creed [of the Mass])

The introductory part of this work[54] is, to a great extent, a repetition of the prologue to the previous work. Its purpose is then stated. It will examine five points — the different meanings of *symbolum*, its meaning in the terms *Apostles' Creed* and *Nicene Creed*, the authors of these Creeds, the difference between them, their conformity. He accepts the tradition, recorded in Rufinus of Aquileia[55] and Isidore of Seville[56] that the Apostles' Creed owes its origin to the apostles, each contributing a section. He states that the Blessed Virgin and Mary Magdalene were present at its composition.

He explains the Nicene Creed phrase by phrase and frequently word by word. He gives a wealth of philosophical and theological background. He treats of the heresies that are at variance with its teaching. In this, as in his Commentaries in general, we see Alan at his best, both as writer and teacher.

Super symbolum Quicumque (On the Creed 'Quicumque . . .')

This is a poem in elegiacs.[57] His handling of this metre is definitely superior to what we find in the *De planctu* and the ter-

---

[54] Ed. N. M. Häring, "A Commentary on the Creed of the Mass by Alan of Lille," *Analecta Cisterciensia* 30.2 (1974) 281-303.

[55] *Commentarium in symbolum apostolorum,* PL 21.237.

[56] *De ecclesiasticis officiis* 2, PL 83.815-816.

[57] Ed. N. M. Häring, "A Poem by Alan of Lille on the pseudo-

minology shows a kinship with the *Anticlaudianus*. The *Quicumque* emphasises the Unity and Trinity of God, the Incarnation, the two Natures in one Person in Christ, His redemptive Death, His Resurrection and Ascension into Heaven, His Second Coming for the final judgement, the salvation of the just and damnation of the unjust. Alan expands this material. He introduces philosophical explanations, references to the Blessed Virgin, quotations from Scripture, a quotation from Virgil, a reference to his teacher, Gilbert of Poitiers, and the inevitable remarks on the relationship between Faith and Reason.

Expositio cuiusdam super orationem Dominicam (A Commentary by Someone on the Lord's Prayer)

This is a very full treatment of the Lord's Prayer.[58] Alan maintains that the Apostles' Creed essentially contains all that we are to believe. He likewise maintains that the Lord's Prayer contains in essence all the blessings of heaven and earth that we can hope for or expect. He examines all the different forms of prayer, the relation between the Lord's Prayer and the contemplative and active life. He discusses the various positions we adopt when praying. With regard to praying on one's knees, he has some strange and some interesting remarks. Kneeling promotes tears

---

Athanasian Creed," *Revue d'histoire des texts* 4 (1974) 226-238. Until 1963 this creed was part of the Office of Prime on certain Sundays. It was not written by Athanasius. The heresies against which it was directed and the heresies that find no echo in it indicate that it was written between 380 and 430. Its author is not known. It may have been St. Ambrose (ca. 339-397).

[58] Ed. N. M. Häring, "A Commentary on the Our Father by Alan of Lille," *Analecta Cisterciensia* 31.1 (1975) 149-177. For a discussion of the authenticity of the work, see 150-156.

(of repentance, I presume), since there is a *naturalis affectio* between the eyes and knees. It is, moreover, a natural position; the infant in the womb rests with his head between his knees according to the teaching of medical science (*physica*). For this reason he postulates an etymological connection between *genae* (cheeks) and *genua* (knees). Isidore of Seville makes this connection too, but for the opposite reason — the cheeks and knees are oposite each other.[59]

In the formal part of the commentary he treats each of the seven petitions of the prayer, giving detailed theological, philosophical and ascetical insights on practically every word.

Expositio Prosae de angelis (Explanation of the *Prosa* on the Angels)

The *Prosa* is a composition in rhythmic prose, written as a Sequence for the feast of St. Michael.[60] It is attributed to Notker in PL 131.1018-1019.[61] Alan attributes it to Gerbertus.[62]

The text used by Alan differs in minor details from any of the traditional texts. Alan uses the *Prosa* as a basis for a disquisition on a favourite subject, the various hierarchies, their work and their knowledge of God. This matter is treated also in the *Quoniam homines* and in the *Hierarchia*.

---

[59] *Etymol.* 11.108.

[60] d'Alverny, *Textes inédits* 194-217.

[61] See W. von den Steinen, *Notker der Dichter und seine geistige Welt* (Bern 1948) 334ff.

[62] Gerbertus (ca. 940-1003) was a brilliant scholar and inventive genius. He was successively Archbishop of Rheims, Archbishop of Ravenna and Pope with the title of Sylvester II. Bizarre stories appeared about him during his life and after his death. For full account, see Sheridan *Anticl.* 108, note 84.

Hierarchia (Hierarchy)

In this work[63] Alan speaks of a three-fold Hierarchy: supercelestial (the Trinity), celestial (the Angels), subcelestial (ecclesiastical). The celestial Hierarchy is treated in detail. The distinction he makes between the knowledge of the three hierarchies is worth noting. Theosophy is the wisdom of God. Theophany is the Angels' knowledge of God. Theology is man's knowledge of God.

De arte praedicatoria (On the Art of Preaching)

This work contains forty-eight sermons on various subjects.[64] The text in Migne is confused and defective. The sermons are Alan's but the compilation of them is later. Not enough research has been done on this work to warrant further statements on it.

Sermones (Sermons)

This work contains eleven complete sermons and a fragment of a sermon, "On the Birthday of St. Augustine."[65] A critical

[63] d'Alverny, *Textes inédits* 219-235.
[64] PL 210.111A-198A. Pope Innocent III (1160-1216) knew of this work. See M. Maccarone, *Lotharii cardinalis De miseria humane conditionis* (Lucca 1955) 80.21. Alan was himself a noted preacher. As in the case of all such, there are traditional stories. One story says that Alan on one occasion omitted his usual prayer to God for help and his salutation to the Blessed Virgin at the beginning of his sermon and for a time lost his power of speech. See E. Martene, *Veterum scriptorum et monumentorum amplissima collectio* (Paris 1729) 6.52. Cf. *Histoire littéraire de la France* 16 (Paris 1892) 412.
[65] PL 210.198B-228D. "Repertorium der lateinischer sermones," *Beiträge* 43.1 (1961) 69-83 lists 227 sermon titles of Alan.

edition of the full text of this sermon and of eight others has been published by M.-T. d'Alverny.[66] There are also critical editions of four other sermons: "For the Day of the Assumption of the Blessed Virgin,"[67] "On St. Peter,"[68] "On the Contempt of the World,"[69] "On a Theme from Virgil."[70] Non-critical editions of two sermons are found in B. Hauréau.[71]

Epistola magistri Alani quod non est celebrandum bis in die (Letter of Master Alan that Mass is not to be celebrated twice on the same day)

This letter[72] was written to his "venerable friend, P." The P. may well be Peter Cantor who was interested in this point of discipline.[73] Two practices are condemned: outright bination and

[66] *Textes inédits* 241-306.

[67] P. Glorieux, "Alain de Lille docteur de l'Assomption," *Mélanges de science religieuse* 8 (1951) 16-18.

[68] L. Hödl, "Eine unbekannte Predigtsammlung des Alanus von Lille in Münchener Handschriften," *Zeitschrift für katholische Theologie* 80 (1958) 516-527.

[69] M.-T. d'Alverny, "Un Sermon de Alain de Lille sur la misère de l'homme," in *The Classical Tradition, Literary and Historical Studies in Honor of Harry Caplan*, ed. W. Luitpold (Ithaca 1966) 515-535.

[70] M.-T. d'Alverny, "Variations sur un thème de Virgile dans un sermon d'Alain de Lille," in *Mélanges offerts à André Piganiol*, ed. R. Chevallier (Paris 1966) 1517-1528.

[71] A Lenten sermon in *Mémoires de l'Academie des inscriptions et belles lettres* 32 (Paris 1886) 18-19 and a Christmas sermon in *Notices et extraits* 6 (Paris 1893) 194-195.

[72] d'Alverny, *Textes inédits* 290-294.

[73] PL 205.110A. J. A. Dugauquier, ed., *Pierre le Chantre, Summa de sacramentis et animae consiliis*, Analecta mediaevalia Namurcensia 7 (Louvain 1957) 2.411.

the fusion of two Masses into one, e.g. beginning with a Mass of the Day and changing to a Mass of the Dead.

Liber poenitentialis (Work on the Sacrament of Penance)

This work is a manual for confessors, who sorely needed it if we are to believe the introductory remarks.[74] In one place Alan says that priests are spiritual physicians and should pattern their approach to the penitent after the practice of worldly physicians.[75] There follows a short and delightful account of the "bedside manner" of the competent medical practitioner. Among other things he identifies with the patient (*se conformat infirmo*): this must be one of the earliest references to the "how-are-we-today?" approach. There follows a well-detailed account of the physician's method of obtaining a case-history, his diagnosis and his remedies which appear to be restricted to prescribing a diet.

De sex alis cherubim (On the Six Wings of the Cherubim)

This work[76] is based on Isaias 6:1-10. Isaias had a vision of the Lord sitting on a throne. Above him were Seraphim (not Cherubim), each with six wings. They kept calling, one to

[74] There are two redactions of this work. The shorter one is in PL 210.279-304 and in an edition by J. Longère, "Alain de Lille, Liber poenitentialis, les traditions moyenne et courte," *Archives* 32 (1965) 169-242. The longer one is edited by J. Longère, *Alain de Lille, Liber poenitentialis*, 2 vols., Analecta mediaevalia Namurcensia 17, 18 (Louvain 1965). For the incompetence of confessors, see *Sermo ad scholares*, ed. d'Alverny, *Textes inédits* 274.

[75] PL 210.285C; ed Longère 2.25.

[76] PL 210.269A-280C.

another, "Holy, holy, holy is the Lord of hosts; the whole earth is full of His glory." The prophet realized his own sinfulness and the sinfulness of the men with whom he associated and he acknowledged this sinfulness. One of the Seraphim came to him with a burning coal and touching his mouth with it, told him that his sins were forgiven and that, though God did not wish it, He must forgive the sins of the people if they turned to Him. Alan explains the vision and then logically goes on to refer each of the five feathers of each of the six wings to the Sacrament of Penance, man's means of obtaining forgiveness. Part of the work has been at times attributed to St. Bonaventure[77] and part of it to Clement of Llanthony. There seems to be no reason to doubt its authenticity and no necessity to divide it into two separate works as some suggest.[78]

De fide catholica contra haereticos (On the Catholic Faith, Against Heretics)

This is a work against heretics.[79] It is in four books and a book is devoted to each of four heretical bodies, the Albigensians, the Waldensians, the Jews, the Mohammedans.[80] The text is in very poor condition.

[77] The work was probably confused with the *De sex alis seraphim* of St. Bonaventure: *S. Bonaventurae opera omnia*, ed. Aloysius Lauer (Quaracchi 1898) 8.131-151.

[78] L. Hödl, *Die Geschichte der scholastischen Literatur und der Theologie der Schlüsselgewalt*, Beiträge 38.4 (1960) 232.

[79] PL 210.307c-430a.

[80] V. Cilento, *Alano di Lilla* 68-71; J. Russell, "Interpretations of the Origins of Medieval Heresy," *Mediaeval Studies* 25 (1963) 26-53; C. Thouzellier, *Hérésie et hérétiques* (Rome 1969); D. Berger, "Gilbert Crispin, Alan of Lille, and Jacob Ben Reuben: A Study in the Transmis-

Sermo de sphera intelligibili (Discourse on the Intelligible Circle)

This work[81] begins from the much-discussed statement, already found in *Regula* 7: "God is a circle whose centre is everywhere and whose circumference is nowhere."[82] Four types of Being are discussed: Actual Being, Primordial Matter, Forms, the Divine. There is a type of knowledge corresponding to each type of Being.

Literary Works

Liber parabolarum (Book of Parables)

This is a short work in elegiacs consisting of a series of proverb-like statements with very definite scriptural and classical echoes.[83] The maxims are practically all of a moral nature or, more correctly, the second line of each couplet gives a moral application to the general maxim of the first line. Maxims dealing with the same subject are collected together and the work could be a ready-reference source for one in search of pithy statements to suit any occasion. Works specializing in the dicta of wordly wisdom had a great vogue from Hesiod to com-

---

sion of Medieval Polemic," *Speculum* 49.1 (1974) 34-47; J. M. Trout, "Alan the Missionary," *Citeaux* 26 (1975) 146-154.

[81] d'Alverny, *Textes inédits* 297-306.

[82] PL 210.627A. The statement goes back to the *Book of the XXIV Philosophers*, Beiträge 25 (1927) 208.

[83] PL 582A-594C.

paratively recent times. They were committed to memory, made their way through every stratum of society and furnished quotations for many who had no idea of their source. It is not surprising that this was for long the most popular work of Alan. There were two French and two German translations of it and it was quoted by many famous men, including Rabelais.[84] Even today Glorieux considers the *Parables* "a near classic."[85] In general, however, works of this kind are no longer popular; these sententious pearls of wisdom are treated as clichés. We can agree with G. Raynaud de Lage that we now find the *Parables* tiresome but that should not dispose us to think that the work cannot have come from an author we like. Raynaud de Lage points out that the work is stylistically flat.[86] The flatness, however, is confined to the second line of the couplets, which tends to be anticlimactic and marred by "fillers" (*eo, ibi, idem*, etc.) introduced to accommodate the metre. The rigidity of the structure demanded for this line is largely responsible for the "fillers" and partially explains the anticlimactic element. It would seem that the author collected and elaborated a number of proverbs. These he put in dactylic hexameters. To each hexameter he added a pentameter line giving the hexameter a moral application. One cannot read the work without being continually reminded of Alan. There are

---

[84] *Gargantua* Ch. 14, *Oeuvres de François Rabelais*, ed. A. Lefranc (Paris 1913) 1.141. Alan's work is referred to as *Alanus in parabolis*. There is a tradition that Charles I of England, shortly before his death, said, "He who lies on the ground can fall no further." These words, once incorrectly attributed to Ovid, come from *Parables* 584A.

[85] Article in *New Catholic Encyclopedia* 1.239.

[86] *Alain de Lille, poète* 16.

verbal similarities with his other works. The rare twelfth-century Arabic derivative *cifr* is found in the *Parables*.[87] This word literally means "zero" and figuratively "useless," "of no consequence," "a nothing." It is found in *The Plaint of Nature* referring to the bat[88] and in the *Anticlaudianus* referring to the letter H.[89] In the *Parables* Alan is talking of the vagaries of an incompetent writer who finds himself in difficulties both as regards matter and arrangement. He says that "he is delighted to find himself involved in figures that signify nothing and is often anxious to get ahead of himself." There is too a strong resemblance between the thoughts and terminology of *Parables* 594A-C, *De arte praedicatoria* 117A-B and the Sermon, *Memorare novissima tua*.[90] Apart from these verbal similarities we recognize Alan's interest in schools and teaching, his preoccupation with fire, water, waves, storms, his fear of heights, his love of youth, his idea of the role chance plays in life, and his desire for peace. There seems to be no reason for doubting the authenticity of the *Parables*.

Rhythmus de incarnatione Christi (Poem on the Incarnation of Christ)

This work views the Incarnation from the standpoint of the Seven Liberal Arts and shows that it defies all the laws of Nature.[91]

---

[87] PL 210.586C. Alan seems to have been the first to use the word in a Latin work.

[88] PL 210.436D.

[89] 2.438.

[90] D'Alverny, *Textes inédits* 267-273.

[91] PL 210.577A-580A; M.-T. d'Alverny, "Alain de Lille et la

Rhythmus de natura hominis fluxa et caduca (Poem on the Transitory and Mortal Nature of Man)

Man passes away like the grass of the field. He should remember this and direct his life accordingly.[92]

Anticlaudianus

The full title of this work is *Anticlaudianus de Antirufino*, "The antithesis of Claudian's *'Against Rufinus'.*"[93] Claudian had told the tale of Rufinus, the completely evil man. Nature realises that she has failed to produce the perfect man. She longs to achieve this objective. She calls a council of the Virtues and puts her proposition before them. They realise that their powers are limited. They can create the man's body but not his soul. That must come from God. Prudence is persuaded to undertake

---

'Theologia'," in *L'Homme devant Dieu, mélanges offerts au Père de Lubac*, vol. 2 (Paris 1964) 126-128.

[92] PL 210.579A-580C; G. M. Dreves and C. Blume, *Ein Jahrtausend lateinischer Hymnendichtung* (Leipzig 1909) 1.238.

[93] PL 210.488D-574D; T. Wright, *Alani Anticlaudianus*, in *The Anglo-Latin satirical poets and epigrammatists of the twelfth century*, Rolls Series 59.2 (London 1872) 268-428; R. Bossuat, *Alain de Lille, Anticlaudianus, texte critique avec une introduction et des tables* (Paris 1955). Translated with commentary: W. H. Cornog, *The 'Anticlaudianus' of Alain de Lille, Prologue, Argument and Nine Books Transl. with an Introduction and Notes* (Philadelphia 1935); J. J. Sheridan, *Alan of Lille, Anticlaudianus, Translation and Commentary* (Toronto 1973) — this has an Introduction on the life and works of Alan, a Bibliography and an Index; translation with introduction by W. Rath, *Alanus ab Insulis, Der Anticlaudian, übersetzt and eingeleitet*, in *Aus der Schule von Chartres*, vol. 2. (Stuttgart 1966).

the journey to heaven to ask for a soul. The Seven Liberal Arts produce a chariot for her. The Five Senses are the horses. She sets out. When she reaches the limits of our Universe, she needs further help. Theology and later Faith come to her assistance. She reaches the throne of God, obtains the Soul and returns to earth. A perfect body is fashioned from the Four Elements. The soul is united to it. The Perfect Man exists. Allecto, one of the Furies, hears of his existence. She mobilises the Vices to war against him. The Virtues rally to his support. In the ensuring battle the Vices are defeated. The New Man is supreme and the Virtues have an assured home on earth.

In the Prose Prologue to this work Alan states that it can be approached on three levels — A Tale of Adventure, A Tale with a Moral, or An Allegory. The allegory has been variously interpreted. Throughout the book the emphasis is on knowledge. It seems to centre on the Chartrian ideal of integrating the Liberal Arts, Theology and Faith to give man perfect knowledge. It is written against a background of Platonism and the man with perfect knowledge would be the man of perfect virtue. The allegory can best be referred to man's eternal search for knowledge.[94]

Vix nodosum (I can hardly undo the knotty knot)

This is a poem of 148 lines in Goliardic verse.[95] Its authenticity has been questioned. The resemblance to other works of Alan is striking. Even a casual reading shows its affinity with the section

---

[94] See Sheridan, *Anticl.* 23-38.
[95] N. M. Häring, "The poem *Vix nodosum* by Alan of Lille," *Medioevo, Rivista di storia della filosofia medievale* 3 (1978) 165-185. This includes a translation into English by J. J. Sheridan.

on love in the *De planctu* (IX). It is filled with conceits, unusual words and phrases that are favourites of Alan: comparison of the rose and Celtic nard, of clay and precious stones (*Anticl.* 2.10-11), the use of grammatical terms (*positiva, superlativa*) to compare objects, the description of the adulteress (*De planctu*, IX), the use of *sincopare* to describe the murder of a husband by an adultress, such words as *neronizans* and *protheatur*, the use of the term *bos sophistica* in reference to Pasiphae (*De planctu*, VIII). These are but a few of the examples that could be cited. It is hard to imagine an imitator who could reproduce Alan's style, vocabulary, metaphors and tone so successfully. I think that Alan wrote it.

The poem deals with the relative merits of the love of a *virgo* and a *matrona*. Sex is described in terms that are raw, and often disgustingly vulgar. I think that it is a very early work of Alan and that in later years he took from it words and descriptions that caught his fancy and worked them into more mature productions.

Doubtful Works

Quinque digressiones cogitationis (The Five Ranges of Knowledge).

This short work is edited by M-T d'Alverny, *Textes inédits* 313-317. The five ranges of knowledge are sense, imagination, reason, intellect, understanding. Above these comes faith. The work is nowhere specifically attributed to Alan. However, its vocabulary, its Chartrian flavour and its turns of expression indicate that Alan may well be the author. See d'Alverny, ibid., 181-183.

Summa de sacramentis (Summa on the Sacraments)

Totus homo (The Entire Man), the opening words of the text, are generally added to the title. The work is a detailed treatment of four Sacraments: Baptism, the Eucharist, Penance and Matrimony. It has been edited by P. H. Betti, *Spicilegium Pontificii Athenaei Antoniani* 7 (Rome 1955). One manuscript attributes the work to Alan. It is difficult to form an opinion as to whether this work was written by Alan. There are striking parallels between passages in it and in other works of Alan. Many of them can be explained on the grounds that different authors were using the same known sources. There are obvious divergences, but corruption of texts could explain some of these. Otho of Sankt-Blasien does not list this work, but he does not list the *Summa Quoniam homines* either and makes it plain that he is not giving a complete list. See p. 1 supra.

Betti in his excellent *Introductio* comes to the conclusion that Alan is not the author. The arguments pointing to Alan as author are to be found in O. Lottin, "La Summa de sacramentis — Totus homo. Est-elle l'oeuvre d'Alain de Lille?" *Psychologie et morale aux xiiᵉ et xiiiᵉ siècles* 6 (Gembloux 1960) 107-117.

DE PLANCTU NATURAE (ON THE PLAINT OF NATURE)

Date

What evidence we have for the date of the *Plaint of Nature* is internal, scanty and inconclusive. Peter of Poitiers dedicated his *Sententiae* to William of Blanches Mains, Archbishop of Sens from 1168 to 1176.[96] In this work he has the sentence *in ipso vestibulo questionis excubat vestigium solutionis*.[97] In the *Plaint* Alan has the phrase *huius questionis solutionem in vestibulo excubare demonstrans (showing that the answer to the question was ready and waiting at the door)*.[98] There is some reason for thinking that Peter of Poitiers wrote his work before 1170.[99] The *Plaint* was written before the *Sententiae*.

The *Ars versificatoria* of Matthew of Vendôme and the *Plaint* show definite interdependence. However, the nearest we can come to dating the *Ars* is that it was written before 1175. Moreover, M.-T. d'Alverny has pointed out that we cannot be absolutely sure as to which work came first.[100]

R. Bossuat regards the *Anticlaudianus* as the logical sequel to the *Plaint* and dates the latter 1179-1182.[101] The *Anticlaudianus* may be called a sequel to the *Plaint* but it most certainly is not an immediate sequel. In the *Anticlaudianus* we have a self-assured, self-possessed writer who produces a work with logical development, smooth transitions, a certain restraint in the use of Rhetoric and a calm dignity. P. Duhem thought that a somewhat close connection in time was indicated between the two works since both contain the same theories about the relative positions

---

[96] P. S. Moore and M. Dulong, *Sententiae Petri Pictaviensis* 1 (Notre Dame, Ind. 1943) 1.

[97] P. S. Moore, J. N. Garvin, M. Dulong, *Sententiae Petri Pictaviensis* 2 (Notre Dame, Ind. 1950) 165.61-62.

[98] See VIII infra. The same phrase is in the *Vix nodosum* 42-44, ed. Häring 180.

[99] P. S. Moore, *The Works of Peter of Poitiers* (Notre Dame, Ind. 1936) 39-41.

[100] *Textes inédits* 34.

[101] *Alain de Lille Anticlaudianus* 13.

of Venus, Mercury and the Sun.[102] However, his argument is based on a reading of *superjecta* in II, p. 84 *infra*. The correct reading is definitely *interiecta*. The *Plaint* is an important work and was to have a far-reaching influence. Nevertheless, one cannot escape the conclusion that it may be a display piece. The author revels in every device of Rhetoric. He at times tortures the Latin language to such an extent that one is reminded of some of Joyce's English. He so interweaves the ordinary, etymological and technical signification of words that, when one extracts the meaning of many a section, one despairs of approximating a satisfactory translation. One wonders if he is deliberately trying to be more recondite than Bernardus Silvestris.[103] However one must admit that in many sections one encounters a forcefulness, an enthusiasm and a ring of sincerity that is seldom, if ever, equalled in Alan. In addition, the important sections have a unique originality. One feels that one can learn more about Alan, the man, from the *De plactu* than from the rest of his works combined. These factors more than compensate for the oddities and difficulties of his diction.

This work shows that he was still far from the development of theme and the consistency of character which he later evidenced in the *Anticlaudianus*. Nature is the heroine of the *Plaint*. However, the degeneration of man is due to a fatal and inexcusable fault on her part. She had been appointed by God as "His Substitute,[104] His vice-regent," to ensure that there would

---

[102] *Le Système du monde* 3 (Paris 1915) 228-229. See Reynaud de Lage, *Alain de Lille, poète* 24, note 44.

[103] In the *De plactu* Alan had found his métier and he revelled in it. P. Glorieux, "Alain de Lille, le moine" 52.

[104] The strong term *pro-dea* is used.

be no deviations in the natural order. This office she fulfilled faithfully for some time. Then comes the astounding explanation for the basis of the change for the worse on Earth. She needed help in the work and, moreover, she had decided to withdraw from our Universe to live a life of complete happiness "in the delightful palace of the ethereal region."[105] She abandoned her God-given post. Man's degeneration was due to Nature's abandonment of her post in favour of an incompetent delegate. Alan never questions this decision on her part. The more mature questioners in Peter of Compostella's *On the Consolation of Reason*, to which Alan owes much,[106] would never have allowed Nature's explanation to go unchallenged. Perhaps I have unduly emphasised this flaw. The *Plaint* cannot be judged entirely from the point of view of a literary work.

There is a further point. G. Raynaud de Lage lists one hundred and eleven manuscripts of the *Plaint*.[107] Of these only six belong to the thirteenth century. The same number of manuscripts is listed for the *Anticlaudianus*.[108] Of these four definitely belong to the twelfth century, two are possibly twelfth century, and thirty-two are from the thirteenth century. At the beginning of this Introduction I mentioned writers, from ca. 1220 to ca. 1270, who spoke in praise of Alan. Some of these

---

[105] See IX infra.

[106] I have followed P. Blanco Soto, "*Petri Compostellani de consolatione rationis*," Beiträge 8.4 (1912) 19-21; M. Manitius, *Geschichte der lateinischen Literatur des Mittelalters* 3 (Munich 1931) 154-155 and others in thinking that Peter of Compostella antedated Alan. Maria Gonzalez-Haba, *La Obra De consolatione rationis de Petrus Compostellanus* (Munich 1975) argues for a much later date for the work.

[107] *Alain de Lille, poète* 182-184.

[108] Ibid. 184-186.

refer to various works of his and in every case the *Anticlaudianus* is mentioned. There is not one reference to the *Plaint*. It would seem that it had no great impact on his contemporaries and immediate successors. This seems strange when we consider the great influence it was to have later.

I am convinced that a very long interval separates the *Anticlaudianus* from the *Plaint*. While deeply conscious of the danger of error, I would date it ca. 1160-1165.

Genre

The *Plaint* belongs to the type of literature called Menippean. This name derives from Menippus of Gadara (ca. 225 BC). It is interesting to note that he was the originator of the serio-comic style in which humorous expression was given to philosophical views. His prose was interspersed with verse. Varro, Seneca and Petronius cultivated this genre in antiquity.[109] Martianus Capella, Boethius and Peter of Compostella represent later writers of this type who had a deep influence on Alan.

Argument

The poet speaks. All joy has left him and he is beset by grief. This arises from the current contempt for Nature's laws in regard to sex and generation. Faced with this, he cannot maintain silence: he must sing his song of sorrow. Homosexuality is rampant. Man has become like a grammarian whose interest is in Figures of Speech and poor ones at that, or like a logician who resorts to an unjustified form of Conversion. However beautiful

[109] Quintilian 10.1.95; J. Wight Duff, *Roman Satire* (Hamden, Conn. 1964) 84-105.

and attractive women may be, they are inferior to men. Now
they have lost even their attractions. The great lovers of old are
no more (I).

The poet in a trance-like state[110] sees a maiden glide down
from heaven. She is graced with every natural beauty in its
highest perfection. Yet her tear-bedewed face bespeaks her suffering.

A crown on her head represents the stars, paying special attention to the Zodiac and its constellations, each of which is
represented by a precious stone. Below these constellations a set
of seven gems represent the Planets. The gems, with the exception of those representing the Northern Circumpolar Stars, wax
and wane and the precious stones show the variation of movement of the Planets. Thus the diadem and crown produce "an
image of the firmament."

Her dress is forever changing colour. On it are pictured the
various birds of the air. Comments are made on their habits or
peculiarities. Fish and land-animals appear in the same way on
her tunic. Flowers are pictured on the lower part of her shoes.
There is a surmise that herbs and trees had their place on the upper part of her shoes and on her undergarments (II).

There one could see representations of the rose, the white narcissus, the lily, thyme, a stream with quiet murmur,[111] the columbine, the violet, the basilisca. Some of these things with which
Spring clothes the meadows have a practical value[112] (III).

---

[110] The dream motif gives a writer great latitude and freedom. The
beginning, sequence and end of a dream are beyond his control.

[111] The fact that this is a dream must explain the *murmuring* stream
among pictures of flowers.

[112] The idea of things being useful, as well as beautiful is typical of
Alan. Cf. his description of the Garden of Nature, *Anticl.* 1.74-75,
Sheridan, 47.

The maiden's beauty is again emphasised. There is a brief account of her producing images on slate tablets, images that disappear as soon as they appear. An account is given of her arrival in a chariot drawn by Juno's birds, accompanied by a man who aids the woman-driver. The splendour of the ensemble (or possibly of the maiden alone) dazzles the poet. Now comes the main theme. All nature[113] proceeds to celebrate the maiden's arrival. The sun and stars shine more brightly, an eclipse of the moon is removed.[114] A storm that has been raging subsides. The birds stage some kind of gymnastic game. Juno's long-dead passion for Jupiter is rekindled.[115] The sea, where a storm has just been raging, grows calm. The fish try to show their joy. From the stream come maidens with gifts for the visitor. Earth was at its Spring and dressed in flowers to greet the maiden. The trees in full foliage inclined their tops in adoration. Nymphs come from the woods with gifts. Prosperpine decides to resume her residence on earth so as to meet the maiden. Land animals frolick in welcome. In a word everything in the universe pays court to the maiden and seeks her favour (IV).

Spring is now here and renews everything. Flowers grow and

---

[113] Fire, water, earth and air, the four elements, are to contribute their share to the celebration. Cf. Bern. Silv. 2.9.30ff. (see full reference, n. 120 infra).

[114] Apparently the dream motif allows the sun, moon and stars to be visible simultaneously.

[115] Why are these two introduced here? Juno was a foundress of marriage and the protectress of the mother and child at birth. Jupiter was her brother and husband. It is intended to suggest that normal sex is trying to reassert itself? Does it mean that the natural bond of marriage should be proof against all obstacles? Juno's life had been one act of jealous revenge after another against Jupiter for his extramarital affairs: Ovid, *Met.* 1.601-624; 2.425-488; 3.253-562; 9.21-22, 292-300; 10.155-161. She is now willing to forgive all this.

come to bloom, making earth like the heavens. The sun, with all his benefits, begins to exert his influence. The days grow long, the flocks grow lively, the birds are heard again as are the chattering streams with their silvery sheen (v).

Despite the beautiful surroundings, the maiden still shows signs of grief. She approaches the poet who is so affected by her that he falls into a trance. She helps him regain his faculties. She is astounded by the fact that he does not recognise her. She points out that he owes everything he has to her — his existence, humanity, senses, beauty, reason and memory. She has made him in the image and likeness of the Universe. As the planets in retrograde motion go contrary to the normal revolution of the stars, so does sensuality in man run counter to reason.[116] In the Universe we have the Creator above the firmament, angels in the air, man on earth: in man wisdom is in the head, magnanimity in the heart, desire in the loins. The sun's heat brings life to earthly things, the heart's warmth enlivens the rest of the body. In the Universe the moon is the cause of many humours, so too is the liver in man. The Universe has its seasons from the childhood of Spring to the death of Winter, so too does man pass gradually from childhood to old age. The maiden emphasises that all her accomplishments are achieved under divine guidance and help. Finally she mentions her name. She is Nature. She is involved in all generation and birth. There is, however, a second birth, a regeneration that comes directly from God. We know of it by Faith. The poet falls down in adoration before Nature and tenders profuse apologies for his previous failure to recognise and honour her. He has some questions for her and goes on to ask them (vi).

[116] See ii, note 40.

The poet compliments Nature by reference to her power, her gifts and the universal honour paid her. He then asks why she has come to earth and what is the cause of her grief (vii).

Nature is surprised that the poet cannot see the reasons. She proceeds to wash away his doubts with a flood of rhetoric.[117] Every created thing obeys her laws with the exception of man, the one whom she has most benefited. He is leagued with a Venus who in turn has deserted her true role and may be compared to a grammarian who ignores rules and abounds in solecisms. Thus unnatural sex has become rampant. She bewails the honours and privileges she has conferred on man. She refers specifically to Helen of Troy, Pasiphae, Myrrha, Medea and Narcissus.[118] Sex deviates are classified. Nature explains her violent reaction to sex perversion and excuses her strong language. She has come to reform man and punish him if he proves intransigent.

The poet then asks why Nature attacks homosexuality among men with such bitterness, seeing that the poets attribute the same defect to the gods, for example Jupiter, Bacchus and Apollo. Nature's answer concentrates on the poets. Their works are naked falsehoods made attractive by artistic appeal, or falsehoods dressed in a cloak of probability. Falsehoods about the defects of the gods make men too tolerant of such faults in themselves. Other poetic works are false at the literal level but

[117] Nature responds to this question with a preamble so long that, by the time the answer is reached, one has forgotten the question, a fault that Alan was later to attribute to the arrogant man (xiv, p. 153).

[118] Two of these are odd choices. Pasiphae and Myrrha were in no way accountable for their unnatural passions. Perhaps the Greek concept that "the doer must suffer" (Aeschylus, *Choephoroi* 313), regardless of intention or responsibility, is operative here.

contain within a truth of deep significance. Still other works are historically true but are interspersed with entertaining fictions. Poets who write about a plurality of gods or crimes committed by them are to be equated with Arrhius and Manichaeus. The others can be accepted.

The poet's next question is: "Why are there rents in the part of your garment that represents man?" The answer is that vicious men have attacked Nature and torn off pieces of her garment to keep for themselves. "Why," persists the poet, "have men become so vicious?" Nature introduces her reply by stating that, as far as possible, she will try to use refined language to describe loathsome objects. God created the world from nothing. He established peace and harmony among its elements. The continuation of the world was to depend on a birth-death cycle. He appointed her as His vice-regent, to see to it that like should spring from like and life should go on. For a time she faithfully discharged her office. The work proved too much for her. To carry it out perfectly she needed a sub-delegate and, moreover, she decided to withdraw from earth and live in the undisturbed peace of the ethereal regions. She delegated Venus to take her place. Venus would be aided by her husband Hymenaeus and their son, Desire.

The mention of Desire prompts the poet, who has heard much of his power, to ask for more detailed information (VIII).

Nature begins by describing Desire in nineteen lines of strained oxymora. She then goes on to detail his powers over one and all, the changes he can effect in men and women, the crimes he can induce them to commit and the one and only remedy is to flee when Venus approaches (IX).

Nature goes on to explain that Desire is basically good. Her strictures have dealt with his excesses. She must now return to her account of the fate of the world under Venus' rule. She had given Venus explicit instructions and a detailed blueprint. Sexual unions were to be strictly between males and females. The male was to be to the female as an adjective is to a noun. The relationship between them should be akin to the relationship which a transitive verb effects between its subject and object, which exists between the terms of a syllogism, between a subject and predicate. Venus would have to face the arguments of the Fates and was given sufficient training in Rhetoric to deal effectively with them. Venus was to interpret her instructions literally, avoiding analogy, metonymy and Figures of Speech in general.

For a while all went well but Venus ultimately became bored with the eternal sameness of her work. She forsook her husband, Hymenaeus, to carry on an affair with Antigenius. A child, *Sport* (*Jocus*), was born. A comparison is made between Desire, Venus' legitimate son, and Sport. From Sport came all sorts of perversions.

There are other vices that run counter to Nature and she offers to give details in an elegiac ode (x).

Justice is gone, crime abounds, fraud is everywhere and in a decadent age does not even try to conceal itself. Children cannot trust their parents nor can brother trust brother. Respect for law and righteousness makes a man a laughing-stock. Man is just an irrational animal (xi).

The poet would like a treatment of each vice individually. Nature becomes a little confused. She indicates that she will first deal with Gluttony as it has a connection with lust. In what seems to be an attempt to avoid a too abrupt transition, she points out that the daughters of a once dead Idolatry are trying to resurrect their mother. Among these daughters is Bacchilatria (Worship of Bacchus, the Wine-God). She now goes on to deal with drunkenness which works its way through every social stratum, affecting even prelates in the recitation of the Divine

Office. Gluttony comes next. The poet describes gluttons' devotions to the stomach, their disgusting practices and their elaborate feasts. She describes them for the most part in a metaphor couched in terms drawn from banking and debt-collecting.

Avarice (Nummulatria, Worship of Cash) is now treated. Money is all-powerful, it outclasses eloquence, martial valour, Logic, Rhetoric, chastity, poetry, knowledge. However, it is far inferior to wisdom. She brings every good. However much others may revere money, do you trample on it and pursue prudence.

The poet begs Nature to stigmatise Avarice still further (xII).

Avarice ruins personal friendships at every level, causes truces to be broken and fosters war. It feeds on itself and ever increases. It really makes man a beggar, since he is forever seeking further riches. It destroys his peace of mind. He is beset by imaginary fears and the dread of loss is as great as an actual loss. His money brings him no happiness since he refuses to use it. He will not even buy decent food. He gouges money out of the poor and is immune to any feeling of pity. His soul lies buried with his coins. These are his gods. Riches in themselves are not to be despised. It is the irrational attitude towards them that is reprehensible. The rich man can easily make a mistake, too, by trying to procure friendship by gifts. Only a hypocritical friendship can be gained in this way (xIII).

Nature goes on to deal with Arrogance.[119] In some of the best

---

[119] *Arrogance* is not the exact equivalent of the Latin *arrogantia*. One of the commonest meanings of *arrogantia* is appropriating, or laying claim to, something that does not belong to one. This is the aspect of *arrogantia* most emphasised by Alan.

characterisation in the work, there is a description of the arrogant man with his affected diction, his solemn silences, his personalised actions, his unconventional gestures, his over-attention to dress. Some make obviously false claim to a distinguished ancestry. Others, though patently unlearned, speak on subjects that would call for the mind of an Aristotle. Still others affect a courage that they are far from possessing. They must be different, silent while others talk, serious when others are merry — in a word always differing from others in speech, manners, gestures, hair-style, stance and gait. Considering man's life, from birth to death, he has little to justify his arrogance.

Now comes Envy, the daughter of Pride. She ruins and corrupts men and destroys their peace of mind. She refrains from attacking those who are evil and concentrates her assaults on the good and the prosperous. The remedy is to identify with one's fellow-man in his joys and sorrows.

Flattery comes next. Flatterers concentrate on the rich and on the powerful in church or state. Their object is to elicit gifts and their praise is proportionate to the gifts. They have no respect for truth. They are cheats.

The poet now asks for some maxims to help him avoid the vices mentioned (XIV).

Restrain your appetite for food. Drink sparingly and add a generous proportion of water to your wine. Let your food be plain and your meals not too frequent. This will restrain the ardour of Cupid. Restrain your eyes. This too will help. Do not hoard your money. Let it be of use to yourself and others. See to it that your gifts promote what is right. Fight the pride, vanity and destructive powers within you by meditating on the toils of life and the certainty of death (XV).

Hymenaeus makes his appearance and is described in detail.
On his clothes is painted a representation of marriage. Though
the painting had faded somewhat, one could see there the chief
characteristics of marriage: marital fidelity, indissolubility, the
joy and celebration surrounding a marriage ceremony.
Hymenaeus is attended by a band of musicians but their instruments are silent in sympathy with their master's sadness.

In succession Chastity, Temperance, Generosity and Humility
make their appearance. Chastity, Temperance and Humility are
described in detail and an account given of the message for man
to be found in the pictures on their garments. Generosity is dealt
with in a more summary fashion.

Nature addresses these Virtues. She knows why they are here:
the vices of men have driven them from earth. She identifies
with their sufferings and promises that evil men shall be punished. Her power, however, is limited. She needs the aid of
Genius. Hymenaeus will go with an official document asking
him to come. The document is set forth. Hymenaeus makes
ready to leave. He asks the musicians to bestir themselves and
supply some music (xvi).

Some twelve musical instruments are mentioned and
evaluated. The effect of most of them on man is described (xvii).

Nature speaks in general terms of the wrongs done her by men
and goes on to single out one in particular. He had been
favoured with noble lineage, high offices and learning. He had
only one vice, Prodigality. In Platonic fashion Nature explains
that this one vice wrecks everything. Generosity is saddened by
the man's forthcoming punishment. His vice is but the
misemployment of her gifts to him. Nature reiterates her
Platonic stand. Generosity agrees.

Genius comes on the scene. He is described in detail. He holds a pen in his right hand and a parchment in his left. He continuously draws pictures emphasising his connection with birth. He changes the pen to his left hand and draws pictures of some of his products that have not turned out so well. Truth, daughter of Nature and Genius, is standing by. She is described in detail. Opposite her stands Falsehood, bald, ugly and in rags.

Genius addresses Nature, expressing his agreement with her ideas and his readiness to lend his aid. He dons his official robes and reads the sentence of excommunication. This would be the punishment for men who sinned against Nature. The attendant maidens have had candles in their hands. Their flame dies out. The mirror with its visions is withdrawn. The poet awakes from his ecstasy (xviii).

Interpretation

Until comparatively recently very little beyond a literal approach would suffice for an interpretation of the *Plaint*. There was a force or power called *physis* by the Greeks and *natura* by the Romans. Ultimately this force was personified. The basic idea of Natura was the production of something. Through her power things came into being, developed, grew old and passed out of existence. Her domain was extended to embrace all mundane phenomena. She controlled all animal and plant life, the movement of the planets and stars, the waters in the ocean, in clouds or on earth, the seasons with their heat and cold. Alan's predecessor, Bernardus Silvestris, had gone thus far.[120] Alan

---

[120] *Bernardus Silvestris De mundi universitate libri duo sive megacosmus et microcosmus*, ed. C. Barach and J. Wrobel (Innsbruck 1876; reprinted Frankfurt a.M. 1964). Translation: W. Wetherbee, *The Cosmographia of Bernardus Silvestris* (New York and London 1973).

decided to extend the power of Natura to the moral order, in other words, to man, the only being with free will and the power to act against the laws that Natura had imprinted on his heart. Influenced by the Chartrian synthesis of the Mosaic account of creation in Genesis with the theory of the Four Elements from Plato, Alan theorised that God created the world and then appointed Natura as His substitute and vice-regent, to be in full charge of the operation of the Universe and in particular to ensure that by like producing like all living creatures should increase and multiply according to the injunctions in Genesis 1. For a time all went well. Then Natura sub-delegated her power to Venus. She gave her explicit and detailed instructions as to how she was to fulfill her office. Again for a time all things went well. Then Venus lapsed. She entered an adulterous union with Antigenius and bore an illegitimate son called (by antiphrasis) *Sport*. From him originated unnatural sex practices and in connection with these came a host of vices. Things got so bad that Natura returned to outlaw and excommunicate those indulging in these vices.

What lies behind all this? One could be near-literal and claim that Alan saw around him a world where vice was rampant at every level of society. At this juncture we have a choice. Alan was a genuine reformer and wanted to write something that might induce the evil-doers, or at least some of them, to mend their ways and forewarn the good against the pitfalls of vice. This motive is explicitly set forth in the *Plaint*.[121] The alternative

---

Brian Stock, *Myth and Science in the Twelfth Century* (Princeton 1972) is invaluable for an understanding of Bernardus Silvestris and the background of Alan.

[121] We may note here his insistence on prophylactics against, and remedies for, habits of vice.

would be that Alan had just discovered that literature was his *métier* and found in the world around him material for a Menippean Satire in which he could display his virtuosity in prose and verse. His claims to be a reformer are the satirists' traditional defence of their genre. I would like to quote Gilbert Highet here:

> Satire . . . may be loosely defined as a piece of verse, or prose mingled with verse, intended both to entertain, and to improve society by exposing to derision and hatred the follies, vices and crimes of men. Among its salient characteristics are spontaneity (real or apparent), topicality, ironic wit, coarse humour, colloquial language, frequent intrusions of the author's personality or *persona*, and incessant variations of tone and style.[122]

This could be a fair description of the *Plaint*. To sum up here, Alan chose the Nature story to give him scope for a Menippean satire. Moreover, in the *Anticlaudianus* he specifically stated that the intellectually mature reader would find an allegory there.[123] When in the *Plaint* he asks Nature about the rents in her garments, she emphasises in her answer that she is giving a symbolic interpretation.[124] Nowhere in the *Plaint* is anything said to indicate that the whole work is an allegory. In essence the above interpretation that the work is a satire and not a full blown allegory is that of B. Bischoff.[125] However, he thinks that Alan's work is directed against one ecclesiastical person "of doubtful morals." This restriction poses problems. The person most bitterly attacked in the work is the man who had been favoured with gifts from Fortune, Prudence, Magnanimity and Generosity and has held more than one high office but had ruined

[122] *Oxford Classical Dictionary* (ed. 1970) 953.
[123] Bossuat 56, Sheridan 41.
[124] See VIII infra.
[125] D'Alverny, *Textes inédits* 43, note 53.

everything by one vice, Prodigality.[126] Plato would maintain that whoever lacks one virtue really lacks all virtues. Christian theology would maintain that the one who deliberately indulges in one serious vice destroys Divine Grace in his soul and is incapable of any virtue on a supernatural level. St. Paul states that if he were to give away all that he possessed but had not love, it would be of no avail to him.[127] Basically Christian and Platonist would agree that all virtue is based on love of, and imitation of, God, the Supreme Being,[128] and love of every good through Him. Ostentatious Prodigality, motivated by a desire to seem a favourite son of Generosity, would destroy the basis of all virtue. Bischoff's theory could gain strength from the adage *corruptio optimi pessima*.

There are difficulties. It is clearly stated that this man was singled out from a number of others for special stigmatisation. Though Alan can be extreme and carry rhetorical exaggeration to great lengths, would he claim that the man, marred by the vice of prodigality, is guilty of irregular sex practices. He could claim that he did not have the supernatural virtue of Chastity but that is something quite different. Could he accuse him of drunkenness, avarice and the host of other vices mentioned?

However, a literal interpretation would normally be out of keeping with a twelfth-century work of this kind. Practically everything written in this vein has a symbolic sense hidden beneath the literal.[129] This approach to literature became

---

[126] See XVIII infra.

[127] 1 Cor. 13:3.

[128] Matt. 5:48; Plato, *Rep.* 484c, 613b; *Theatetus* 176b. For a discussion of this matter see W. Jaeger, *Paideia: the Ideals of Greek Culture* 2 (Oxford 1943) 279-288.

[129] R. Javelet, "Image du Dieu et nature au xii⁰ siècle," in *La filosofia*

popular from the various interpretations of Scripture. When it passed beyond Scripture, it was used as a device by writers who feared undesirable repercussions from a plain literal statement of what they had to say. Others saw in it an imitation of Nature who cloaked her meaning under various coverings. It was finally to become just a literary fashion.

Alan made extensive use of allegory in his interpretation of Scripture, even going so far as to maintain that a literal interpretation of Scripture would involve one in contradictions.[130] This would lead one to expect allegory in his non-scriptural writings. Perhaps Alan was a true and genuine reformer and thought that the dream-motif and the personifications of nature, the virtues and vices which he introduced were enough to satisfy contemporary expectations of allegory in such a work. Against this, however, is the fact that he himself states that in a *fabula* the entire narrative is false *in verbo et non in facto*.[131]

The road to the hidden meaning of an allegory is treacherous with pitfalls. Different predispositions and preconceptions can lead to widely different theories, all of them with some degree of plausibility. The *Plaint* might be interpreted as a religious allegory. The first sojourn of Nature could represent man before the Fall. The administration of Venus could refer to the time between the Fall and coming of Christ. The second coming

---

della natura nel mediaevo, Atti del Terzo congresso internazionale di filosofia medioevale (Milan 1966) 286-296; Brian Stock, *Myth and Science* 31-62; Wetherbee, *Cosmographia of Bernardus Silvestris* 13-16.

[130] PL 210.407C. He had, however, some reservations: see *Regulae* 34, PL 210.637C-D.

[131] *Distinctiones*, PL 210.783C. The idea of *entire* comes from his etymology of *fabula*. He thought it came from the verb, *for*, "I say" and *holon* (which he writes *olon*), the Greek for "all."

of Nature could symbolise the Redemption. In this context it is necessary to understand the doctrine of the Trinity.

The doctrine of the Trinity teaches that God is three divine and distinct persons, Father, Son (or Word) and Holy Spirit, and that all three are one in nature, essence or substance. Yet although the three persons have only one nature, essential attributes of that nature are, by a process known as appropriation, usually attributed to one person rather than to another, thus, power to the Father, wisdom to the Son, goodness to the Holy Spirit. Likewise, although all three persons act together in common out of their one nature in any operation having an effect outside God, creation usually is attributed to the Father, illumination or revelation to the Son or Word, sanctification to the Holy Spirit. All the same, this does not mean that the word Trinity may not be used as the source or subject of any attribute which, in this way, is more generally appropriated to one or other of the three persons. Indeed the term may be used of certain attributes which are really proper to one of the persons as he operates outside God. The attribute of Redeemer, for example, properly belongs to the Son as Man, but, as here in the *Plaint*, the Trinity may be said to have come on earth and to have redeemed the world in as much as it is the first cause of an incarnation and a redemption which it effected through the Son.

God created the Universe and everything in it. The rest of creation was for man's benefit. It contained a large number of things that were different in genus and species, some of which seemed even opposed to one another. Two of its Elements, fire and water, were not only incompatible with, but destructive of, each other. Yet there was peace and harmony there. It was God's plan that life on earth should continue by a cycle of death and birth. For the human race birth was to take place by a union of man and woman and this was to be the closest and most important of unions. For a time this idyllic condition perservered.[132]

Then came the Fall. Man lost supernatural Grace.[133] God determined that the birth-death cycle should continue. However, He warned woman that although child-bearing and birth would become painful, she would still be drawn to her husband.[134] The generally accepted theory was that the impulses placed in man by God when he created him would remain, but that his intellect would be darkened, his will weakened and he would be subjected to a strong inclination to evil. The departure of Nature symbolises man's loss of God's Grace. The gates were now open for the entry of vice of every kind.

The direction of man was now taken over by Venus.[135] Weakened man succumbed to vice. Idolatry made its appearance and in its wake the other vices.[136] Every vice mentioned in the

---

[132] Gen. 1:1-2:24; *Plaint* VIII infra.

[133] Nature and grace were closely allied in twelfth-century thought: M.-D. Chenu, *La Théologie au douzième siècle*, Études de philosophie médiévale 45 (Paris 1957) 295.

[134] Gen. 3:16.

[135] John Scotus, in his *Annotationes in Marcianum* 8, 8 gives three interpretations of Venus. Considered from the point of view of the physical, she represents the seed of all living things found in this world. In a moral sense, allied with this, Venus represents the naturally good powers given to good men who will use them as they should. Finally, dealing with men after the Fall, she can deteriorate and lead them into evil lust. See ed. C. Lutz, *Johannis Scotti Annotationes in Marcianum* (Camb., Mass. 1939) 13.

[136] Idolatry is first mentioned in Leviticus 19:4 and there are some seventy references to it in the OT. Alan strains so hard to connect every vice with Idolatry that the OT influence is obvious.

Plaint is referred to again and again in both the Old and New Testament. It is worth noting that those in charge of the theocratic Jewish state came in for a large measure of blame as do the Prelates in Alan. Amongst the most detested of vices was sodomy. It led to the destruction of one city.[137] Rulers were blamed for tolerating it and praised for suppressing it.[138] Of particular interest here is a passage in St. Paul.[139] He points out that those who had had no law to guide them could have known God by his invisible nature manifested in the things created by Him. They had the law of God "written on their hearts." They ignored it and indulged in idolatry, worship of the creature instead of the Creator.[140] This brought the curse of God on them. The first curse mentioned is lesbianism and homosexuality, "exchange of natural relations for unnatural." Then came greed, malice, envy, murder, strife, deceit, slander, arrogance, boasting; men became foolish, faithless, heartless, ruthless. He adds a word of warning for the ones who "judge those who do such things and yet do them" themselves.[141]

Finally conditions so deteriorated that practically all virtue had disappeared from earth.[142] God, Who loves goodness and wishes to reform the evil-doer, came to the rescue. The Trinity[143]

---

[137] Genesis 18-19.

[138] 3 Kings 14:24; 15:12; 22:47; 4 Kings 23:7.

[139] Romans 1:18-2:24. Note especially 1:26-27.

[140] This could be symbolised by Venus' liaison with Antigenius.

[141] It is hardly necessary to point out that every vice referred to by St. Paul and Alan is mentioned again and again in Scripture. For Paul see Romans 1:18-2:24.

[142] In *Tractatus Magistri Alani De virtutibus et vitiis*, Alan states that all virtues have their foundations in Nature (ed. O. Lottin, "Le Traité," *Mediaeval Studies* 12 (1950) 27).

[143] Symbolised by Nature, Genius and Truth.

came on earth. Supernatural virtues are to return, the good are to be encouraged and given new strength and helps.[144] Appeals, remonstration and threats are to be directed towards those affected by vice. Those of them who prove irreformable are to be set apart and visited with punishments consonant with their crimes.

Professor W. Wetherbee treats the question of allegory in the *Plaint*.[145] He aptly refers many passages to various elements in religion. A most interesting feature is his explanation of much of the allegory as referring to the failure of poetry. He has not gone into the matter in detail. Alan has a section, explicit but too brief, dealing with poets and poetry.[146] It seems to me that there would be an element of inconsistency in having such a passage literally referring to this subject and so much more of the work an allegory oriented in the same direction. The idea in itself is a fascinating one and we can only hope that Professor Wetherbee returns to it and treats it with the detail and documentation of his invaluable Introduction to the *Cosmographia*.

I feel certain that others could find and defend other allegorical interpretations. Is the search for allegory being carried too far? Perhaps in the 1160s, Alan, who had written learned prose works, discovered his poetic potential. He cast

---

[144] The idea of Redemption as a complete restoration of Original Justice is not uncommon in the twelfth century: M.-D. Chenu, *La Théologie au douzième siècle*, (Paris 1957) 289-308.

[145] "The Function of Poetry in the 'De Planctu Naturae' of Alain de Lille," *Traditio* 25 (1969) 87-125; *Platonism and Poetry in the Twelfth Century* (Princeton 1972) 188-211. In the latter work I find myself in difficulties by reason of a lack of any reference, primary or secondary, for many of the statements made.

[146] VIII infra.

about for a subject. Nature, with its ramifications, was a popular subject of discussion. One has but to glance at the 787 pages of *La Filosofia della Natura nel Medioevo* in *Atti del Terzo Congresso Internazionale di Filosofia Medioevale* (Milan 1966), to realize that speculation about Nature loomed large in current discussions. Psychologically Alan was a reformer: "improve or perish" is a constant theme in his writings. He is forever in search of defects.[147] He saw around him a world in which the natural virtues were seemingly ignored. Perhaps he chose this as the subject of his work, using the Trivium to symbolise the defects he mentions and giving little thought to any elaborate underlying allegory.[148]

BACKGROUND

Nature

Aristotle gives seven meanings for "Nature."[149] For us the seventh is the most important. He states: "Processes of generation and growth are called 'Nature' because they are motions

---

[147] Nature herself confesses her failures in *Anticl.* 1.214-265, Sheridan 54-56.

[148] Theagenes of Rhegium (ca. 525 BC) was the first grammarian to attempt an allegorical interpretation of Homer's *Theomachy*. The practice spread and indeed is still with us. Nevertheless, competent scholars think that even stories about the Cyclops, Sirens, Circe, Scylla and Charybdis etc., which once seemed obvious allegories, are nothing more than "tall tales" told by Carthaginian merchants to credulous, superstitious Greek sailors to keep them away from lucrative trading in the western Mediterranean.

[149] *Metaphysics* 5.4 (1014b16-1015a19).

derived from it." He divided the Universe into the heavens and the world of Nature and when he speaks of Nature he has the world of the four elements in mind. Nature is the principle of order in the sublunary world and is thus a connection between the sublunary world and God. For Plato the world-soul links the eternal world with the terrestrial. Plotinus accepts Plato's idea of a world-soul but develops it still further. Here we find the One, self sufficient and the source of all things. The first emanation of the One is *nous*, the divine mind. In this are all the ideas and exemplars of all things. From *nous* comes the world-soul. Plotinus postulates two world-souls. One of these contemplates *nous* and receives reflections of the ideas there, the other passes them on to matter and generates the beings of the terrestrial world. This second world-soul is Nature.[150]

In Macrobius' "Golden Chain of Being"[151] we have an account of the Neoplatonic theory of the workings of the world-soul. It creates bodies based on exemplars from the fount of *nous* and endows them with mind. It first creates the celestial bodies and in the terrestrial sphere endows man, and man alone, with as much mind as he is capable of. Nature is the sum total of all that comes into being by the operation of the world-soul. Only the things in the sublunary world are subject to change, decay and death. Here too, however, the four elements, out of which all material things are made, are not diminished; they change forms. Thus the material universe is itself immortal.[152] Nature takes part in human reproduction, protecting the seed that has been planted.

[150] *Enneades* 3.8.4, ed. P. Henry and H.-R. Schwyzer, *Plotini opera* (Paris and Brussels 1951) 1.398.

[151] *Comm.* 1.14.15. Cf. Homer, *Iliad* 8.19.

[152] Macrobius, *Comm.* 2.12.10-11.

In Chalcidius Nature is the intermediary between the exemplar and matter. It is the life-giving principle of the world-soul working on matter. Nature's operation extends to all things that are born, grow and die. Asclepius explains that the continuity of mortal beings is guaranteed by the sex instinct which God implants in them.[153]

With Boethius we come to teaching on Nature that is easier to understand and more relevant to the *De planctu*. We might sum up his teaching by saying that Nature, examined and understood by reason, is the surest guide to everything worthwhile. The greatest of studies is that which directs its attention to the secret workings of Nature.[154] The nature of everything does that which is proper to it, is mixed with no contrary effects and repels all opposition.[155] By her laws she guides all things, keeps the world in order and binds things together with a knot that cannot be untied. Her influence cannot be eradicated. Given the proper circumstances the tame lion or the caged bird will revert to their natural instincts. Each thing obeys a law of Nature and follows a course that leads to a circle of birth and death.[156] In living creation, the love of life comes from Nature and also the desire for propagation.[157] Finally, nothing that follows Nature opposes God.[158]

---

[153] Ed. A. Nock and A. Festugière, *Corpus Hermeticum* (Paris 1945) 2.321.

[154] *De consolatione philosophiae* 1.M.2; Stewart-Rand 134.

[155] Ibid., 2.Pr.6.54-57; Stewart-Rand 210.

[156] Ibid., 3.M.2.1-38; Stewart-Rand 232-234.

[157] Ibid., 3.Pr.11.53 ff.; Stewart-Rand 280.

[158] Ibid., 3.Pr.12.56-57; Stewart-Rand 290.

Bernardus Silvestris

Few works have been subjected to as many interpretations as the *Megacosmus* and *Microcosmus* of Bernardus Silvestris.[159] The work is divided into two books. In the first, the *Megacosmus*, Nature approaches Noys (*Nous*) and complains about the sad condition of matter[160] and begs Noys to produce from it a more refined and orderly world. Noys agrees. The four elements are separated; she gives matter forms from the divine ideas and brings the world-soul into existence. A long account is given of the contents of the newly-formed Universe.

An explanation is then given of this Universe. It is a living animal, animated by the world-soul which gives life to all created things. The world-soul is an emanation of Noys, the divine and eternal mind of God. It will produce souls and it will be the work of Nature to provide bodies for these souls.

The second book, the *Microcosmus*, deals with the formation of man who is to be the masterpiece of creation. Noys instructs Natura to seek out Urania and Physis. Natura sets out on her journey. At the outer limit of the created universe she encounters Genius, who gives forms to created things in such a way that each is distinguishable from the other. Urania agrees that she will accompany Natura back to earth, bringing man's soul with her. First, however, they ascend to the abode of the super-essential God and pray for help in accomplishing their purpose.

They set out. They pass the planets. They find Mercury fashioning Hermaphrodites. They recognise Venus' power to stir up desires for pleasure and see her child, Cupid, at her

[159] See above, n. 120.
[160] The term *silva* or *hyle* is used to describe matter.

breast. They rest on the moon and there Urania explains the heavens to Natura. Finally, they reach Granusion, the abode of Physis. It is a beautiful, paradise-like garden and everything in it bestirs itself to welcome Natura. Noys appears with further instructions about the man that is to be formed. He will be a little world, an image of the greater world. He will be able to understand the cause of earthly phenomena. He will be master over all things on earth. The rest of creation will serve him and provide for his needs. Urania fashions his soul from the world-soul, Physis prepares the body, Natura unites the soul and body.

Scripture

The Hebrew vocabulary did not have a word corresponding to our word "Nature." The only intermediary between God and man was the Law. The word *physis* is not found in the Septuagint, the Four Gospels or the Acts of the Apostles.[161] It is only when the teachers of Christianity come in contact with Greeks and Romans that we find the word used. St. Paul says: "When the Gentiles, who have no law, carry out the precepts of the law by the directions of nature, though they have no law to guide them, they are a law to themselves. They show that the obligations of the law are imprinted on their heart."[162] This is a significant statement of the power of Nature as a moral guide.

---

[161] *Natura* is found in a few instances in the ot Vulgate. Some of these are attempts to tone down references to bodily functions. Others are due to the fact, well known to many a translator, that a word, not current in the author's time, may nevertheless be the best means of expressing his idea.

[162] Rom. 2:14-15.

Nature can take the place of the Law that regulated the conduct of the Jews.

Such is a very brief outline of *Natura* before she appeared in the *De planctu*. It is in Alan of Lille that she reaches full stature. Alan of Lille himself gives eleven definitions of Natura.[163] She herself describes her role in detail in the *De planctu* itself.[164] Perhaps the best summary of her role in the universe is in G. Raynaud de Lage: "C'est Dieu même qui a institué tout un réseau de causes secondes, qui a défini leur domaine en même temps qu'il a orienté leur action; mais, une fois, le système constitué, le Créateur respecte son autonomie et normalment n'intervient pas dans son fonctionnement. Nature représente ce système, personnifie la régularité et la continuité de son action, résume l'orientation correcte de ses tendances dans l'ordre moral comme dans l'ordre physique, reflète enfin l'autorité divine qui lui a été déléguée et qui justifie la rayonnement dont le poète l'a parée."[165]

Genius

There are few words in Latin with as many shades of meaning as "Genius." Etymologically, the word is connected with

---

[163] *Distinctiones*, PL 210.871A-D.
[164] Section IX.
[165] *Alain de Lille, poète* 67. For further information see ibid. 59-88; G. D. Economou, *The Goddess Natura in Medieval Literature* (Cambridge, Mass. 1972); R. G. Collingwood, *The Idea of Nature* (New York 1960); Tullio Gregory, *Anima mundi. La Filosofia di Guglielmo di Conches e la scuola di Chartres* (Forence, 1955) 175-246; *La Filosofia della natura nel medioevo, Atti del Terzo congresso internazionale di filosofia medioevale* (Milan 1966).

gignere, to bring forth, to give birth to. Its basic idea is the production and protection of life.

In antiquity the role of Genius most emphasised was that of tutelary deity. Each mortal had a *genius* assigned to him at birth.[166] Horace's answer to the question as to why brothers differ so much in character was: "the Genius alone knows — that companion who rules our star of birth."[167] Genius for some became identified with the Greek "daimōn," especially the "daimōn" that exerted so powerful a moral influence on Socrates.[168] The Genius adhered closely to each individual, so closely that it would be impossible to escape him for even a moment.[169] There was a belief that a ghost was the Genius of the dead person.[170] The Christian teaching on Guardian Angels would make the theories on the good Genius quite intelligible to the twelfth century.

The second aspect of Genius that calls for attention is his connection with the generative process. A fragment of Valerius Soranus, preserved by Augustine,[171] speaks of Genius as "a God who is in charge of, and has power over, the birth of all things." Isidore states: "They give him the name of Genius because, so to speak, he has power over the birth of all things, or from the fact

---

[166] Later theories were to speak of two *genii*, one inclining man to good, the other to evil. Cf. Persius 4.27; H. D. Brumble, "The Role of Genius in the *'De planctu Naturae'* of Alanus de Insulis," *Classica et mediaevalia* 31.1-2 (1970) 314.

[167] *Epistles* 2.2.188; cf. Seneca, *Epistles* 101.1.

[168] Apuleius, *De deo Socratis* 15, ed. G. F. Hildrebrand (Leipzig 1842) 2.144.

[169] Censorinus, *De die natali liber* 3, ed. O. Jahn (Hildesheim 1965) 7.19-8.2.

[170] Arnobius, *Adversus nationes* 3.41, CSEL 4.139.6-10.

[171] *De civitate Dei* 7.13. CSEL 40.5.1.a., 321.9-10.

that he brings about the birth of children. Thus the beds, prepared for the newly-wed husband, were called 'genius' couches.''[172] Other references show that newly-weds performed rites in honour of Genius.[173] Their object was that the marriage might be blessed with offspring. Festus quotes Aufustius to the effect that: "Genius is a son of the Gods and the sire of men, the one from whom men are born. Thus he is called my Genius because he generated me."[174] Censorinus spoke of those who thought that after marriage there were two genii in the household, one for the husband and another for the wife.[175]

This brings us to Bernardus Silvestris. When Natura and Urania came to Granusion, they found there, among other things, two genii. The work entrusted to them was to keep the human race in existence.[176] The terminology shows that they are the guardians that help the male and female genitalia to fulfill their purpose. Bernardus has one other reference to Genius.[177] When Natura came to Aplanon she found there a Genius skilled in drawing shapes and forms. To him was assigned the task of giving individual shapes and forms to beings coming into existence, so that no two should be identical or indistinguishable from each other.

It can easily be seen that Genius has a very close kinship with Nature, particularly with Nature as described by Alan in the *De*

---

[172] *Etymologiae*, ed. W. M. Lindsay (London and New York 1913) 8.11.88-89.

[173] Arnobius, *Adversus nationes* 2.67, CSEL 4.102.25-27.

[174] Ed. W. M. Lindsay, *Sexti Pompei Festi De verborum significatu quae supersunt cum Pauli epitome* (Leipzig 1933) 84.

[175] Censorinus, *De die natali liber*, ed. Jahn 7.7.

[176] 2.14.159-170.

[177] 2.3.92-100.

planctu. Both have the same interests — that like shall produce like, that sexual relations shall follow the norms of Nature, that those born shall grow up to live a life in accord with Nature as understood by right reason, that the human race shall not die out. Nature may well call Genius her other self. Genius gives the final form to the things of Nature. It is only to be expected that he shall give the final form to her decree of excommunication.

One final remark may be appropriate here. With the use of words such as anathema and excommunication, Alan has entered the realm of ecclesiastical law. Men are excommunicated for breaking certain laws of God. God does not personally pronounce the excommunication. His priest does that. This process is followed by Nature. She has her priest, Genius, read the document of excommunication.[178]

Literary Antecedents

The *Timaeus* of Plato is basic for the *De planctu*. From it comes, directly or indirectly, the account of the structure of the Universe and of man, the little copy of the Universe. We find there a detailed description of man, his mind and body, his internal organs and their significance, the tension between intellect and passion and man's five external senses. It is not hard to see that the *Timaeus* supplies the foundation for the *De planctu*.[179]

Boethius' *De consolatione philosophiae* is the literary model for the *De planctu*. The parallelism between them is close. In

---

[178] See D. N. Baker, "The Priesthood of Genius: A Study in the Medieval Tradition," *Speculum* 51.2 (1976) 277-291.

[179] The footnotes in the Translation will identify many specific borrowings from the *Timaeus*.

both a woman appears. Comments are made on the fine workmanship and material of the garments. Both garments show a rent. Neither woman is at first recognised and each is surprised at this. Both expatiate on the favours they have conferred on the person to whom they appear. Both are forced to reveal their identity. In each instance it is decided that the conversation will proceed by a question-and-answer routine. Both decry poetry as a guide to a happy life. In both we find requests that statements, but dimly understood, be clarified and that subjects, treated generically, be explained more specifically.

Beyond this general agreement in format we find many resemblances in details: the imperviousness of the ass to music, the rotation of seasons, the changing face of Nature, man's resemblance to a fortress, the perpetual hunger of the rich for further possessions, the warning that intemperance lays man open to other vices, the theory that the punishment of the vicious helps to reform them and serves as an example for others.

The *Megacosmus* and *Microcosmus* of Bernardus Silvestris was well known to Alan. Nature, in her search for Urania and Physis, came to Anastros and was fascinated by its charm and beauty. The description of Anastros in Bernardus supplied Alan with his description of the place to which Nature retired when she withdrew from earth. In both Bernardus and Alan we have an account of the efforts made to form soul and body in such a manner that a successful "marriage" between them might be possible. In both emphasis is laid on the value of memory. Alan took over and developed Bernardus' account of the planets. In particular we should note the latter's reference to Mercury, who was fashioning Hermaphrodites and to Venus who, with Cupid at her breast, gave rise to generative impulses. When Nature in

Bernardus reached Granusion, the place shone with an added lustre and everything took on a festive appearance to welcome her. Everything on earth welcomed Alan's Nature in the same way. Most of the phenomena mentioned in Bernardus 2.10 find a place in Alan. Physis foresaw difficulties in the formation of man and feared that the defects in *silva* might be reflected in him. All that could be hoped for was that his basic nature would be sound. Physis' fears were justified. Man did fail. This is the point where the *De planctu* takes up the tale.

Alan of Lille

The Plaint of Nature

I

Metre 1

I turn from laughter to tears, from joy to grief, from merriment to lament, from jests to wailing,[1] when I see that the essential decrees of Nature are denied a hearing, while large numbers are shipwrecked and lost because of a Venus turned monster, when Venus wars with Venus and changes "hes" into "shes" and with her witchcraft unmans man. It is not a case of pretence begetting a show of grief or faked tears giving birth to deceit: it is not an act, but rather an ache, that is in labour or, rather, actually giving birth. The Muse implores, grief itself orders, Nature begs that with tears I give them the gift of a mournful ditty.[2]

Alas! Where has Nature with her fair form betaken herself? Where have the pattern of morals, the norm of chastity, the love of modesty gone? Nature weeps, moral laws get no hearing, modesty, totally dispossessed of her ancient high estate, is sent into exile. The active sex shudders in disgrace as it sees itself

---

[1] Metre is Elegiac. For opening lines see James 4:9; *Anticlaudianus* 4.450-452, Sheridan 134.

[2] Alan is punning on *dolus* and *dolor*. He is insisting that his grief is real and probably had Horace, *A.P.* 102-103 in mind. The idea that certain conditions demand that the poet use his poetic power goes as far back as Pindar, *Nem.* 4.56.

degenerate into the passive sex.[3] A man turned woman blackens
the fair name of his sex. The witchcraft of Venus turns him into
a hermaphrodite.[4] He is subject and predicate: one and the same
term is given a double application.[5] Man here extends too far the
laws of grammar. Becoming a barbarian in grammar, he
disclaims the manhood given him by nature. Grammar does not
find favour with him but rather a trope. This transposition,
however, cannot be called a trope. The figure here more correctly falls into the category of defects.[6]

[3] Alan begins to describe homosexuality in terms of grammar. The
use of grammatical terms to express sexual ideas dates as far back as
Nero (54-68 AD). Lucilius describes the relationship between Menander,
the grammarian, and his pupil's mother, Zenonis, in terms of "cases,
conjunctions, figures and conjugations" (*Anthologia Graeca, The
Greek Anthology*, trans. W. Paton [New York 1918], vol. 4, no. 139).
This practice was to continue. See P. Lehmann, *Die Parodie im Mittelalter* (Stuttgart 1963) 107-108, 223-224. Grammar was very much to
the fore in the twelfth century and attempts were made to use it in the interpretation of Scripture and the explanation of theology. See M.-D.
Chenu, "Grammaire et théologie aux xiie et xiiie siècles," *Archives* 10
(1935/6) 5-28.

[4] Hermaphroditus, son of Hermes and Aphrodite, was fused against
his will with a nymph, Salamacis; Ovid, *Met.* 4.285-379. Pliny *N.H.*
7.3.34 states that such beings are born, that they had once been considered as portents but in his day were regarded as entertainments.

[5] Man is described as subject, woman as predicate. Cf. vɪɪɪ, note 26.

[6] Figures of Speech are not nearly so common in Latin as they are in
English. Even when found, they are often accompanied by some soften-
ing word or words, such as *quasi* or *ut ita dicam*. Quintilian 1.5.5 maintains that it is often difficult to distinguish between a Figure of Speech
and a barbarism or solecism. See *Anticlaudianus* 2.422, Sheridan 86.
Alan is here playing on the literal meaning of *translatio* and its technical

That man, in whose case a simple conversion[7] in an Art causes Nature's laws to come to naught, is pushing logic too far. He hammers on an anvil[8] which issues no seeds.[9] The very hammer itself shudders in horror of its anvil. He imprints on no matter the stamp of a parent-stem: rather his ploughshare scores a barren strand.[10] The one who has used the dactylic measure of

---

meaning in Rhetoric. For the latter, see Boethius, *In Topica Ciceronis commentaria* 3, PL 64.1107B-1108A; Otto of Freising, *Gesta Frederici I imperatoris*, MGH SS 20.355.39-43; J. Jolivet, *Arts du langage et théologie chez Abélard*, Etudes de philosophie médiévale 57 (1969) 76-77.

[7] Conversion means the interchange of the subject and predicate terms in a proposition. Simple conversion changes "All A is B" to "Some B is A." Conversion by contraposition changes "All A is B" to "All non-B is non-A": Boethius, *De syllogismo categorico*, PL 64.804A. Alan is here describing the homosexual in terms of logic. In the *Anticlaudianus* 6.144-156, Sheridan 161, he shows that the Virgin Birth transcends all laws of logic.

[8] The anvil was used to signify any kind of formative work: studies in Rhetoric, Tacitus, *Dialogus de oratoribus* 20.4; studies in Philosophy, Sidonius Apollinaris, *Ep.* 4.1.3, W. B. Anderson, *Sidonius, Poems and Letters* (Loeb Texts, London and Cambridge 1965) 2.26; studies in Poetry, Horace, *A.P.* 441; Sidonius, *Ep.* 4.8.5, pp. 92-94. Cf. Alan, *Anticlaudianus* Prose Prologue, Sheridan 39. Here the hammer typifies man.

[9] It may seem strange to speak of an anvil producing seeds. Alan would have seeds of fire in mind. The ancient writers spoke of seeds of various elements, even of stones. Lucretius 6.201, 444, 507, 841; Verg., *Aen.* 6.6. The anvil here typifies woman.

[10] Cf. Virg., *Aen.* 4.212; Ovid, *Heroides* 5.115; *Carmina Burana* 77.3, edd. A. Hilka and O. Schumann 2.53. The phrase was proverbial for useless labour.

Venus fares ill in iambics where a long syllable cannot be followed by a short.[11]

However much all man's good looks bow humbly down to woman's beauty, being ever inferior to it in fair grace, however much beauty of countenance serves the daughter of Tyndareus,[12] and comely Adonis[13] and Narcissus[14] are overcome and worship her, she is herself despised, though that fair face may carry the day and her godlike form maintain that she is a goddess for whose sake the thunderbolt would lie idle in Jupiter's right hand, every string of Phoebus'[15] harp would grow slack and inactive, a freeman would become a slave and Hippolytus[16] would sell his personal chastity to enjoy her love.

Why do so many kisses lie fallow on maidens' lips while no

---

[11] Matthew of Vendôme likened the male genitalia to a dactylic foot ($-\cup\cup$), Ars versificatoria 79-80, ed. E. Faral, Les Arts poétiques du xiie et du xiiie siècle (Paris 1923) 27. Horace describes an iambic foot as "a long syllable followed by a short" (syllaba longa brevi subiecta), A.P. 251. Alan fuses both ideas to emphasise the impossibility of normal relations between homosexuals. The subjecta of Horace is reflected in the patitur of Alan.

[12] Helen of Troy. Her abduction by Paris led to the Trojan war.

[13] A very beautiful youth, beloved by Aphrodite and slain by a boar. Ovid, Met. 10.519-739; Anticl. 6.226; 7.4, Sheridan 164, 174.

[14] A beautiful youth, son of Cephisus and Liriope. He fell in love with his own reflection, pined away, died and was turned into a flower of the same name. Ovid, Met. 3.342-510; Anticl. 2.14, 7.42, Sheridan 66, 174.

[15] Apollo, patron of music. Anticl. 2.351, 5.267, Sheridan 82, 146.

[16] Hippolytus had no interest in sex. His stepmother, Phaedra, became enamoured of him. He rejected her. She committed suicide, leaving a note accusing him. When his father, who was absent, returned, he banished Hippolytus and used one of three wishes given him by Poseidon to ensure his doom. A sea monster terrified Hippolytus'

one wishes to harvest a crop from them? If these kisses were but once planted on me, they would grow honey-sweet with moisture, and grown honey-sweet, they would form a honeycomb in my mouth.[17] My life breath, concentrating entirely on my mouth, would go out to meet the kisses and would disport itself entirely on my lips so that I might thus expire and that, when dead myself, my other self might enjoy in her a fruitful life.[18]

No longer does the Phrygian adulterer[19] chase the daughter of Tyndareus but Paris with Paris performs unmentionable and monstrous deeds. No longer does Pyramus cleave to Thisbe[20] through a cleft in the wall: the little cleft of Venus has no charm

---

horses. He fell from the chariot, was dragged by the horses and injured to such an extent that he died in a very short time. The *Hippolytus* of Euripides and the *Phaedra* of Seneca deal with this theme. Cf. *Anticl.* 1.150, 7.115, Sheridan 51, 176.

[17] Cf. Matthew of Vendôme, *Ars Versif.* 1.56.26, ed. Faral, *Arts poétiques* 130.

[18] *Felici* here has its basic meaning of "fertile" or "fruitful." In the background is the idea of a man continuing to live in his offspring.

[19] Paris. Troy belonged to Phrygia and *Phrygian* is used of many things pertaining to Troy.

[20] These lovers lived next door to each other in Babylon. Their parents opposed their romance, but they succeeded in communicating through a chink in the wall of the houses. They planned to escape and arranged a meeting place. Thisbe was first to reach it. She was scared by a lioness and ran, dropping her cloak, which the lioness tore into shreds. When Pyramus came and saw the torn cloak, he thought that she was dead and killed himself. She came back to the meeting place, saw the dead body of Pyramus and killed herself. Ovid, *Met.* 4.55-166; Anon., *Piramus et Thisbe*, ed. Faral, *Arts poétiques*, 331-335, from Gervais de Melkley, *Ars versificaria*.

for him. No longer does the son of Peleus[21] belie the actions of a maiden and so prove to maidens that he is a man.

Yet the man who sells his sex for love of gain makes a miserable return to Nature for her gift to him. Men like these, who refuse Genius his tithes and rites, deserve to be excommunicated from the temple of Genius.[22]

[21] Achilles. When the troops were mustering for Troy, Achilles' father or mother persuaded him to hide in Scyros, dressed as a girl. While there he had an affair with Deidameia and she bore him a son, Neoptolemus. He was discovered by Ulysses who "placed among the women's wares arms that would attract a man." Achilles grasped these, thus belying the actions of a woman: Ovid, *Ars am.* 1.689-696; *Met.* 13.162-170; *Anticl.* 9.265, Sheridan 211. It is hard to see that Achilles "sold his sex" by disguising himself as a woman to gain exemption from war. There were ancient references to affairs between Achilles and Patroclus and Achilles and Troïlus, but it is not likely that Alan knew of these.

[22] See Introduction, pp. 59-62.

II

Prose 1

As in mournful tones I kept repeating these elegiacs,[1] a woman glided down from an inner palace[2] of the impassible world and could be seen hastening her steps in my direction. Her hair shone with no borrowed sheen but with one special to itself and, presenting an image of light-rays, not by mere resemblance but by a native lustre surpassing the natural, it made the maiden's head image a star-cluster. A twofold hair-band, parting the hair, did not ignore the regions above nor disdain to grant earth a caressing smile. What one might call a length of lily-white path, forming a crosswise demarcation,[3] separated the

[1] Cf. Boethius, *De con. phil.*, Pr. 1.1, ed. H. F. Stewart and E. K. Rand (London and New York 1926) 130.

[2] Ovid, *Met.* 1.168ff., represents the gods as living in palaces fronting on the Milky Way and calls these dwellings "palaces of the high heavens."

[3] *Decusata.* Cicero in his *Timaeus* has a verb *decussavit* which the Greek original shows to mean "form in the shape of an X" (X = 10): *Timaeus* 6, *M. Tullii Ciceronis opera quae supersunt omnia,* ed. J. Baiter and C. Kayser (Leipzig 1864) 8.137. Columella uses the word with the same, or approximately the same, meaning: *De re rustica* 4.17.6, 4.24.8, ed. H. B. Ash (Loeb Texts, Cambridge, Mass. 1948) 1.392, 414. This meaning is found in Firmicius Maternus, *Consultationes Zacchaei et Apollinii* 1.4, ed. G. Morin, Florilegium *Patristicum* 39 (Bonn 1935) 10.27 and in Martianus Capella, 1.37, 2.208, 8.823, *De nuptiis Philologiae et Mercurii libri VIII*, ed. A. Dick (Stuttgart 1925; repr. with

struggling locks.[4] The fact that it ran crosswise did not, I maintain, cause a defect in her looks but was a protection for her beauty. A comb of gold, gathering the golden hair into a well-ordered movement, was surprised to find an appearance in unison with itself. For the impression of the colour that bordered the gold of the comb on either side baffled and misled the eyes.[5]

Her forehead,[6] spreading to a smooth surface of generous width, lily-like in its milk-white hue, seemed to vie with the lily. Her brows, starlike in their golden radiance, not thickened to bushiness nor thinned to over-sparseness, enjoyed a mean between both extremes. The serene peacefulness of her eyes, caressing in their friendly sparkle, brought with them the freshness of twin stars. Her nose, balsam-like in its sweet

---

additions by Jean Préaux, Stuttgart 1969) 23.19, 77.19, 433.24. It seems to have this meaning in Jerome, *In Hieremiam prophetam*, 31.9, ed. S. Reiter, CSEL 59 (1913) 385.4. Confusion was caused by the fact that another *decusare* appeared, a verb formed from *decus* and meaning "to ornament" or "to adorn": "Vita sancti Deicoli," *Acta sanctorum Januarii*, Johannes Bollandus (Paris, Palmé, n.d.) 2.563r; Odo of Cluny, *De vita sancti Gerardi* 1.12, PL 133.650C. I think that this is the verb found in most, if not all, places in the *De planctu*. However, I have adopted whichever meaning best suits the context.

[4] *Anticl.* 1.273, 3.17, Sheridan 56, 91. Alan seems preoccupied with hair in his description of both men and women. This derives from the *Timaeus* 76c-D. The brain is all-important. The skull protects it and for safety's sake the hair serves "as a light roofing for the part around the brain." By its connection with the brain, it enjoys a very important role.

[5] The colour of the golden comb blended so completely with the colour of the hair that one could not tell them apart. Cf. Matthew of Vendôme, *Ars versif.* 1.56.7, ed. Faral, *Arts poétiques* 129.

[6] See description of Prudence in *Anticl.* 1.220ff., Sheridan 56ff.

fragrance, neither unduly small nor abnormally prominent, made an outstanding contribution to her beauty of countenance. The nard of her mouth served her nose choice feasts of fragrance. Her lips, rising in gentle swell, challenged the recruits in Venus' army to kiss them. Her teeth by a certain uniformity in colour resembled a configuration in ivory. The brilliant fire of her cheeks, set aglow by tint of roses, by its charming radiance gave her face a friendly expression. For, with a pleasant lustre, the red of her face, wed to the white of muslin, showed the effects of a harmonious mixture. The smooth and refined chin, more distingushed than shining crystal, took on the sheen of silver.

Her neck, quite normal in length and moderately slender, prevented its nape from being close-wed to the shoulders. Her apple-like breasts gave assured proof of the fullness of youth with its charms. Her arms, shining from afar for the viewer's delight, seemed to call for embraces. The gentle curve of her flanks, impressed with the stamp of due moderation, brought the beauty of her whole body to perfection.

As for the other things which an inner chamber hid from view, let a confident belief declare that they were more beautiful.[7] For in her body lay hidden a more blissful aspect to which her face showed the introduction. However, as her countenance revealed, the key of Dione's daughter[8] had not opened the lock of her chastity. Great though the delight of her beauty was, tears inexplicably sought to wipe out the beauty of her smile. For tears, flowing stealthily from the well of her eyes, gave notice of

---

[7] Ovid, *Met.* 1.502: "What is hid, he deems more beautiful." Alan uses this idea again and again in his descriptions. See xvi, note 12.
[8] Venus.

the throb of internal pain. Moreover the face itself, turned towards the ground in chaste modesty, bespoke an injury done the maiden in some form or other.

A reddish royal crown and diadem, glittering with circling gems, flashed like lightening above her head.[9] Its material, gold, was not counterfeit, did not fall in corruption below gold's estate, did not deceive the eyes with hollow sheen; rather, the purest form of gold furnished its essence. With wondrous circlings and unceasing revolutions, this diadem wandered from east to west, but repeatedly made its way back to its place of origin. As it eternally kept up this practice, its movement, because of its excessive tendency to seek again its point of origin, seemed rather ridiculous.[10]

Some of the afore-mentioned gems at times brought to our eyes wonderous new light from the renewed brightness of their radiance, at times seemed, by the departure of their sparkle, to have gone into exile from their home in this diadem.[11] Other gems, set firm in their base, ever maintaining a twinkling vigil, kept eternal watch.[12] Amongst the former, a bright circle, representing the curve of the zodiac, glittering with necklaces of

[9] All the heavenly bodies unite to form a crown for Nature.

[10] There is a play on words here. There is a fallacy in logic called *petitio principii*, "begging the question." Strictly speaking, the frequently adduced example of a syllogism, "All men are mortal, John is a man, therefore John is mortal," involves *petitio principii*, since the major assumes what has to be proved. If the major is changed to "Man is mortal" the fallacy disappears. Literally *petitio principii* means "seeking the beginning" or "going back to the origin." The simile is somewhat far-fetched.

[11] Stars that are visible only at certain times of the year.

[12] The Northern Circumpolar Stars. These are visible the year round. The number visible depends on the latitude of the viewer. Cf. *Anticl.* 5.1ff., Sheridan 136.

precious stones, cut short the kisses of the stars that touched it on either side.[13] In this circle a band of twelve gems, by their pre-eminence in size and their privileged position in brightness, seemed to demand special consideration above the others.[14]

In the front part of this diadem three precious stones glowed

[13] He is probably referring to constellations, such as Ophiuchus, that have some of their stars inside the Zodiacal belt.

[14] The Signs of the Zodiac. Their arrangement in the diadem seems based on the Square of Opposition in Aristotelian logic:

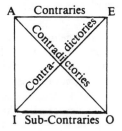

A (All P is S) and E (No P is S) are contraries: I (Some P is S) and O (Some P is not S) are sub-contraries. A (All P is S) and O (Some P is not S) are contradictories, as are E (No P is S) and I (Some P is S). Jos. Gredt, *Elementa philosophiae Aristotelico-Thomisticae* 1 (Freiburg i.B 1929) 49.

The arrangement of the Signs of the Zodiac seems to be:

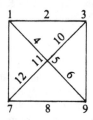

The order of the Signs would be: Leo, Cancer, Gemini, Aquarius, Capricorn, Sagittarius, Taurus, Aries, Pisces, Virgo, Libra, Scorpio.

in front of the other nine, shining with a pride and daring that are reflected in their names.[15]

By its light the first stone[16] imposed the sentence of exile on night and by its warmth on Winter. For in it, as the pleasantly deceptive picture showed, the image of an image of a lion flashed forth. The second stone,[17] but not second to the first in light, glowing forth from a bolder position in the above-mentioned section, seemed to look down on the rest of the stones with a certain attitude of disdain. In it as the picture, ap-ing truth,[18] showed, a crab[19] seems to be following himself when,

[15] *Antonomasia* is a figure of Rhetoric in which some description of a person is substituted for his or her name, e.g. Pelides (son of Peleus) for Achilles, Tyndaris (female descendant of Tyndareus) for Helen of Troy. Quint. 8.6.29. The first three stones represent the constellations Leo, Cancer and Gemini. The Lion is a universally accepted symbol of courage. The Crab (Cancer) bravely came to the aid of the water-snake that was being attacked by Hercules. A Roman tradition regarded the Twins (Gemini) as warriors. Dion. Halic., *Ant. Rom.* 6.13.1-3. Moreover Pollux was said to have been a boxer; Ovid, *Fasti* 5.700; Bern. Silv. 1.3.45; *Anticl.* 6.230, Sheridan 164.

[16] The constellation Leo (23 July — 23 August). Alan must be refer-ring to the light and warmth of July and August. Leo is at its best for viewing in March and April. Cf. *Anticl.* 5.32, Sheridan 138.

[17] The constellation Cancer (21 June — 22 July). This constellation is a faint group. Alan must be thinking of the bright days of June and July. Cf. *Anticl.* 5.32, Sheridan 138.

[18] *Veritatis simia*, "an ape of truth." The Platonic question as to the relationship between artistic representation and truth was much in Alan's mind. Plato maintained that the world of Art is "three removes from Nature." To take Plato's example: We have a number of beds. However, there is only one real bed which is the Form or Idea of bed, created by God and existing in a supramundane world. The carpenter copies this bed. The painter or poet copies the carpenter's bed: *Rep.* 10.597c-e. Cf. *Anticl.* 1.122-130, Sheridan 49.

[19] The fish, the crab, is supposed to be able to travel forwards and

in feigned imitation, he goes backward as he goes forward and forward as he goes backward. The third stone,[20] by the overflowing riches of its brightness, made up for the impoverished splendour of t? stone on the opposite side.[21] In it, as the faithful representation in the picture showed, the shades of Leda's children, showing goodwill in a mutual embrace, went their way.

Following this arrangement, three stones, enjoying a second-grade position, had taken up their abode in a diagonal position.[22] The first of these, giving the impression of tears by little drops of moisture, gave itself a sad expression by a kind of imaginary weeping. In this stone, the cruet of the youth of Ida,[23] as the appearance of the sculptured image of an attendant showed, sighed forth a flowing stream. The second stone, driving out the guest of heat from its kingdom, by its icy numbness, claimed Winter as its guest. In this stone the picture had woven for Capricorn[24] a tunic of faked fleece of goat-hair. The third stone, wearing a countenance of crystal-clear light, with his ban-

---

backwards with equal ease: Isid., *Etym.* 3.71.26; Bern. Silv. 1.3.126. *Imitatoria confictione* is a somewhat odd combination. In his *Summa* 10a Alan describes four types of resemblances; *Imitatoria* refers to resemblance in action: *Summa Quoniam homines* ed. P. Glorieux, *Archives* 20 (1953) 147. Alan means that the diadem was revolving and Cancer, while revolving with the diadem, manifested an additional revolution of his own.

[20] The Gemini, Castor and Pollux, were twin sons of Tyndarus and Leda. Cf. *Anticl.* 5.17, Sheridan 136-137.

[21] Pisces, a faint constellation.

[22] *In contradictoria parte.* See note 14 supra.

[23] The Youth of Ida is Ganymede, who became cup-bearer to the Gods. The cruet of the Youth of Ida is the constellation Aquarius (20 Jan. — 18 Feb.): Isidore, *Etym.* 3.71.2; cf. *Anticl.* 5.14, Sheridan 136.

[24] Capricorn (22 Dec. — 15 Jan): Isidore, *Etym.* 3.7.31; *Anticl.* 5.34, Sheridan 138.

ner of cold heralded the approach of Winter. In this stone the old man of Haemonia,[25] keeping his bow ever taut, threatened to wound but never fulfilled his threats by giving them effect.

Revelling in the light that favoured the other side, three attractive, clear gems delighted the eyes. The first of these, blazing with the purple tint of a rosy hue, brought a vision of roses to the eyes. In it a bull,[26] bearing aloft his insignia on his head, seemed to thirst for battle. Another gem, by its special blend of light, enriched the sisters in its band with its pleasing charm. In it a ram,[27] proud of the decorations on his forehead, demanded the leadership of the flock. The third gem, displaying the green of the emerald, contained a remedy that revived the sight of the eyes. In it fish,[28] swimming in an imaginary river, repeatedly carried out an exercise natural to them.

On the other diagonal[29] a set of three stones of starlike beauty sparkled with sweet smile. The first of these stones, shining with the noon-day light of a golden sun, showed forth the charm of

[25] Sagittarius (22 Nov. — 21 Dec.). He was originally the Thessalian Centaur, Chiron. Haemonia is a poetical name for Thessaly. Astronomers say that the centre of the Universe is somewhere in this constellation. Cf. *Anticl.* 5.14, Sheridan 136.

[26] The constellation Taurus (20 April — 20 May): Isid., *Etym.* 3.71.24; *Anticl.* 5.36, Sheridan 138.

[27] The constellation Aries (21 March — 19 April): Isid., *Etym.* 3.71.23-24.

[28] The constellation Pisces is represented by the *smaragdus*. Pliny, 37.16.63-64, deals with the soothing effects of the *smaragdus* on the eyes. He adds Nero "used to watch the fights between gladiators in a smaragdus." See Pliny, *Natural History*, ed. D. Eicholz, (Loeb Text, Cambridge, Mass. 1962) 10.212ff. and notes; U. T. Holmes, "Medieval Gem Stones," *Speculum* 9 (1934) 195-204.

[29] *Contradicente latere.* See Square of Opposition, note 14 supra.

never-failing beauty. In it, as the image-figure in the sculpture showed, Astraea,[30] by a certain priority due her brightness, entered the lists with the stars. The second stone, neither abounding in an overflow of brilliance nor begging sparklets for impoverished brightness, rejoiced in a modest flash. In it, in keeping with the principles of pictorial art, scales,[31] with their balanced tongue, guaranteed a decision on weights. The third stone, forever changing its appearance, now promised the blessings of fair weather, now clothed itself in clouds of darkness. In it, the form of a scorpion[32] shining forth promises laughter with its face, tears with the sting in its tail.

Below the abodes of these twelve stones, a set of seven gems,[33] forever maintaining a circular motion, in a marvellous kind of

[30] The constellation Virgo (23 Aug. — 22 Sept.): Isid. *Etym.* 3.71.28. Astraea, daughter of Jupiter and Themis, ruled the world during the Golden Age. When man became corrupt she left earth and returned to the heavens (Ovid, *Met.* 1.150; Juvenal 6.14-20). Nature will later tell a story of her own actions that is identical in some details with that of Astraea. Virgil, *Ecl.* 4.4ff., sings of Astraea's return to earth.

[31] The constellation Libra (23 Sept. — 22 Oct.): Isid., *Etym.* 3.71.29; *Anticl.* 5.33, Sheridan 138.

[32] The constellation Scorpio (23 Oct. — 21 Nov.): *Anticl.* 5.33, Sheridan 138. For the sting in the scorpion's tail, see Apocalypse 9.10.

[33] The seven Planets of medieval times — Sun, Moon, Mercury, Venus, Mars, Jupiter, Saturn. The gems are based on the description of the High Priest's vestments in Exodus 28.14-19, the stones of the heavenly city in Apoc. 21.19-21 and Martianus Capella's description of the crown of Juno in 1.74-76 (ed. Dick 34.5-35.4). See Hildebertus, *Carmina minora* 10.42 (Teubner 1969) 34. They are also found in Peter of Compostella, *De consolatione rationis*, ed. P. Blanco Soto 69.10-70.3. Marginal notes there refer the Sun (carbuncle), Jupiter (agate), Saturn (diamond) and Mars (asterite) to the four Cardinal Virtues — Prudence, Justice, Temperance, Fortitude. The gems of Venus (sapphire), Mercury (hyacinth) and the moon (crisolite) are referred to the three

merriment busied themselves with a verisimilar dance.[34] Nor was
this dance without its own sweet harmony: now it sports in semitones; now it blossoms forth in sonorous intermediate tones;
now with fuller range it advances to a melodious diapason. This
harmony with its drumming tones awakes our sensuousness as
we listen, and thus brings to our eyes the prelude to sleep.[35] But
since a moderate amount of sound lessens the impact on the ear
and an excessive amount causes a loathing, our ears were
revolted and grew torpid from the over-abundant supply of
sound.

Although these seven stones were not held in subjection to the
diadem itself by any bonds of union, yet never did they, by
absenting themselves, leave the sets of stars above bereft. The
stone farthest away was a diamond:[36] greedier than the others in

---

Theological Virtues — Faith, Hope and Charity. It should be noted that
these gems do not correspond exactly with the names given them in
English.

[34] Peter of Compostella, ed. P. Blanco Soto 55.6-7. Reference to the
ordered movement of the stars as a dance goes back far: Plato, *Tim.*
40c; *Epin.* 982E; Lucian, *De saltatione* 17.

[35] The Music of the Spheres: Macr., *Comm.* 2.3.1ff. refers to Plato's
statement (*Rep.* 10.617b) that a Siren sits on each of the spheres.
Macrobius adds that the divinities are thus provided with song. For the
"prelude to sleep" see Plato, *Tim.* 45D. Cf. *Anticl.* 4.332-369, Sheridan
130-135.

[36] Exodus 28.19; Pliny 37.15.55-61; Mart. Cap. 1.75, ed. Dick 35.8;
Marbod of Rennes, *Liber de gemmis*, PL 171.1739B-1740B. The *adamas* is
noted for its hardness, Isid., *Etym.* 12.1.14, 16.13.2-3. It represents
Saturn. Saturn had the longest orbit and slowest motion of any planet
known in medieval times. Its sidereal period is 29½ years. Its mean
synodic period is 378 days. This means that, when Earth passes Saturn
and makes a complete orbit, it will overtake Saturn in about 13 more
days. When Earth passes Mars it will make two full orbits plus approx-

tread, more lavish in inactivity, it spent an excessive amount of time in the orbit of its wide circuit. It was inert from frost, arising from a cold so great that its affinity with the nature of what originated it established that it was sprung from the star of Saturn. The second star was an agate.[37] By the proximity of its course to the others it became a closer associate of them: it transformed the hostility of some into goodwill and, by the influence of its royal power, it turned the childlike attachment of others into mature friendship. This charming accomplishment gave proof that this stone belongs, by a close kinship of nature, to the star of Jupiter. The third stone was an asterite. In it the king of steel had pitched camp and the effects of the star of Mars were there concentrated by a certain extension of his qualities.[38]

---

imately 50 days before it overtakes it again. Saturn was considered cold, unfriendly and ill-disposed towards natural and normal things: Ptolemy, *Tetrabiblos* 3.157, ed. F. E. Robbins (Loeb Text, Cambridge, Mass. 1940) 340-347; Mart. Cap. 8.852, 853, 856, 861, ed. Dick 448.10; 449.2, 12, 17; 450.16; 454.4; Bern. Silv. 2.5.45-73; *Anticl.* 4.462-483, Sheridan 134-135.

[37] Exod. 28.19; Pliny 37.54.139-142; Marbod, PL 171.1741A-1742A; Peter of Compostella, ed. Blanco Soto 69.15. *Achates* represents Jupiter, the friendly planet, exercising a beneficial influence on everything that comes in contact with it. Ptol., *Tetr.* 3.161.163, ed. Robbins 347-353; Isidore of Seville, *Etym.* 16.11.1 refers to its use by magicians to quell storms and stop the flow of rivers; Bern. Silv. 2.5.73-101; *Anticl.* 4.441-462, Sheridan 134.

[38] *Astrites.* Pliny has *asteria* and mentions an *astrion* and *astriotes* and states that all three are similar in their power of reflecting sunlight: 37.47.131-37.50.134. Alan's form probably comes from Mart. Cap. 1.76, ed. Dick 35.10. Isidore has the form *asterites* (*Etym.* 16.10.3). The name seems to have come from the Greek *asterĕs*, a mythical precious stone. Cf. Ps-Democritus, ed. M. Berthelot, *Collection des anciens alchimistes grecs* (Paris 1887) 50.14; D. Eichholz (Pliny, *Nat. hist.*,

Dreadful with its menacing appearance of lightning, it threatened the others with destruction. The fourth stone was a ruby.[39] This, bearing the image of the sun, outlawed by its shining candle the shadows of night and gave peaceful sleep to its brothers when their lamps were extinguished. Now, by the royal authority of its sovereignity, it bade the others to follow bypaths, now it granted them power of undisturbed movement.[40] A sapphire, joined to an amethyst, keeping close to the ruby's path and serving it like attendants, was never robbed of a view of the light mentioned above. Separated by a short distance from the sun, they run around his orb together with him or follow him, or one star following him grants the other the favour of preceding him.[41] By tendencies in nature, one of these two stars showed the

---

37.47.141) thinks that it may be "a very pale star-sapphire." The reading best supported is *calybis principatu*, not *caloris*. Chalybs meant steel and war-weapons of steel. This fits Mars, the god of War.

[39] *Carbunculus.* Exodus 28.18; Pliny 37.25.92-118; Isid., *Etym.* 16.14.1; Marbod PL 171.1754A-B. Denotation is not too definite. It probably includes rubies, red garnet and probably red spinel.

[40] Reference here is to retrograde motion of the planets. The speed of Earth is greater than that of the outer planets and its orbit is shorter. Thus, for example, Earth overtakes and passes Mars. As one views this from Earth, Mars seems to slow down as Earth approaches it, stop momentarily as Earth passes it, reverse its course as Earth leaves it behind and finally resume its regular motion. The apparent reversal is not over the exact course that Mars has followed but in a narrowish loop. The optical illusion was first explained by Johann Kepler (1571-1630). Cf. *Anticl.* 2.112-114, 4.37-39, Sheridan 70, 118.

[41] Sapphire and amethyst: Exod. 28:18, 39:11, 39:12; Pliny 37.38.119-120; 37.40.121. These stones represent Venus and Mercury. In classical times, Venus when west of the sun, was called *Lucifer*, the morning star. When east of the sun, it was called *Hesperus*, the evening star: Cic., *De. nat. deor.* 2.20.53. The same terminology is used today.

influence of Mercury, the other, that of Dione's daughter.[42]

The last stone was a pearl.[43] Lying nearest the edge of the reddish-glowing crown, shining with borrowed light, it begged support for its brightness from the ruby. This pearl was at times close to the above-mentioned light when waxing, when waning it pays homage to the rays of its light as though to the ruby and in submission begs that, once again adorned with light from above, it may carry around the insignia of its renewed brightness. At times, with the aid of regular reinforcements, it nurses the injuries to its damaged orb; at times bereft of its special light, it bewails the loss of its special dignity. Silvered over with crystalline brightness, it paralleled the performance of the star of the moon. The dignity of the above-mentioned diadem is highlighted by the brilliance of all these stones and in itself it produces an image of the firmament.

Her dress, woven from silk-smooth wool, kaleidoscopic in its various colours, served the purpose of a robe of office for the maiden. Changing circumstances, which substituted one hue for another, altered the garment with a varied display of colour. At first whitened to the brightness of the lily, it dazzled the eyes. Secondly, as though moved to repentance and struggling to

---

Alan shares the role between Venus and Mercury. Astronomically this is feasible as Mercury, when visible, trails the setting sun down the sky or rises before it in the morning. However, it is visible for so short a time that its role as morning or evening star is hardly worth considering. Cf. *Anticl.* 2.126.132, Sheridan 70-71.

[42] Venus.

[43] Apoc. 21:21; Pliny 9.54-59, 107-123; Marbod, PL 171.1766A-B. This gem is treated only incidentally in Pliny 9. He is really dealing with fish. In 17.6.15-16, he shows contempt for it. Alan is here referring to the moon: cf. *Anticl.* 2.133-169, Sheridan 71.

amend, it shone forth in a blood-red colour. Thirdly, at the peak of perfection, it gladdened the eyes with an emerald green. This garment, however, was woven so exceedingly fine that it evaded the searching eyes and its material reached such a degree of fineness that it and air shared the same nature. On it, as the eye would image a picture seen in a dream, was a packed convention of the animals of the air.[44]

There the eagle,[45] assuming first the form of a youth, secondly that of an old man, thirdly returning to his former state, makes his way back from Nestor to Adonis.[46] There the hawk,[47] gover-

---

[44] For soothing effect of green, see note 28 supra. For the convention of birds, cf. Chaucer, *The Parliament of Fowls* 316-371. This work has been the victim of as many interpretations as the *De planctu*.

[45] Psalm 102:5; Hugh of Fouilloy, *De bestiis et aliis rebus*, PL 177.55A. Hugh's work on birds is found in Migne 177 among the "doubtful works of Hugh of St. Victor." See M. Manitius, *Geschichte der lateinischen Literatur des Mittelalters* (München 1931) 3.277; H. Peltier, "Hugues de Fouilloy," in *Revue du moyen âge latin* 2 (1946) 41-42. The eagle is also mentioned in Matthew of Vendôme, *Ars versif.* 111, ed. Faral, *Ars poétiques* 149.45; T. H. White, *The Book of Beasts, being a Translation from a Latin Bestiary of the Twelfth Century* (London 1954) 105; *Physiologus latinus*, ed. F. Carmody (Paris 1939) 8.19; Theobaldus, *Physiologus*, ed. P. Eden (Leiden and Cologne 1972) 29.31. There is no ancient tradition of renewal of youth for the eagle and the authors who refer to it may be describing a renewal of plumage which is probably the correct interpretation of Psalm 102.5.

[46] Nestor was the garrulous but lovable old man in Homer. It is to be hoped that Alan did not accept Ovid's statement that he was over two hundred years. This arises from a misunderstanding of *Iliad* 1.250, where Nestor is said to have survived "two generations" i.e. about sixty years. For Adonis, see above, I, note 13.

[47] Pliny 10.9.22; Isid., *Etym.* 12.7.55-56; Bern. Silv. 1.3.453; Peter of Compostella 59.16; Hugh of Fouilloy, PL 177.21D; White, *Book of Beasts* 138-139.

nor of the aerial city, with the violence of a tyrant demanded
tribute from his subjects. There the kite,[48] playing the role of a
hunter, with his stealthy stalk acted the part of a hawk. There
the falcon[49] stirred up a civil war in the aerial city against the
heron,[50] but not with sides equally balanced. For when you beat
and I am just beaten, that should not be classified as a fight.[51]
There the ostrich,[52] rejecting life in a busy world, leading a life of
solitude, turned hermit, so to speak, haunted the deserts'
wilderness. There the swan,[53] the herald of his own death, pro-
phesied the end of his life by the strains of his honey-sweet lute.
There Nature rained down on the peacock[54] a flood of beauty so
great that you would think that she herself lived a beggar after-

---

[48] Pliny 10.12.28; Bern. Silv. 1.3.469; Hugh of Fouilloy, PL
177.41D-42A; White, Book of Beasts 103.

[49] Peter of Compostella 59.15; Isidore, Etym. 12.7.57; Sidonius
Apollinaris, Ep. 5.5.2., ed. W. Anderson, (Loeb Text, Cambridge,
1965) 2.182.

[50] Pliny 10.69.164; 11.52.140; 18.87.363; Bern. Silv. 1.3.445; Isid.,
Etym. 12.7.21 (where Lucan is quoted); Peter of Compostella 59.17;
Hugh of Fouilloy, PL 177.47B.

[51] Juvenal 3.289.

[52] Job 30:29; Isaias 13:21; 34.13; Jeremiah 50:39; Pliny 10.1.1; Isid.,
Etym. 12.7.20; Bern. Silv. 1.3.470; Peter of Compostella 59.19; Hugh
of Fouilloy, PL 177.35D; White, Book of Beasts 121; Physiologus
latinus, ed. Carmody 24.48.

[53] Statius, Silvae 5.3.81; Pliny 10.32.63; Bern. Silv. 1.3.447; Hugh of
Fouilloy, PL 177.53C; Matthew of Ven. Ars versif. 1.111, ed. Faral, Arts
Faral, Arts poétiques 149.32; White, Book of Beasts 118.

[54] 3 Kings 10:22; 2 Par. 9:21; Ovid, Met. 2.532; Fasti 6.177; Pliny
10.23.45; Isid., Etym. 12.7.9, 48; Peter of Compostella 60.4; Hugh of
Fouilloy, PL 177.53C; Matthew of Ven. Ars versif. 1.111, ed. Faral Arts
poétiques 148.23-24; White, Book of Beasts 149.

wards. There the phoenix[55] dead in himself, brought to life again in another phoenix, by some miracle of Nature raised himself from the dead by his death. There the bird of concord,[56] offering tithes of her offspring, paid her tax to Nature. There the sparrow[57] was reduced to the minimal height of the dwarf, while the crane,[58] on the other hand, rose to the height of the over-sized

[55] Pliny 10.2.3-5; Bern. Silv. 1.3.449; Peter of Compos. 59.27; Hugh of Fouilloy, PL 177.48B; White, *Book of Beasts* 125; *Physiologus latinus*, ed. Carmody 9.20.

[56] This is the stork according to the reading (*ciconia*) in Migne, PL 210.436A and the account in Peter of Compostella 59.28. Hugh of Fouilloy, PL 177.43Bff. refers to the peaceful coexistence of storks with other birds, the close relationship between parents and chicks and the kind nature of the birds. Cf. Ambrose, *Hexaemeron* 5.16.55, PL 14.244A; Pliny 10.31.61-62; Isid., *Etym.* 12.7.16-17; White, *Book of Beasts* 117. There is a tradition recorded (but questioned) by Vincent of Beauvais that the stork gives one of its offspring, as tribute, to the owner of the land where it has nested: *Speculum doctrinale*, lib. 15, cap. 153 (Douai 1624) 1481. This explains the "tithes of her offspring" mentioned by Alan here.

[57] Matthew 10:29; Luke 12:6; Pliny 10.52.107; 10.54.111; Isid., *Etym.* 12.7.68; Hugh of Fouilloy, PL 177.23B; Bern. Silv. 1.3.467; Matthew of Vendôme, *Ars versif.* 111, ed. Faral, *Arts poétiques* 149.41.

[58] Pliny 7.2.26-27; 10.30.58-60; Isid., *Etym.* 12.7.14-15; Hugh of Fouilloy, PL 177.40D; Bern. Silv. 1.3.456. The pygmies, a fabled race, were ever at war with the cranes but were always defeated: Arist., *Hist. anim.* 8.12.597ª 4-8; Pliny 4.11.44-45; Aul. Gell. 9.4.11. Giants and dwarfs together form a frequent picture in twelfth-century literature. They are generally mentioned in contexts where ancients and moderns are being compared. Thus it is said that the moderns can see further than the ancients as they stand, or sit, on their shoulders like dwarfs on the shoulders of giants. The origin of the phrase has given rise to much discussion. John of Salisbury attributed it to Bernard of Chartres: *Metalogicon* 3.4, *Joannis Saresberiensis episcopi Carnotensis*

giant.[59] There the barnyard cock, like a common man's astronomer, with his crow for a clock announces the hours. There the wild cock, scorning the inactivity of his domestic kin, set out for faraway places and roamed the woodland regions.[60] There the horned owl,[61] prophet of grief, sang in advance psalms

---

Metalogicon, ed. C. Webb (Oxford 1929) 136. It may, however, antedate Bernard: E. Jeauneau, "Nani gigantum humeris insidentes. Essai d'interpretation," *Vivarium* 5.2 (1967) 79-99. I am indebted to Professor Brian Stock for calling my attention to a scene described in Ordericus Vitalis, *The Ecclesiastical History* 8.17, ed. M. Chibnall (Oxford 1973) 4.237-250. To judge from this, it seems quite likely that the seeds of the phrase may well be found in Breton folklore of the eleventh century. Bernard of Chartres, a Breton, may have developed the idea.

[59] Many MSS have here a sentence: "There the pheasant, having borne the stresses of his native isle, came to our shores to be the delight of princes."

[60] The intelligene of the barnyard cock is emphasized in Job 38:36; Pliny 10.24.46-49; Hugh of Fouilloy, PL 177.33Bff.; Vincent of Beauvais, *Speculum doctrinale* 15.159 (Douai 1624) 1486. Pliny states that the lion fears the cock. The lion came to represent the devil (Ezechiel 2:25; 1 Peter 5:8). Thus evil spirits, that roam by night, flee at the crowing of the cock. Reference to cock-crow is frequent in Church Hymns: Ambrose, *Analecta hymnica* 50.4; Prudentius, *Liber cathemerinon*, ed. J. Bergman, CSEL 61 (1926) 1. There may be an echo of this in *Hamlet* act 1, sc. 1. Bernardus Silvestris, 1.3.462-463, identifies the wild cock with the pheasant.

[61] *Bubo*, the screech-owl, is mentioned in Leviticus 11.17; Virgil, *Aen.* 4.461-462; Ovid, *Met.* 5.539-552; Pliny 10.16.34-35; Isid., *Etym.* 12.7.39; Hugh of Fouilloy, PL 177.45A; Bern. Silv. 1.3.477. *Noctua*, the night-owl is mentioned less frequently: Leviticus 11:16; Baruch 6.21; Pliny 10.19.39; 18.87.362; White, *Book of Beasts* 113. For difference between these owls, see Isid., *Etym.* 12.7.40. For reference to Nature's drowsiness in fashioning the night-owl, cf. *Anticl.* 1.153-157, Sheridan 51.

of lamentation for the dead. There the night-owl grew filthy in a midden of such ugliness that one might think that Nature had been drowsy when she fashioned him. There the crow,[62] that knows beforehand what is to come, wasted his time in silly chatter. There the magpie, painted an undefinable colour,[63] forever maintained a sleepless devotion to argument.[64] There the jackdaw, with marvellous thievery, gathered a treasure of knickknacks and gave proof of his innate avarice.[65] There the dove,[66] intoxicated with Dione's sweet curse, was toiling in the

[62] Virgil, *Geor.* 1.388 and Horace, *Od.* 3.17.3 speak of the crow foretelling rain by its cries. Bernardus Silvestris 1.3.467 refers to its long life. Hugh of Fouilloy, PL 177.96c mentions its long life and prophetic powers. Cf. White, *Book of Beasts* 142-143; Matthew of Vendôme, *Ars versif.* 111, ed. Faral, *Arts poétiques* 149.43.

[63] In Greek and Latin an animal was described by its predominant colour. They did not have our "black-and-white" and such combinations. The areas of white and black in the magpie are so equal that they could not assign it a colour. This is the meaning of *dubiam* in Bern. Silv. 1.3.468.

[64] The nine daughters of Pierus and Evippa challenged the Muses to a contest in song. They were defeated and became insulting. They were turned into magpies but their former gift of speech and love of argument remained: Ovid, *Met.* 5.294-678; Pliny 10.59.118-119; Isid., *Etym.* 12.7.46; Matthew of Vendôme, *Ars versif.* 111, ed. Faral, *Arts poétiques* 149.32.

[65] Arne betrayed her native Siphnos for gold. She was turned into a jackdaw and retained her former greed. Ovid, *Met.* 7.465-468. Cf. Cicero, *Pro Flacco* 76; Pliny 10.41.77; Isid., *Etym.* 12.7.35; Peter of Comp. 60.5; Matthew of Vendôme, *Ars versif.* 111, ed. Faral, *Arts poétiques* 149.39.

[66] Osee 7.11; Pliny 10.52.104. Doves are sacred to Venus, Ovid, *Met.* 13.673; 15.386; Matthew of Vendôme, *Ars versif.* 111, ed. Faral, *Arts poétiques* 148.25. They draw her chariot, ibid. 14.596. Cf. Isid., *Etym.* 12.7.61; Bern. Silv. 1.3.458. Hugh of Fouilloy has several sections treating of the dove as a symbol of everything good (PL 177.15a-20d).

Cyprian's wrestling arena. There the raven,[67] with repulsive and shameful jealousy, did not admit that his offspring were his children until, in a sort of argument carried on with himself, he established this by proof from their black colour. There the partridge shrank, now from the attacks of the powers of air, now from the snares of huntsmen, now from the warning barking of dogs.[68] There the duck,[69] together with the goose,[70] obeying the

[67] Psalm 146:9 and Job 38:41-43 seem to imply that the raven neglects his offspring. Alan seems to attribute this to doubts on his part as to whether they are really his legitimate offspring, since he uses the word *zelotypia*, a rare word found only in two sections of the Old Testament, Numbers 5:14-30 and Ecclesiasticus 26:8-9. In Numbers it refers to rites open to a husband who doubts his wife's fidelity; in Ecclesiasticus it is used to describe the lack of peace in a home with a jealous wife. Cf. Juvenal 6.279. The proof from their black colour may echo the fable that the raven, who had the gift of speech, was once white but was changed to black for his treachery: Ovid, *Met.* 2.534-541. Pliny, 10.60.121-124, has a story of the life, death and funeral of a talking raven. However, Bernardus Silvestris (1.3.473-475) seems to indicate that the raven forgets where the nest with his young is and presumably would not take food to any nest until he had identified his own. Vincent of Beauvais' account agrees with Alan: *Speculum Naturae* 16.61 (Douai 1624) 1192.

[68] The partridge fares ill in Pliny 10.51.99-103; Isid., *Etym.* 12.7.63; Hugh of Fouilloy, PL 177.49B. Emphasis is laid on his sexual excesses and aberrations. This may derive from Arist., *Hist. anim.* 9.8.613^{b}25-614^{a}25 The references in Alan are deductions from Ovid, *Met.* 8.256-259, where it is stated that the partridge "does not lift her body high in flight . . . but flutters along the ground." Indeed Aristotle mistakenly thinks that the partridge is entirely incapable of flight. A dog can jump high enough to pull a partridge out of the air. Matthew of Vendôme is interested in the bird's value as food: *Ars versif.* 111, ed. Faral, *Arts poétiques* 148.30.

[69] Pliny 8.41.101; 18.87.362; Isid., *Etym.* 12.7.51; Bern. Silv. 1.3.466; Hugh of Fouilloy, PL 177.97B; White, *Book of Beasts* 151-152.

[70] Pliny 10.26.51-58; Isid., *Etym.* 12.7.52; Hugh of Fouilloy, PL

same laws of life, wintered in their native stream. There the turtle-dove,[71] bereft of her mate, scorning to add further verses to her love song, rejected the joys of a second mating with another. There the parrot fashioned on the anvil of his throat a mint for human speech.[72] There the quail,[73] failing to recognise the deception in inflection of speech, was deceived by the trickery of an imitative voice. There the woodpecker,[74] the architect of his own little home, using his beak as a pickaxe, built his cottage in a holm-oak. There the meadow-pipit, eschewing the role of stepmother, took to her mother's breast the offspring of another, the cuckoo, to be her own son. She was, however, repaid with a death-dealing reward: she recognised her step-son

---

177.46D-47B; Bern. Silv. 1.3.476. It seems to be the wild duck and wild goose that are in question here. Cf. Ovid, *Met.* 11.773 where *anas fluvialis* is used for wild duck.

[71] Pliny 10.52.105; 30.21.68; Isid., *Etym.* 12.7.60; Bern. Silv. 1.3.463; Peter of Comp. 60.1; Hugh of Fouilloy, PL 177.25C-D; Theobaldus, *Physiologus* 68-69; Matthew of Vendôme, *Ars versif.* 111, ed. Faral, *Arts poétiques* 148.27; White, *Book of Beasts* 145-146.

[72] Pliny 10.57.116-117; Isid., *Etym.* 12.7.24; Bern. Silv. 1.3.472; Peter of Comp. 59.25; Hugh of Fouilloy, PL 177.94D; Matthew of Vendôme, *Ars versif.* 111, ed. Faral, *Arts poétiques* 148.19; Anon., *Isidorus Versificatus* 93, ed. Hünemörder 113; White, *Book of Beasts* 112-113.

[73] This bird is prized as food and can be lured by a decoy: Pliny 10.33.65-69; Bern. Silv. 1.3.463; Peter of Comp. 59.25. There may be a reference to the belief that migrating quails seek a bird of some other species to lead them: Isid., *Etym.* 12.7.65; Hugh of Fouilloy, PL 177.49D; White, *Book of Beasts* 148-149.

[74] Pliny 10.20.40-41; Isid., *Etym.* 12.7.47; Bern. Silv. 1.3.463; Hugh of Fouilloy, PL 177.95D; Matthew of Vendôme, *Ars versif.* 111, ed. Faral, *Arts poétiques* 49.37; White, *Book of Beasts* 148-149.

but did not get to know her son.[75] There the swallow,[76] returned from his migration, covers with mud a nest-home beneath a beam. There the nightingale,[77] renewing the lament for her defloration, makes excuses for her dishonoured chastity as she

[75] Pliny 10.11.25-27, uses *coccyx* for the cuckoo. He regards it as a transformed hawk but describes its parasitic habits. Cf. 18.66.249. Of the some one hundred and twenty-seven species of cuckoo, forty-seven are parasitic. The parasitic cuckoo lays an egg in the nest of another bird and removes one of the other bird's eggs. The young cuckoo hatches in twelve days, usually before the other eggs in the nest. It removes the other eggs or chicks from the nest. It is cared for by its foster-parents until it can fly. Alan states that it lays its egg in the nest of the *curuca* (or *curruca*). What is the *curuca*? Some manuscripts of Juvenal 6.275 have a reading *curruca* describing a husband hoodwinked by an adulterous wife. Such a one could presumably be carrying the adulterer's child. Did Alan have this reading? Aristotle, *Hist. anim.* 6.7.364ᵃ2, mentions the *hypolais* as one of the birds whose nest hosts the cuckoo's eggs but the identity of this bird has not been established. I have translated the word as meadow pipit for no better reason that that I remember from my boyhood that the cuckoo's preference for this bird's nest caused the meadow pipit to be called *banaltra na cuaiche*, "the cuckoo's nurse."

[76] Pliny 10.34.70-71; 49.92; 55.114; Isid., *Etym.* 12.7.70; Peter of Comp. 60.9; Hugh of Fouilloy, PL 177.42A.

[77] Tereus, King of Thrace, was married to Progne, daughter of Pandion, King of Athens. Progne was anxious that her sister, Philomela, should visit her. Tereus went to bring her. He fell in love with her and when they reached Thrace he raped her, shut her up in a hut and cut out her tongue to insure silence. She wove the story into a piece of embroidery and sent it to her sister, Progne. Progne brought her to the palace and in revenge they killed Itys, Progne's son by Tereus, and served his flesh to her husband. When he sought to take vengeance on them, Philomela was changed into a nightingale and Progne into a swallow: Ovid, *Met.* 6.438-670; Bern. Silv. 1.3.459; Peter of Comp. 59.31; Matthew of Vendôme, *Ars versif.* 111, ed. Faral *Arts poétiques* 148.15.

plays a sweet harmony. There the lark,[78] like a celebrated harpist, gifted with the art of song, not from a study of technique but from Nature's teaching, displayed a beak with a harp's power. She separated tones into subtle particles, kept dividing semitones until they reached indivisible units. There the bat,[79] a hermaphrodite among birds, held a zero rating among them.[80] These living things, although they had there a kind of figurative existence, nevertheless seemed to live there in the literal sense.

Muslin, with its white colour faded to green, which the maiden, as she herself later explained, had woven without seams, was not cheapened by common material but was gay with delicate workmanship. It served the purpose of a mantle and, entwined with many an intricate pattern, gave the impression of colour reflected on water. In it a story in pictures gave an account of the nature of aquatic animals, dividing them into their various kinds.

There the whale,[81] with his long cragged outgrowths, vied with the rocks and with the impact of his turreted body, rammed ships, the sea's little towns. There the sea dog,[82] adding a two-fold con-

---

[78] Pliny 11.44.121; Bern. Silv. 1.3.466; Peter of Comp. 59.31; Matthew of Vendôme, *Ars versif.* 111, ed. Faral, *Arts poétiques* 148.22.

[79] Pliny 10.81.168; 11.62.164; Isid., *Etym.* 12.7.36; Peter of Comp. 60.10; Hugh of Fouilloy, PL 177.95c; White, *Book of Beasts* 140-141. The bat was regarded as part bird, part mouse.

[80] *Cifr.* This is a rare twelfth-century Arabic derivative. Literally it means "zero" and figuratively "useless." It is found also in Alan's *Liber parabolarum*, PL 210.586c and in the *Anticlaudianus* 2.438, Sheridan 87.

[81] Pliny 9.2.4, 5.12-14 (where sinking of ship is mentioned), 15.41; Isid., *Etym.* 12.6.8; Peter of Comp. 58.28; Theobaldus, *Physiologus* 56-59.

[82] Pliny 9.55.10; Ambrose, *Hexaemeron* 5.2.5, CSEL 32.143.16; Isid., *Etym.* 12.6.5; Peter of Comp. 59.5. Alan may be thinking of the title of Ausonius' *Epigrammata* 13, *De lepore capto a cane marino*: PL 19.827c.

fusion to the equivocal indication of barking in his name by never resorting to barking,[83] chased the hares[84] of his own element in the sea-glades. There the sturgeon,[85] set apart by his noble body, offered the blessed boon of his flesh for the tables of kings. There the herring,[86] the most common of fish, by his wide availability relieved the hunger of the poor. There the

[83] Meaning is somewhat obscure. Barking (*latratio*) strictly refers to dogs. However it is used at times to refer to things that have little connection with a dog's bark. It is, for example, used to designate the roaring waves in Silius Italicus 5.397 and Statius, *Achill.* 1.451. Thus the term is equivocal and not univocal. Peter of Compostella states that the sea-dog does not bark. Alan may mean that, despite his name, barking cannot be attributed to him either univocally or equivocally. Cf. *Summa Quoniam homines*, 10, 73, ed. P. Glorieux, *Archives* 20 (1953) 49, 221.

[84] Pliny 9.72.155; 32.1.8; Isid., *Etym.* 12.6.23. This fish is said to be poisonous even on contact.

[85] *Sturgio.* This is probably from the Low Latin *sturio.* The classical word is *acipenser.* Pliny, 9.27.60, states that it had lost its esteem. Its former high rating is obvious from Cicero, *Tuscul.* 3.18, *De fin.* 2.8; Horace, *Sat.* 2.2.47.

[86] *Allec.* Variants include *alec, hallec, alex, halex.* The common use of the word is for the sediment of a fish, *garum*: Pliny 31.8.95. It, or a diminutive of it, *halecula,* is used to denote an unidentified saltwater fish: Columella, *De re rustica* 6.8.2; 8.15.16; Isid. *Etym.* 12.6.39. There is a theory that the German *häring,* "herring," comes from *halex*: *Deutsches Wörterbuch* ed. J. Grimm and W. Grimm, Band 4, Abt 2 (Leipzig 1877) 1104-1105. Around 1520 L. Andrewe identified *alec* with the herring: "Extracts about Fish," iii, from Andrewe's "The noble lyfe and natures of man, Of bestes serpentys fowles and fisshes y be moste knowen," in *The Babees Book*, ed. Fred J. Furnivall, EETS OS 32 (London 1868; reprint, New York 1969). Alan's reference to the wide availability of the *allec* and its role as a staple in the diet of the poor aptly describes the herring.

plaice[87] with the sweet taste of his flesh made up for the absence of meat in the austerity of Lent. There the mullet[88] with the sweet inducements of his flesh proved attractive to the palate as an appetizer. There the trout entered the bights and when christened in the open sea was called a salmon.[89] There the dolphin,[90] appearing as a prophet, foretold the billowy storms that lay ahead for ships at sea. There a sirenian,[91] a fish in the loins, was seen to have a human face. There the moon robbed of its own light, like one in envious rage, avenged her own deprivation on the shellfish and they, as though in the throes of a new moon, paid the penalty for the moon's impoverishment.[92] The middle section of

[87] This is from the Old French *plaiz*, which goes back to the *platessa* of Ausonius, *Epist.* 4.60, MGH *Auct. Ant.* 5.2.161. Cf. Bern. Silv. 1.4.436; Peter of Comp. 59.7.

[88] The bearded mullet was highly prized by connoisseurs. In the reign of Tiberius three mullets fetched a price of 30,000 sesterces: Suet., *Tib.* 34. On another occasion Tiberius put up for auction a 4½ pound mullet that had been presented to him. It was sold for 5,000 sesterces. However, the bidders, Apicius and Octavius, were activated by more than an appreciation of the fine quality of the fish: Seneca, *Ep.* 95.42. Cf. Pliny 9.30.64-67; Isid., *Etym.* 12.6.25; Bern. Silv. 1.3.435; Peter of Comp. 59.8; Pseudo-Hugh of St. Victor, PL 177.106A; White, *Book of Beasts* 203.

[89] *Trucula*, diminuative of *tructa*: Isid., *Etym.* 12.6.6. "Salmon": Pliny 9.32.68; Ausonius, *Idyll* 10, PL 19.889A; Bern. Silv. 1.3.437; Peter of Comp. 58.32.

[90] Pliny 9.7.20-10.23; Isid., *Etym.* 12.6.11; Bern. Silv. 1.3.417; Peter of Comp. 58.31; Pseudo-Hugh of St. Victor, PL 177.105C; White, *Book of Beasts* 200.

[91] Bern. Silv. 1.3.428; Peter of Comp. 58.29; Theobaldus, *Physiologus* 60-61; Pseudo-Hugh of St. Victor, PL 177.78A; White, *Book of Beasts* 134-135.

[92] For the effect of the moon on *conchylia*, see Cicero, *De divinatione* 2.33; Horace, *Sat.* 2.4.30; Statius, *Silvae* 4.6.11; Bern. Silv. 1.3.423-424.

the cloak had been assigned to these inhabitants of the sea
regions. The remaining section of the mantle showed many fish
that were strangers to the sea and, roaming the various streams,
had taken up their abode in a homeland of fresh water.[93]

There the pike,[94] relying on the commands of a despot rather
than the demands of merit, imprisoned his subjects in the
dungeon of his own belly. There the barbel,[95] renowned for a
body of no mean size, lived on friendly terms with the lowliest of
the fish. There the shad,[96] spring-time's companion, which,
when in season, offers the delights of his truly delicious flavour,
waited on man's taste. There the lamprey,[97] pierced with many a
window-like opening, was studiously working on prologues to

[93] Bern. Silv. 1.3.431-432.

[94] Ausonius, *Idyll.* 10, PL 19.889C (= *Mosella* 122, MGH *Auct. Ant.*
5.2.86). Later writers were not to share Ausonius' distaste for the pike:
Dialogus Ratii et Everardi, ed. N. M. Häring, "A Latin Dialogue on the
Doctrine of Gilbert of Poitiers," *Mediaeval Studies* 15 (1953) 268-269.
Cf. Bern. Silv. 1.3.422 and 438; Peter of Comp. 59.9; Pseudo-Hugh of
St. Victor, PL 177.106A. Despite separate listings by Bern. Silv., it is
probable that *lucius* and *lupus* both refer to the pike: White, *Book of
Beasts* 202, note 4.

[95] Ausonius, *Idyll,* 10, PL 19.889C; Bern. Silv., 1.3.419; Peter of
Comp. 59.10. This fish attains a weight of 50 lbs. His weight and the
four fleshy filaments hanging from his mouth would make him by far
the most formidable of the fresh water fish mentioned.

[96] Ausonius, *Idyll.* 10, PL 19.899C; Bern. Silv. 1.3.437; Peter of
Comp. 58.33.

[97] Pliny 9.81.171; Isid., *Etym.* 12.6.42-43; Bern. Silv. 1.5.410;
Pseudo-Hugh of St. Victor, PL 177.108C; White, *Book of Beasts* 209.
Elaborate banquets began with a serving of lamprey: Pliny 35.46.162.
Alan maintains that gluttony is the gateway to other vices, pp. 174-175
infra. Cf. Alcuin, *De virtutibus et vitiis*, PL 101.633C.

passion for diners. There the eel,[98] imaging a serpent, was believed, because of a certain similarity of traits, to be the
serpent's grandchild. There the perch,[99] mailed with javelins of
thorn, was less afraid of the attacks of the pike. There the chub
regained by his scrofulous head what he lost by the spareness of
the lower parts of his body.[100] These figures, exquisitely imprinted on the mantle like a painting, seemed by a miracle to be
swimming.

A linen tunic,[101] with pictures from the embroider's art, concealed the maiden's body beneath its folds. This tunic, bestarred
with many a colour, gathered into folds to make the material
heavier, sought to approximate the element, earth. On the first
section of this garment, man, divesting himself of the indolence
of self-indulgence, tried to run a straight course through the
secrets of the heavens with reason as charioteer. In this section
the tunic had suffered a rending of its parts and showed the effects of injuries and insults.[102] In the other sections, however, the
parts had sustained no injury from division or discord in the

---

[98] Pliny 9.38.74; Pseudo-Hugh of St. Victor, PL 177.108A; White,
Book of Beasts 209. *Anguilla*, "the eel," was thought to be a derivative
of *anguis*, "a serpent."

[99] Pliny 9.24.57; Ausonius, *Idyll*. 10, PL 19.889B (= *Mosella* 115, MGH
Auct. Ant. 5.2.85); Bern. Silv. 1.3.435.

[100] Cato, *De re rustica* 158.1; Ausonius, *Idyll*. 10, PL 19.888D
(= *Mosella* 85, MGH *Auct. Ant.* 5.2.85).

[101] Genesis 37:3.

[102] The rending of the garment goes back to Boethius' description of
Philosophia in *De cons. phil.* Pr. 1.22-24 (Stewart-Rand 130ff.). There
it signifies the injury done Philosophia by various sects. Here it denotes
the injury done to Nature by man. Cf. *Anticl.* 1.313-315, Sheridan 58.

beautiful harmony of their unbroken surface.[103] In these a kind of magic picture made land animals come alive.

There the elephant,[104] rising on high in the size of his prodigious frame, increased by manifold interest the body deposited with him by nature. There the camel,[105] ugly with the peaks on his scrofulous body, serves man's purposes like a hired servant. There horns, taking the place of a helmet, seemed to equip the buffalo's[106] head for war. There the bull,[107] harassing the earth with his hooves, thundering with bellows, foretold the lightning stroke of his attack. There the oxen,[108] eschewing the belligerence of the bulls, gaped like country bumpkins engaged in menial tasks.

[103] All animals, except man, follow the instincts given them by Nature.

[104] Pliny 8.1.1; Isid., *Etym.* 12.2.14; Bern. Silv. 1.3.205; Peter of Comp. 57.10; Pseudo-Hugh of St. Victor, PL 177.72B; Theobaldus, *Physiologus* 64-67; White, *Book of Beasts* 24-28.

[105] Pliny 8.26.67; Isid., *Etym.* 12.1.35; Bern. Silv. 1.3.205; Peter of Comp. 57.10; Pseudo-Hugh of St. Victor, PL 177.90B; White, *Book of Beasts* 79-80.

[106] Pliny 8.15.38. He regards *bubalus* as a vulgar and mistaken name for *urus*, the *auroch*, a now extinct species: Isid., *Etym.* 12.1.33; Bern. Silv. 1.3.206; Peter of Comp. 57.17; Pseudo-Hugh of St. Victor, PL 177.90A; White, *Book of Beasts* 78.

[107] Pliny 8.70.181-182; Isid., *Etym.* 12.1.29; Bern. Silv. 1.3.217; Peter of Comp. 57.16; Pseudo-Hugh of St. Victor, PL 177.89D; White, *Book of Beasts* 77.

[108] Pliny 8.70.176-180; Isid., *Etym.* 12.1.27-30; Bern. Silv. 1.3.219; Pseudo-Hugh of St. Victor, PL 177.90A; White, *Book of Beasts* 77. Alan attributes to the ox the qualities that Peter of Compostella assigns to the ass, 57.14-15 and the quiet ox took the place of the gentle farm horse of later times.

There the horse,[109] urged on by his impetuous mettle, joining his rider in battle, broke a lance with the enemy. There the ass,[110] offending our ears with his idle braying, as though a musician by antiphrasis, introduced barbarisms into his music. There the unicorn,[111] lulled on a virgin's breast, in his sleep passed into the repose of death at his enemy's hand. There the lion,[112] gently murmuring tuneful rumblings in his cubs' ears, by a wondrous magic song of nature, lit up the spark of life. There the bear,[113] bringing forth with difficulty her shapeless offspring through the portals of her nose, fashioning them by licking them over and over with the stilus of her tongue, gave them an improved

[109] Pliny devotes a great deal of space to horses: 8.64-67, 154-167. He has a very high regard for their intelligence: Isid., *Etym.* 12.1.43-48; Bern. Silv. 1.3.213; Peter of Comp. 57.13; Pseudo-Hugh of St. Victor, PL 177.91B; White, *Book of Beasts* 84-88.

[110] Pliny 8.68.167; Columella, *De re rustica* 7.1.1-3. The name *asinus* was by antiphrasis connected with the Greek *aeidein*, to sing. In addition the ass was regarded as the least responsive of all animals to music: Aul. Gell. 3.16.13; Jerome, *Ep.* 27.2, CSEL 54.224.4. *Distinctiones* PL 210.712B-C has many meanings for "ass"; Bern. Silv. 1.3.213; Peter of Comp. 57.14; Pseudo-Hugh of St. Victor, PL 177.91A; White, *Book of Beasts* 82.

[111] Psalms 21:22, 28:6, 77:69, 91:11, Isaias 34:7; Pliny 8.30.72, 11.106.255; Anon., *Isidorus Versificatus* 43, ed. Hünemörder 109. *Unicornis* was adopted as a Latin equivalent of the Greek *monokeros*. The animal is legendary and seems to have been confused with the rhinoceros, the wild ox and various species of antelope.

[112] Pliny 8.17.42-58; Isid., *Etym.* 12.2.5; Bern. Silv. 1.3.209; Peter of Comp. 57.19; Pseudo-Hugh of St. Victor, PL 177.56D; Theobaldus, *Physiologus* 24-27; Anon., *Isidorus Versificatus* 37-40, ed. Hünemörder 108; White, *Book of Beasts* 7-11.

[113] Pliny 8.54.126-127; Isid., *Etym.* 12.2.22; Bern. Silv. 1.3.209; Pseudo-Hugh of St. Victor, PL 177.67B-68D; White, *Book of Beasts* 45-46.

appearance. There the wolf,[114] adopting the role of a highwayman, by lying in hiding, deserved to swing aloft on gallows row. There the panther,[115] rampaging in more open robbery, hunts the herds of cattle not only with his pelt but with his own special essence. There the tiger,[116] with frequent shedding of innocent blood, violently attacked the citizen of the cattle-state. There the wild ass,[117] throwing off the slavery of the tame ass, freed by the decree of nature, lived on the proud mountain tops. There the boar,[118] with his flashing armour of teeth, sold his own

[114] Isid., *Etym.* 12.2.23-24; Bern. Silv. 1.3.215; Peter of Comp. 57.27; Pseudo-Hugh of St. Victor, PL 177.67B-68D; White, *Book of Beasts* 56-61. Alan describes the wolf in terms used by Peter of Compostella to describe the hare: 57.30-31.

[115] Pliny 8.22.63, 10.94.202; Bern. Silv. 1.3.215; Peter of Comp. 57.21; Pseudo-Hugh of St. Victor, PL 177.69D-72B; Theobaldus, *Physiologus* 70-73; White, *Book of Beasts* 14-17. The names "pard," "leopard" and "panther," refer to the same animal. The common belief was that a panther gorged himself, slept for three days, awoke and belched, giving forth a very sweet smell which attracted all animals except the dragon. This is the *substantia* referred to by Alan. The leopard also chooses a spot where his skin will blend with the leaves or grass around him and waits for his prey. This is the hunting "with his pelt" that Alan mentions.

[116] Isid., *Etym.* 12.2.7; Bern. Silv. 1.3.210; Peter of Comp. 57.22; Pseudo-Hugh of St. Victor, PL 177.83B-C; Anon., *Isidorus Versificatus* 47, ed. Hünemörder 109; White, *Book of Beasts* 12-13.

[117] The wild ass is frequently mentioned in Scripture: Job 6:5; 11:12; 24:5; 39:5; Psalm 103:11; Ecclesiasticus 13:23; Isaias 32:14; Jeremias 2:24; Daniel 5:21; Osee 8:9; Pliny 8.46.108, 8.69.174; Isid., *Etym.* 12.1.39; Bern. Silv. 1.3.221; White, *Book of Beasts* 82-84.

[118] Virgil, *Geor.* 3.249; Ovid, *Met.* 8.773; Tibullus 4.3.2-3; Pliny 18.1.2; Isid., *Etym.* 12.1.27; Bern. Silv. 1.3.210; Pseudo-Hugh of St. Victor, PL 177.89C; Peter of Comp. 57.23; White, *Book of Beasts* 40-42.

life to the hounds at the price of many a gash. There the dog,[119] harassing the breezes with imaginary wounds,[120] bit the air with persistent snapping of teeth.

There the stag and doe,[121] fleet with speed of foot, saving their lives by keeping ahead, cheated the chasing dogs out of their unfair bites. There the goat,[122] clad in a skilful pretence of wool, seemed to offend our nose with a four day stench.[123] There the ram,[124] dressed in a more noble robe of office, rejoicing in a plurality of wives, robbed marriage of its dignity. There the little fox,[125] ridding himself of the stupidity of a beast, ardently

[119] Pliny 8.61.142; Isid., *Etym.* 12.2.25-26; Bern. Silv. 1.3.223; Pseudo-Hugh of St. Victor, PL 177.65c, 86B; White, *Book of Beasts* 61-67.

[120] Cf. *Anticl.* 1.130, Sheridan 122.

[121] Isid., *Etym.* 12.1.18; Bern. Silv. 1.3.207-208; Peter of Comp. 57.29; Pseudo-Hugh of St. Victor, PL 177.64A, Theobaldus, *Physiologus* 49-51; White, *Book of Beasts* 37.

[122] Hor., *Ep.* 1.18.15-16; Isid., *Etym.* 12.1.15; Bern. Silv. 1.3.211; Peter of Comp. 57.26; Pseudo-Hugh of St. Victor, PL 177.63B; White, *Book of Beasts* 40-42.

[123] John 11:39; cf. Hor., *Od.* 1.17.7.

[124] The ram is mentioned more frequently than any other animal in Scripture. He was the animal most frequently offered in sacrifice. Sacrifice of rams was also a Roman practice: Varro, *De lingua latina* 6.12; Virgil, *Aen.* 7.175; Pliny 34.19.80; Tac., *Hist.* 5.4. There may be an echo of this in Alan's *trabeatus*, "in robes of office." Cf. Isid., *Etym.* 13.1.11; Peter of Comp. 57.25; White, *Book of Beasts* 73-74.

[125] Persius 5.117; Hor., *Ars poetica* 437; Isid., *Etym.* 12.2.29; Bern. Silv. 1.3.217; Peter of Comp. 57.28; Pseudo-Hugh of St. Victor, PL 177.59A; Theobaldus, *Physiologus* 44-47; White, *Book of Beasts* 53-54. See *Reynard the Fox, The Epic of the Beast* by William Caxton — text modernised by W. P. Stallybrass (London-New York, 1924?).

sought the superior cunning of man. There the hare,[126] seized
with a fit of black fear, terrified not of sleep but of the paralysis
of fear, dreamt of the approach of hounds. There the rabbit,[127]
tempered the rage of the cold for us with his pelt and with his
own flesh fought off hunger's attack on us. There the squirrel,[128]
disdaining to be wed to an inferior cloth, was joined to purple by
the elegant stitch of matrimony. There the beaver,[129] to avoid
suffering complete dismemberment of his body by his enemies,

[126] Hor., *Ep.* 2.35; *Od.* 1.37.18; Isid., *Etym.* 12.1.23; Bern. Silv.
1.3.220; Peter of Comp. 57.30. The meaning is not too clear. According
to Cato hare's flesh induced prolonged sleep: quoted by Diomedes, *Ars
grammatica*, ed. H. Keil 1.362.22-23. Alan may mean that the hare is
not so much afraid of sleep as of becoming a somnific dish.

[127] I can find no other reference to the value of the rabbit in fur-
nishing food and clothing. Most references to them are far from com-
plimentary. They are accused of undermining cities and causing famine
by ruining crops: Pliny 3.5.79, 8.43.104, 8.81.217; Solinus 23.12, ed.
Mommsen 105.3.

[128] *Cisimus* or *scisimus*. Bern. Silv. 1.3.230. For want of something
better and influenced by the suggestions in the *Medieval Latin Word-
List* (Oxford 1934) and the *Lexicon mediae et infimae latinitatis
Polonorum* 2 (Wrocklaw-Kraków-Warszawa 1959) I am translating this
by "squirrel," the normal Latin for which is *sciurus*: Pliny 8.57.138;
11.100.246.

[129] There are frequent references to the belief that the beaver was
hunted for valuable medicine that could be extracted from his testicles
and that, when closely chased, he bit off his testicles and left them to his
pursuers with the hope that, satisfied with these, they would abandon
the chase: Cicero, *Pro Scauro* 2.5; Juvenal 12.34; Pliny 8.47.109,
32.13.26; Peter of Comp. 57.24; Pseudo-Hugh of St. Victor, PL
177.61A; Anon., *Isid. Versif.* 45-46, ed. Hünemörder 109. The last mentioned envisages either a male beaver pursued a second time (or if not
that, a female beaver) and trying to show his pursuers that he no longer
has what they are seeking.

cut off his hindmost parts. There the lynx[130] enjoyed such clearness of sight that compared with him the other animals seemed to be blear-eyed. There the marten[131] and the sable,[132] by the excellence of their skins, brought to perfection the imperfect beauty of the mantles that called for their help.

A presentation akin to a stage production offered these representations of animals as a delightful feast, so to speak, for the eyes of the beholders. I did not establish by any authority that would give certainty what fancies, shown by way of pictures, played on the upper part of the shoes[133] and the underclothing that lay concealed beneath the outer garments. However, as certain helps toward establishing a slim probability indicated, I am inclined to think that a smiling picture made merry there in the realms of herbs and trees. There trees, I think, were now clad in coats of russet,[134] now tressed with leaves of

---

[130] Pliny, 8.57.137; Isid., *Etym.* 12.2.20; Bern. Silv. 1.3.225; Peter of Comp. 57.20; Pseudo-Hugh of St. Victor, PL 177.84B; White, *Book of Beasts* 22.

[131] Old French is *martrine*. Cf. Giraldus Cambrensis, *Topographia Hibernica* 1.24, ed. J. F. Dimock, *Giraldi Cambrensis opera* 5, Rolls Series 21.5 (London 1867) 78. He has *martrinarum*, but see variants and Du Cange 5.290; Bern. Silv. 1.3.231.

[132] Old French is *sable* and is referred to a medieval Latin word *sabelum* or *sabellum*. Du Cange, 7.248, has *sabelum* which he seems to identify with the marten.

[133] Ordinary Roman footwear comprised the *solea* corresponding to our sandal and the *calceus* which covered the entire foot. Alan uses *caliga* which normally means the high boot of a soldier. This would disclaim any softness in Nature and its upper part would be covered by her long garments.

[134] *Purpureus* covers a wide range of colours. We find it applied to the rose-flower (Hor. *Od.* 3.15.15), to dawn (Ovid, *Met.* 3.184), to fire (Stat. *Achill.* 1.161), to blood (Virgil, *Aen.* 9.349), to lips (Hor. *Od.* 3.3.12).

green, were now bringing forth young, fragrant flower-buds, now showing their age in the growing strength of their offspring. But since I know this series of pictures not by the certainty that can be relied on but by the slippery path of probability alone, I pass over this series, leaving it to rest in peace and quiet. The lower parts of her boots, drawing on soft leather for their material, followed the form of her feet so closely that they seemed to have grown on them and in marvellous manner to be branded on them. By the pictures' genius shades of flowers, falling little below truth and reality, were there with their charm.

III

Metre 2

There[1] the beautiful rose, faithfully reproduced, differing but little from its actual appearance, with its own hue matched royal purple and dyed the ground blood-red. There outclassing[2] its fellow-flowers was the delightful, fragrant bloom of Adonis[3] and the noble lily with its silvery sheen enriched fertile field and valleys deep.

There the thyme, aspiring to rival the rest of the flowers, entering the lists with an appearance different from them,[4] vied with the companionable flower of Narcissus,[5] and the droll streams laughed with quiet murmur. The columbine, with its flower-bearing appearance, shone forth as the light-bearer of all

[1] Metre: minor Asclepiads.

[2] *Concludens* has echoes of Rhetoric where it means "to round off a speech."

[3] Very probably the anemone: see Ovid, *Met.* 10.735-739. Later the White Narcissus or Pheasant's Eye was called the flower of Adonis.

[4] Thyme is a shrubby plant and not really a flower. However, it grows in such abundance that it is found wherever there are flowers. Its pleasant odour and the excellence of its honey earned it frequent mention in poetry: Hor., *Od.* 4.2.27; Vergil, *Aen.* 1.440 and *Ecl.* 7.37. For its numerous medical uses see Pliny 21.89.154-157.

[5] Narcissus fell in love with his own reflection in water and his shade still gazes on it in the Stygian pool. This may explain Alan's use of *socius* to qualify the flower into which Narcissus had been transformed.

flowers. The little violet, telling of Spring's leisure-time, a pictured face full of attraction, bestarred the arbutus. Here Nature had ordered to come to life that species of flower which had a leaf with a king's name,[6] yet was never to feel the writer's thumb. These are the riches of Spring and her garb, the beauty of earth and its stars; these the picture brought forth by its powers, giving an image of flowers by a skillfully deceptive art. Spring, lavish in favours, ennobles the meadows with these garments of flowers in bloom. These meadows give linen, these others give purple when the zephyr's right hand has clothed them.

[6] This cryptic description refers to the *basilisca*. In strict Latin its name is *regia* and the English equivalent is adderwort: R. Gunther, *The Herbal of Apuleius Barbarus*, printed for presentation to members of Roxburghe Club (1925) 31-32. The Latin *charta* comes from the Greek *chartes* and means "a leaf of papyrus." In Greek the finest papyri were called *chartai basilikoi*, "royal papyri": Hero, *Automotapoetica* 26.3. In Rome the best papyri came to be called "Augustus." The mention of a plant called "royal" would lead Alan's readers to think of the papyrus, rather than of an obscure plant. The next line comes as an unexpected check to their thoughts. He is here using a Figure of Speech called *Para Prosdokian* ("contrary to expectation") in which the end of a sentence or clause comes as a surprise to the listener or reader.

IV

Prose 2

Although the ornaments of these garments are on fire with the full glow of their splendour, their brilliance suffered eclipse by comparison with the star-like beauty of the maiden. With the aid of a reed-pen, the maiden called up various images by drawing on slate tablets. The picture, however, did not cling closely to the under-lying material but, quickly fading and disappearing, left no trace of the impression behind. Although the maiden, by repeatedly calling these up, gave them a continuity of existence, yet the images in her projected picture failed to endure.[1] The maiden, as we have set forth above, coming from the confines of the heavenly court, was borne to the hut of the passible world in a car of glass. This was drawn by Juno's birds,[2] which were held in check by no jurisdiction of yoke but joined together of their own free choice. However, a man, whose countenance had no flavour of earthliness but rather of the mysteries of the divine, kept a position above the head of the maiden and the chariot and, supplying what is wanting to the female sex, by a series of

[1] Alan here seems to envisage a step on the road towards moving pictures. He seems to say that the images disappeared but very quickly reappeared. An acceleration of this process in regard to a moving object leads to moving pictures. Nature's action here may symbolise the continuation of the human race by the birth–death cycle.

[2] Doves. See II, note 66.

moderate suggestions guided the car on its course.[3] When I was concentrating my rays of vision or, if I may say so, the troops of my eyes, to explore the glory of this beauty, my eyes, not daring to confront the splendour of such majesty and dulled by the impact of brilliance, in excessive fear, took refuge in the war-tents of my eyelids.

At the arrival of the above-mentioned maiden, you would think that all the elements were having a celebration by having, so to speak, their native powers renewed. The firmament, as though lighting the maiden's path with its candles, bade its stars to shine with more than their wonted radiance. As a result the daylight itself seemed to be astonished at this great boldness on their part, when it saw them appear in its sight with too great a show of insolence. Phoebus,[4] too, assuming an unusually gladsome countenance, poured forth all the riches of his light to greet the maiden's arrival. His sister,[5] too, whom he had robbed of her ornaments of brilliance,[6] had her mantle of delight

---

[3] W. Wetherbee, *Platonism and Poetry in the Twelfth Century* 191, sees a reference here to the divine *ratio* that guides Nature. This would be a sublime concept both philosophically and poetically. However the contrast is between *homo* (a man) and *feminei sexus* (the female sex). There is nothing to indicate that it is specifically the sex of Nature that is in question and the insertion of *supplendo* between *sexus* and *feminei* is some indication that he is making a generic statement. Moreover, Alan held no high opinion of woman's ability: cf. *Anticl.* 3.282, 410, 515, Sheridan 103, n. 59. What we have here may be no more than a reference to women's inability to operate a chariot.

[4] The sun.

[5] Diana, the moon.

[6] This could refer to a miraculous stoppage of an eclipse. However it would seem that in Alan's vision sun, moon and stars are giving their brightest light simultaneously.

restored her and was ordered to go forth to meet the approaching maiden.

The air, wiping off the clouds with their tear-laden appearance, smiled on the maiden's steps with the benediction of a fair countenance. This had at first been ruffled by the mad blast of angry Aquilo,[7] but now found rest on the propitious bosom of Favonius.[8] The birds, by some inspiration of nature, played a pleasing game[9] with their wings and in their faces showed reverence for the maiden. Juno, who for a long time had scorned the playful touches of Jupiter,[10] was so intoxicated with joy that, with the uninterrupted fore-play of her eyes, she kept inviting her husband to the enticements of love.

The sea, that beforehand had been raging with tossing waves, now keeping a solemn holiday in honour of the maiden's arrival, promised unbroken calm and quiet. For Aeolus[11] had chained the storm-winds in his prisons to prevent them from stirring up a greater than civil[12] war in the maiden's presence. The fish, swimming on the surface of the water, in so far as the slowness of their natural senses allowed, proclaimed the arrival of the maiden with a certain festive gaiety. Thetis, too, marrying

---

[7] The wet, stormy North Wind.

[8] The soft, gentle West Wind.

[9] Peter of Compostella 54.25.

[10] Juno was frequently at odds with Jupiter over his indiscriminate love affairs: Ovid, *Met.* 1.588-600, 2.422-440, 2.858-3.3, 3.260-272, 4.611, 6.109-113, 9.23, 13.143-145. There is a play here on *iovales tactus* which can mean "playful touches" or "touches by Jupiter."

[11] God of the Winds: Virgil, *Aen.* 1.52-75; Ovid, *Met.* 14.223-224.

[12] Cf. Lucan 1.1.

Nereus, decided to conceive a second Achilles.[13] Maidens,[14] whose beauty would not only rob man of his reason but would also force the heavenly beings to forget their divinity, emerged from the stream-beds and like tributaries presented their queen with little gifts of aromatic nectar. When the maiden had graciously received these, she showed the maidens her love for them by the clasp of long embraces and oft-repeated kisses.

Earth, for long stripped of its ornaments by plundering Winter, acquired a purple garment of flowers from the bounteous spirit of Spring, lest, dishonoured in ragged attire, she might present an improper appearance to the eyes of the tender maid.

Spring, too, skilled craftsman in the weaver's art, wishing to show greater happiness in applauding the maiden's approach, wove garments for trees, which let down their foliage-tresses and bent over in a type of adoration, like a genuflection, offered prayers to the young maiden. Maidens,[15] emerging from the trees, by the light of their beauty enriched the riches of the actual day. In small vessels of cedarwood they brought spices made from types of herbs that have given their names to the spices: by offering these as though in payment of returns due from them, they purchased her favour by their gifts. Nymphs of the dell,[16] their laps filled with flowers, at times with roses coloured the royal chariot the rich red of blood, at times with petals of white

[13] Thetis was a sea-nymph. Nereus was a sea-god. In the vision they were married. Their son would be the "second Achilles." Peleus, father of the real Achilles, was long since dead.

[14] Naiades, water-nymphs. Nymphs were female spirits of Nature, representing the divine power in water, woods, trees and mountains.

[15] Hamadryades, tree nymphs.

[16] Napaeae, nymphs of the wooded vales.

flowers made it shine like a lily. Flora,[17] in lavish mood, presented the maiden with the cotton night-gown she had woven for her husband to earn his embraces. Proserpine,[18] disdaining the marital bed of the lord of Tartarus, returned to her home in the upper world, refusing to be cheated of a face-to-face meeting with her mistress. The land animals, instructed by some force or other in their nature, learned of the maiden's presence and were indulging in some playful frolic. Thus everything in the universe, swarming forth to pay court to the maiden, in wondrous contest toiled to win her favour.

[17] Flora was goddess of flowering plants and tilled fields. Her original name was Chloris. Her husband was Zephyrus, the West Wind: Ovid, *Met.* 5.193-274.

[18] Proserpine was queen of Tartarus. Her husband was Pluto.

V

Metre 3

Flower-bearing[1] Zephyrus had loosed bristling Winter's bonds[2] and by his peace had stilled Boreas'[3] attacks. Laden with a hail of flowers, he rained down the privet and bade its snow-white blooms cover the meadows. Spring, like a fuller with renewed strength, mending the meadow's cloak, set the mantles of flowers afire with the glow of purple. He restored to the trees the foliage-tresses that Winter had shorn, restoring the raiment the latter previously took away. It was the season when Spring's bounteous favour spreads riches in her fields to the applause of the dryads;[4] when the young blooms, as their strength increases, come further aloft leaving their earth-mother behind; when the splendid violet[5] caresses its earth-cradle and with new face seeks a breath of air. It was the time when earth, its surface starred with roses, abounding in constellations of its own, vies with the heavens; when the almond tree[6] bearing the standards of Sum-

[1] Metre: Elegiacs.

[2] Ancient writers spoke of frost and snow as fetters binding the earth: Statius, *Theb.* 5.15; Hor. *Od.* 1.4.10; *Ep.* 1.3.3.

[3] The cold North Wind.

[4] Tree-nymphs.

[5] *Violae speculum.* For connection between *speculum* and *splendor,* see Isid., *Etym.* 19.31.18.

[6] In *Distinctiones* 699ʙ, Alan states that the almond tree is the first of all trees to bloom. Pliny, 16.42.103, states that it blossoms in

mer, foretells his coming and with its flowers indicates the joys of Spring; when the vine, now in bud, entwines itself around the breast of the elm, its husband, and of itself thinks of offspring of its own. The sun's lamp outlaws Winter's shadows and forces all cold to submit to exile. Yet there lay hidden in many a wood the phantom of Winter caused by the shade recently made by the forest's leaves. Now Juno gave to the infant flower her breasts of dew[7] so that, as foster-mother, she may first suckle her children with it. It was the time when the power of Phoebus[8] raises up the dead grass as he bids everything to rise from the tomb; when his merry, smiling face brightens the universe as he wipes the tears of Winter from the face of his world that the flower may entrust itself to the good faith of air and Winter's cold not chafe the infant bloom; when Phoebus visits a world moaning from Winter's numbness and hails it with joyous light; when the prime of youth puts away the old age of time and old-man world begins to be a boy again; when Phoebus robs night of the hours she owns[9] and dwarf day takes the first steps towards becoming a giant;[10] when the flock of Phrixus,[11] rejoicing in its

---

January. Its blossoming can hardly be regarded as a close forerunner of Summer. Perhaps he is referring to the time when its fruit appears, which is March: Pliny, *ibid.*

[7] Juno was interested in the sexual life of women and the survival of the child. Alan has her offering her breasts of dew (= milk) to the infant flower. She is performing some of the functions of Tellus whose work is somewhat akin to her own.

[8] The sun.

[9] Refers to lengthening days and shortening nights.

[10] See II, note 58.

[11] Phrixus was son of Athamas and Nephele and brother of Helle. Athamas later married Ino. She became jealous of Phrixus and Helle. When the corn (which she had roasted) failed to grow, she bribed the

patron, the sun, and paying its dues, prepares a welcome for Phoebus; when Philomena,[12] singing an ode with honey-sweet, lyric voice, solemnly celebrates her Spring. For this festival she plays on the organ of her throat that she may with her own voice proclaim a veritable god. It was the time when the lark with his sweet notes imitates the lyre, flies to the heavens above and holds converse with Jupiter. A silvery sheen decked the frolicking streams and had bade its light to be in the rivers. One could see the many run-offs that chattered forth from the spring and the murmur of its flow was a prologue to sleep.[13] The spring itself with its shining face invited weary men to draw draughts from it.

---

messengers sent to Delphi to say that the sacrifice of Phrixus (and possibly of Helle) was required. The children escaped on a golden-fleeced ram given by Hermes. The ram carried Phrixus to Colchis. Helle fell into the strait and it came to be called Hellespont: Ovid, *Met.* 11.195; Hyginus *Fab.* 1-4.

[12] See II, note 77.

[13] See II, note 35.

VI

Prose 3

Despite the fresh youth of the charming season, by no applause from created nature could the maiden be cheered and moderate her above-mentioned grief. But, lowering the chariot to earth and hallowing the ground with her footprints, she approached me with modest gait. When I saw this kinswoman of mine close at hand, I fell upon my face and stricken with mental stupor, I fainted; completely buried in the delirium of a trance,[1] with the powers of my senses impeded, I was neither alive nor dead and being neither, was afflicted with a state between the two.[2] The maiden, kindly raising me up, strengthened my reeling feet with the comforting aid of her sustaining hands. Entwining me in an embrace and sweetening my lips with chaste kisses, she cured me of my illness of stupor by the medicine of her honey-sweet discourse.

When she realised that I had been brought back to myself, she fashioned for me, by the image of a real voice, mental concepts and brought forth audibly what one might call archetypal words that had been preconceived ideally.[3] She said:

[1] Peter of Compostella 55.19. For *extasis*, see *Summa Quoniam homines*, ed. Glorieux 121.

[2] *Anticl.* 6.76, 98, Sheridan 158, 159.

[3] *Anticl.* 3.343-354; *Summa*, ed. Glorieux 126. Cf. Bern. Silv. 1.2.14; J. Huizinga, *Über die Verknüpfung des Poetischen mit dem Theologischen bei "Alanus de Insulis"* (Amsterdam 1932) 149.

Alas, what blindness of ignorance, what delirium of mind, what impairment of sense, what weakness of reason, have cast a cloud over your intellect, driven your reason into exile, dulled the power of your senses, forced sickness of mind on you, so that your mind is not only robbed of an intimate knowledge of your foster-mother but also that at my first rising the star of your judgement is forced to set as though stricken by some monstrous and unheard-of appearance? Why do you force the knowledge of me to leave your memory and go abroad, you in whom my gifts proclaim me who have blessed you with the right bounteous gifts of so many favours;[4] who, acting by an established covenant as the deputy of God, the creator, have from your earliest years established the appointed course of your life; who of old brought your material body into real existence from the mixed substance of primordial matter; who, in pity for your ill-favoured appearance that was, so to speak, haranguing me continually, stamped you with the stamp of human species and with the improved dress of form brought dignity to that species when it was bereft of adornments of shape?[5] In dealing with that species, I made arrangements for various work-companies of members to serve the body and gave orders that the senses keep vigil there like sentries, so to speak, in the state of the body,[6] so that sighting in advance enemies from outside, they might protect the body against external harassment and thus the entire material body, adorned with the noble pur-

[4] Peter of Compostella 60.33-34.

[5] *Anticl.* 5.291ff., Sheridan 147. Cf. Bern. Silv. 1.1.9-44.

[6] In man there can be found an image of God and His Creation, an image of the Universe, an image of an earthly kingdom. Alan does not always keep these images clearly separated. The images are, of course, interconnected.

ple vestments of nature, might proceed to a marriage alliance
and be joined in a more acceptable union with spirit as a husband and that the husband might not be disgusted by the
baseness of his partner and repudiate the espousals.[7] I also
gave the spirit in you distinctive powers and capacities, lest,
being poorer than the body, it might envy its successes. I
alloted to the spirit the native faculty and power of hunting
down subtle matters in the chase for knowledge and of retaining them when it apprehends them. I stamped it also with the
stamp of ratiocination to separate, with the winnowing-fan of
judgement, vain falsehood from important truth. Through
me, too, the power of recollection becomes your handmaiden
and lays up a treasure, a noble record of knowledge, in the
strong-box of her memory. I have blessed both parts of you,
then, with these endowments so that neither should bemoan
its own poverty or complain of the others' riches.

But just as the above-mentioned marriage was solemnised
by my consent, so, too, at my discretion this marital union
will be annulled.[8] Moreover, my bounteous power does not
shine forth in you alone individually but also universally in all
things. For I am the one who formed the nature of man
according to the exemplar and likeness of the structure of the
universe so that in him, as in a mirror of the universe itself,
Nature's lineaments might be there to see. For just as concord
in discord, unity in plurality, harmony in disharmony, agreement in disagreement of the four elements unite the parts of
the structure of the royal palace of the universe, so too,
similarity in dissimilarity, equality in inequality, like in unlike,

[7] *Timaeus* 30A-B; Bern. Silv. 4.4.9-13.
[8] *Timaeus* 41A-B. Works of God are indissoluble except by His Will.

identity in diversity of four combinations bind together the house of the human body. Moreover, the same qualities that come between the elements as intermediaries establish a lasting peace between the four humours.[9] Just as any army of planets fight against the accepted revolution of the heavens by going in a different direction,[10] so in man there is found to be continual hostility between sensuousness and reason. For the movement of reason, springing from a heavenly origin, escaping the destruction of things on earth, in its process of thought turns back again to the heavens. On the other hand, the movements of sensuality, going planet-like in opposition to the fixed sky of reason, with twisted course slip down to the destruction of earthly things. The latter, then, draws man's mind down to the destruction arising from vice so that he may fall, the former invites him to come to the source of virtue so that he may rise; the one, corrupting man, changes him into a beast, the other has the power to transform man into a god; one illuminates the dark night of the mind with the light of contemplation, the other removes the light of the mind by the dark night of concupiscence; one enables man to hold converse with angels, the other drives him to wanton with brute beasts; one shows the man in exile how to get back to his fatherland, the other forces the one in his fatherland to go into exile. Nor in this matter can the blame for man's nature

[9] Cf. *Exposito cuiusdam super orationem Dominicam* 74, ed. N. M. Häring, "A Commentary on the Our Father by Alan of Lille," *Analecta Cisterciensia* 31.1 (1975) 176; *Anticl.* 2.242-255; 7.1-37, Sheridan 76-77, 173-174; Boeth. *De cons. phil.* M.8.1-4, 16-19 (Stewart-Rand 222); Bern. Silv. 1.2.100-146; William of Conches, *Glosae super Platonem* 58, ed. E. Jeauneau (Paris 1965) 128; M. Baumgartner, *Die Philosophie des Alanus de Insulis*, Beiträge 2 (Münster 1896) 51ff.

[10] See II, note 40.

be laid on my order and arrangement. It was on reason's advice that I arranged such antagonism and war between these contestants, so that if reason could in this debate turn sensuousness into an object of ridicule,[11] the first reward of victory would not be without subsequent ones. For rewards obtained from victories shine more fair than all other gifts. Rewards purchased by toil bring more honour and delight than all gifts given gratis. The one who receives a reward for labour merits higher praise and commendation than he who obtains it while enjoying his leisure. For the work that goes before, infusing a kind of sweetness into the reward that follows, brings a more pleasing recompense to the labourer. In these and in the larger gifts of nature the universe finds its own qualities in man. See how in this universe, as in a noble state, a certain excellence of administration is established by an approved plan of management. For in heaven, as at the pinnacle of an earthly state, the eternal commander has his imperial abode; from all eternity the order had gone out from him that each and every thing should be inscribed and made known in the book of his Providence. In air, as in the centre of the city, the celestial army of angels carry on the battle and, in the capacity of deputies, assiduously extend their protection to man.[12] Man, however, like a foreigner, living on the outskirts of the universe, does not refuse to show obedience to the hosts of angels. In this state, then, God gives commands, the angels carry them out, man obeys. God creates man by his command, the angels by their operation carry out the work of

[11] Acts 19:27; Psalm 37:15; Boeth. *Elench. soph. Arist.* 1.1, PL 64.1008D.
[12] For spirits of a different kind in the lower air, see *Anticl.* 4.271-294; Bern. Silv. 2.7.92-110.

creation, man by obedience re-creates himself. By his authority God decrees the existence of things, by their operation the angels fashion them, man submits himself to the will of the spirits carrying out the operation. God gives orders by his magisterial authority, angels operate by ministerial administration, man obeys by the mystery of regeneration.[13] Our chain of reason extends too far when it dares to lift our discourse to the ineffable secrets of the godhead, although our mind grows faint in sighs for a knowledge of this matter.[14] The image of this perfectly organised state shines forth in man.[15] Wisdom, that gives orders, rests in the citadel of his head and the other powers, like demi-goddesses, obey her as if she were a goddess. For native ability, power of reasoning, as well as the faculty of recalling the past dwell in the various compartments of the head and obey Wisdom with enthusiasm.[16] In the heart, as in the middle of the earthly city, Magnanimity[17] has taken up her abode; she has sworn military

[13] This sounds tawdry and repetitious. The original Latin abounds in the use of words with similarity in sound but difference of meaning: *imperans, operans, obtemperans; creat, procreat, recreat; disponit, componit, supponit; magisterio, ministerio, misterio.* This at least makes an impression, be it favourable or unfavourable.

[14] Human language cannot adequately express God and His attributes: *Anticl.* 5.117-123, Sheridan 141; *Summa*, ed. P. Glorieux 119; Hilary, *De Trinitate* 4.1ff., PL 10.55B; Gilbert of Poitiers, *Commentary on the Pseudo-Athanasian Creed* 55, ed. Häring, *Mediaeval Studies* 27 (1965) 40.

[15] Bern. Silv. 2.13.89-14.9. What follows in Alan is from *Timaeus* 44D, 69B-72D.

[16] *Timaeus* 44D.

[17] *Timaeus* 70A-C; *De arte praedicatoria* 24, PL 210.159C-161B; *De virtutibus et de vitiis et de donis Spiritus Sancti*, ed. Lottin, "Le Traité," *Mediaeval Studies* 12 (1950) 32. Magnanimity is that part of the

allegiance to Wisdom, as commander-in-chief, and carries out operations according to the decisions of Wisdom's command. The loins like the city's outskirts, give the lower portions of the body wilful desires;[18] they do not dare to oppose the orders of Magnanimity but obey her will. In this state, then, the role of the commander is assumed by wisdom, the likeness of the administrator by Magnanimity, while desire appropriates the image of the one obeying. In other things, too, the form of the human body takes over the image of the universe. Just as in the universe the beneficial heat of the sun proves a remedy for whatever is languishing, so, too, in man, the heat proceeding from its base in the heart enlivens and gladdens the other parts of the body. Also, just as in the structure of the universe the moon is the mother of many humours,[19] so, too, in man, the liver sends comparable humours into his members. And just as the moon, when robbed of light from the sun, loses its vigour, so, too, the power of a liver, bereft of enlivening comfort from the heart, grows

---

soul which partakes of courage and spirit and reacts against anything unjust from within or without the body. Without the help of the *Timaeus* and these other works of Alan it would be difficult to understand *Magnanimitas* in the *De planctu*. See R.-A. Gauthier, *Magnanimité* (Bibliothèque Thomiste 28, Paris 1951) 244-247, 265.

[18] *Timaeus* 70D-71E. Plato discusses the relationship between Reason and Desire and states that Desire has little understanding of Reason and less respect for it. The liver is used to scare Desire into submission. Alan relates Desire to Magnanimity and seems over-optimistic about its submission to it.

[19] *Anticl.* 4.362, Sheridan 131; Giraldus Cambrensis, *Topographia Hibernica* 2.3, ed. J. Dimock, *Giraldi Cambrensis Opera* 5, Rolls Series 21.5 (London 1867) 78.

sluggish.[20] And just as in the sun's absence, the air is wrapped in darkness, so too, without the good offices of the heart, the vital power of breath is nullified. However, see how the universe, with Proteus-like succession of changing seasons, now plays in the childhood of Spring, now grows up in the youth of Summer, now ripens in the manhood of Autumn, now grows hoary in the old age of Winter. Comparable changes of season and the same variations alter man's life. When the dawn of man's life comes up, man's early Spring morning is beginning. As he completes longer laps in the course of his life, man reaches the Summer-noon of his youth; when with longer life he had completed what may be called the ninth hour of his time,[21] man passes into the manhood of Autumn. And when his day sinks to the West and old age gives notice of life's evening, the Winter's cold forces man's head to turn white with the hoar frost of old age. In all these things the effects of my power shine forth to an extent greater than words can express. However, for many I have decided to cloak my face in figures in order to protect my secret from being cheapened, lest, if I should grant them an intimate knowledge of myself, what at first had been held in honour by them because they lacked knowledge of it, should when

---

[20] M.-T. d'Alverny thinks that Alan had an interest in medicine and possibly some training in it: *Textes inédits* 105; "Maître Alain — 'Nova et Vetera'," in *Entretiens sur la renaissance du 12ᵉ siècle*, sous la direction de Maurice de Gandillac et Édouard Jeauneau (Paris 1968) 120. His concept of the functions of the liver is widely different from Plato (*Timaeus* 71A-D). He seems to know that it is affected by a failing heart. For list of works on medicine, probably available to Ralph of Longchamps, see *In Anticlaudianum Alani commentum*, ed. J. Sulowski 244-247.

[21] I.e. when he has passed 3.00 p.m. in his day of life.

known be regarded as of less value. For, as the well-known proverb attests: 'The divulgation of what is private gives rise to contempt for it.'[22] A pronouncement, with the authority of Aristotle, trumpets forth that 'whoever reveals secrets to the unworthy lessens their dignity.'[23] But, lest by thus first canvassing my own power, I seem to be arrogantly detracting from the power of God, I most definitely declare that I am but the humble disciple of the Master on High. For in my operations I have not the power to follow closely in the footprints of God in His operations, but with sighs of longing, so to speak, gaze on His work from afar. His operation is simple, mine is multiple; His work is complete, mine is defective; His work is the object of admiration, mine is subject to alteration. He is ungeneratable, I was generated; He is the creator, I was created; He is the creator of my work, I am the work of the Creator; He creates from nothing, I beg the material for my work from someone; He works by His own divinity, I work in His name; He, by His will alone, bids things come into existence, my work is but a sign of the work of God. You can realise that in comparison with God's power, my power is powerless; you can know that my efficiency is deficiency; you can decide that my activity is worthless. Consult the authoritative teaching of theology on whose trustworthiness you should base your assent rather than on the strength of my arguments. According to its reliable testimony man is born by my work, he is reborn by the power of God;[24] through me

[22] Guigo Carthusiensis, *Scala Claustralium* 8, PL 184.480c.

[23] I have failed to locate this quotation in Aristotle. Cf. *Summa*, ed. P. Glorieux 120; *Anticl.* 3.120-125, Sheridan 95-96.

[24] For "creation" and "re-creation," see d'Alverny, *Textes inédits* 200.

he is called from non-being into being, through Him he is led from being to higher being; by me man is born for death, by Him he is reborn for life. But my professional services are set aside in the mystery of this second birth.

Such a birth needs no midwife of my kind. Rather I, Nature, am ignorant of the nature of this birth. When I try to understand these things, the keenness of my intellect grows dull, my enlightened reason is confounded. The intellect is awed by what is not understood; the senses are confused by things beyond sense. Since in these matters (of the second birth) the entire reasoning process dealing with Nature is brought to a standstill, let us, by the power of firm faith alone, pay homage to something so great and mysterious.[25] Nor is it surprising that in these matters theology shows no close kinship with me, since in many instances our paths to knowledge, though not opposite, are different. I establish the truths of faith by reason, she establishes reason by the truths of faith. I know in order to believe, she believes in order to know. I assent from knowledge, she reaches knowledge by assent. It is with difficulty that I see what is visible, she in her mirror understands the incomprehensible. My intellect has difficulty in compassing what is very small, her reason compasses things immense. I walk around the earth like a brute beast, she marches in the hidden places of heaven.

Although it is no part of my office to deal with the above-mentioned matters, yet I allowed my disquisition to range thus far, so that you might not doubt that my power is but a diminutive in comparison with the superlative power of

[25] For faith and reason, cf. *Anticl.* 6.22, 180, Sheridan 156, 162; 7.319, Sheridan 183.

God.[26] But, although my accomplishments fail in comparison with God's power, it, nevertheless, has the advantage when placed side by side with man's power.[27] Thus on the table of comparison, so to speak, we can find three degrees of power and they are termed the *superlative* power of God, the *comparative* power of Nature and the *positive* power of man.[28]

Without one ounce of questioning, all these things bestow on you an intimate knowledge of me. To speak more intimately still, I am Nature who, by the gift of my condescension, have made you a sharer in my presence here and have deigned to bless you with my conversation.

While Nature was revealing aspects of her nature to me in these words and by her instruction, as by an opening key, was unlocking for me the door of her knowledge, the cloudlet of stupor was drifting away from the confines of my mind. By the final instruction, as by some healing potion, the stomach of my mind, as if nauseated, spewed forth all the dregs of phantasy. When I came completely back to myself after my mind's trip abroad, I fell down at Nature's feet and marked them with the imprint of many a kiss to take the place of formal greeting. Then straightening up and standing erect, with humbly bowed head, I

[26] *Diminutam.* This means *diminutive*: Quintilian 1.5.46. Grammarians pointed out that certain diminutives by their meaning involve a comparison — e.g., *grandiusculus*: Donatus, *Ars grammatica*, ed. Keil 4.374.33; Priscian 3.26, ed. Keil 2.101.3-12. Such words are comparatively rare in English. Perhaps "smallish" would serve as an example. The idea of comparison explains Alan's use of "superlative" to describe the power of God.

[27] Alan is fond of this method of praising something that is neither first nor last in rank: *Anticl.* 4.121, 141; 5.420, Sheridan 122-123, 151. Is this an extension of the Aristotelian doctrine of the mean?

[28] Terminology is taken from the comparison of adjectives.

poured out for her, as for a divine majesty, a verbal libation of good wishes. Following this I took refuge in excuses and in humble prayers, seasoned with the sweetness of honey, I craved her indulgence, begging her not to attribute to rash error on my part, not to impute to contemptuous pride or ascribe to poisonous ingratitude the fact that I had performed no joyous or festive rite to greet her arrival. I explained that I had been struck by her appearance as by the emergence of a phantom of something anomalous and monstrous and had been deprived of my senses by the counterfeit death of a trance. I said that it was not surprising that, in the presence of a divinity so great, my mortal covering turned pale, that in the noonday of a majesty so great, my little ray of judgement faded into the twilight of misdirection, that, on the appearance of such bliss, my ragged wretchedness blushed with shame, since the dark fog of ignorance, the dulness that is incapable of controlling shock and frequent impacts of stupor are allied by a certain law of kinship with human frailty, so that from association and cohabitation with them, frail human nature, conditioned by living with them when it was being trained and shaping its attitudes, is wont to be beclouded by ignorance on the first appearance of new things, to be stricken with stupor by the marvels of mighty things and to be injured by shock.

Since this manner of apology was gaining me a favourable hearing from the queen and (a more favourable aspect still) was winning me her good graces and was, moreover, building up my confidence that I could learn more important things, I submitted to her scrutiny an ambiguous matter that was causing a type of mental uncertainty, which by its excessively disquieting influence was shaking the hostelry of my mind. I went on to a question in the following words.

VII

Metre 4

O child of God,[1] mother of creation, bond of the universe
and its stable link, bright gem for those on earth, mirror for
mortals, light-bearer for the world: peace, love, virtue, guide,
power, order, law, end, way, leader, source, life, light, splendour, beauty, form, rule of the world: you, who by your reins
guide the universe, unite all things in a stable and harmonious
bond and wed heaven to earth in a union of peace; who,
working on the pure ideas of Noys,[2] mould the species of all
created things, clothing matter with form and fashioning a
mantle of form with your thumb:[3] you whom heaven
cherishes, air serves, whom earth worships, water reveres; to

---

[1] Metre is Sapphic. This is undoubtedly the finest poetry in the *De
planctu*. For an analysis, see G. Raynaud de Lage, *Alain de Lille, poète*
107-108.

[2] *Nous*, Divine Wisdom. See R. H. Green, "Alan of Lille's Anticlaudianus, Ascensus mentis ad Deum," *Annuale mediaevale* 8 (1967)
3-16.

[3] *Pollex* is derived from *pollere*, "to be powerful." It figures pro-
minently in OT sacrifices: Exod. 29:20; Lev. 8:23-24, 11:14, 17, 25, 28. It
is the strongest of the fingers: Macrobius, *Sat.* 7.13.14; Isid., *Etym.*
11.1.70. There may, however, be an echo of something else here. Alan
has just said to Nature "You, who . . . wed heaven to earth." A marriage engagement was confirmed by having both parties press their
thumbs on a sword.

whom, as mistress of the universe, each and every thing pays tribute: you, who bind together day and night in their alternations, give to day the candle of the sun, put night's clouds to bed by the moon's bright, reflected light: you, who gild the sky with varying stars illuming our ether's throne, fill heaven with the gems of constellations and a varied complement of soldiers:[4] you, who in a protean role, keep changing heaven's face with new shapes, bestow a throng of birds on our expanse of air and control them by your law: you, at whose nod the world grows young again, the grove is frilled with foliage-curls, the land, clad in its garment of flowers, shows its pride: you, who lay to rest and raise on high the threatening sea as you cut short[5] the course of the raging deep so that the ocean's waves may not entomb the sun's face: do you in answer to my plea disclose the reason for your journey. Why do you, a stranger from heaven, make your way to earth? Why do you offer the gift of your divinity to our lands? Why is your face bedewed with a flood of tears? What do the tears on your face portend? Weeping is a sure expression of interior suffering.

---

[4] Probably an echo of *Deus sabaoth*, "God of Hosts," the hosts here being angels: Jeremias 11:20; Romans 9:29; James 5:4.

[5] *Syncopans. Syncope* is a grammatical term for the shortening of a word by omitting a letter or syllable within the word, e.g. *vixet* for *vixisset* in Virgil, *Aen.* 11.118.

VIII

Prose 4

The above-mentioned maiden, then, showing that the answer to this question[1] was ready and waiting at the door,[2] said:

Do you not know what deviation of earthly rotation, what disorder in the wordly order, what carelessness on the part of the world's caretakers, what injustice to justice have forced me to come down from the innermost depths of the secret heavens to the common brothels of earth? If you would, with well-disposed inclination of mind, collect together and store in the treasure-chest of your heart what I would say, I would straighten out the labyrinth of your doubts.

Hereupon, with chastened and restrained voice, I answered in matching vein.[3]

O heavenly queen, there is nothing for which I thirst with greater desire and longing than I do for an explanation of the subject of my inquiry.

---

[1] The series of questions and answers that follow may be a fair picture of a twelfth-century lecture, with what we might consider a somewhat pompous lecturer and students who are pertinacious, mock-modest and at times petulant.

[2] Cf. *Anticl.* 1.423; *Vix nodosum* 43-44.

[3] *Talionem. Talio* originally meant "retaliation in kind" for an injury. It came to mean recompense in kind for a favour: Isid., *Etym.* 5.27.24. Finally, as here, it came to mean like response of any kind.

Then she said:

As all things[4] by the law of their origin are held subject to
my laws and are bound to pay me the tribute rightly imposed,
practically all obey my edicts as a general rule, by bringing
forward the rightful tribute in the manner appointed by law.
However, from this universal law man alone exempts himself
by a nonconformist withdrawal. He, stripping himself of the
robe of chastity, exposes himself in unchastity for a professional male prostitute and dares to stir up the tumult of legal
strife against the dignity of his queen, and, moreover, to fan
the flame of civil war's rage against his mother. Other
creatures that I have equipped with lesser gifts from my
bounty hold themselves bound in voluntary subjection to the
ordinances of my decrees according to the rank of each's activity. Man, however, who has all but drained the entire
treasury of my riches, tries to denature the natural things of
nature and arms a lawless and solecistic[5] Venus to fight
against me. See how practically everything, obeying the edict I
have promulgated, completely discharges the duties imposed
by my law as the raison d'etre of its native condition
demands. The firmament in its daily revolution makes all
things go round with it, not in a frivolous pattern of rotation
but according to the instructions of my teaching: it returns to
the place from which it set out and proceeds again to the place
to which it is going. The stars, too, that shine to give the fir-

----

[4] The section from here to p. 134 sets forth the basis for the theme
of the entire *De planctu*. Nature rules all created things. Man alone
refuses to accept this rule.

[5] *Soloecismus* is a fault in the grammar of a sentence, especially a
lack of concord: Quintilian 1.5.5; 1.5.34.

mament its glory by clothing it with their adornment as they complete the short stays[6] in their journey, traverse in their rotation the many roads allotted to this journey and serve as soldiers in my royal army. The planets, too, in keeping with a decree on arrangement that went out from me, hold the onward rush of the firmament in check as, pressing in the opposite direction, they wander back towards their place of rising. Later they come home again to their course going towards the region of their setting.[7] Air, too, schooled by my teaching, now rejoices in a friendly breeze, now sheds tears as though sympathising with weeping clouds, now grows angry with the brawling winds, now is shaken with the threatening bellows of thunder, now is roasted in an oven of heat, now is made fierce by the cold's severity.

The birds, too, stamped with various natural qualities, by my direction and guidance sail over the waves of the air with oarage of wings[8] and look with heartfelt longing to my instructions. By my intervention as mediator, the sea, joined to earth by firm bonds of friendship and daring not to violate the sanctity of the good faith pledged his sister, fears to stray beyond the limits of a well-defined meandering area into the home-territory of earth.[9] By the decision of my will, however, he now rages in the fury of a storm, now returns to peace and tranquility, now raised by the pride of his swell, he comes to resemble a mountain, now he is straightened out into a level plain. The fishes, bound to me by a vow of recognition, are

[6] The sun is visible every day, the moon is visible for some time most nights, but most stars disappear entirely for long periods.

[7] See VI, note 10.

[8] Virgil, *Aen.* 1.301; 6.19. Cf. *Anticl.* 4.266, Sheridan 127.

[9] *Anticl.* 1.205, Sheridan 53-54.

afraid to modify the norms of my regulations. By my royal edict, too, the rains are wed to earth by a kind of nuptial embrace. Earth, labouring to produce offspring, never ceases in tireless generation to bring the various species of things to birth. The living things of earth, under my arrangement and scrutiny, pledge their obedience in various services. The earth now becomes hoary-headed with rime, now is covered with dark locks[10] of flowers. The grove, too, is now topped with foliage-hair, is now shorn by Winter's sharp razor. Winter also holds the seeds buried deep within the womb of mother-earth, Spring releases them from their prison, Summer brings heat to the crops, Autumn displays its abundance.

But why should I allow the course of my disquisition to range over each and every thing? Man alone turns with scorn from the modulated strains of my cithern and runs deranged to the notes of mad Orpheus' lyre.[11] For the human race, fallen from its high estate, adopts a highly irregular (grammatical) change[12] when it inverts the rules of Venus by introducing barbarisms[13] in its arrangement of genders. Thus

---

[10] *Caesaries* means "dark hair." The Romans regarded dark as a beautiful colour for hair. Alan puts it here in opposition to *albescit*, "grows white," although "dark" does not seem the most fitting designation for flowers.

[11] Orpheus was a Thracian singer and musician, who could charm animals and even exert influence on inanimate objects: Ovid, *Met.* 10.3-154.

[12] *Metaplasmus*. This is the generic term for undue change in the form of a word: Donatus, *Ars gram.* 2.17ff., ed. Keil 4.392ff.; Mart. Cap. 6.325, ed. Dick 149.24.

[13] *Barbarismus*. This is a mistake in the form of a word, e.g. in its gender: Quint. 1.1.5-18.

man, his sex changed[14] by a ruleless Venus, in defiance of due order, by his arrangement changes what is a straightforward attribute of his.[15] Abandoning in his deviation the true script[16] of Venus, he is proved to be a sophistic pseudographer. Shunning even a resemblance traceable to the art of Dione's daughter, he falls into the defect of inverted order.[17] While in a construction of this kind he causes my destruction, in his combination he devises a division in me.[18]

I regret that for the most part I have honoured man's nature with so many graces and privileges, seeing that he disgraces his graces by abuse of propriety, that he disfigures

---

[14] *Tiresiatus.* Tiresias was a Theban seer. He saw snakes coupling, struck them with a stick and was turned into a woman. A repetition of this episode turned him back into a man: Ovid, *Met.* 3.322-331; Hyginus 75.

[15] Martianus Capella 4.362, 383, ed. Dick 167.7, 179.16; Boethius, *Comm. in Porphyrium* 2, PL 64.92C-94D; *In Cat. Arist.* 1, PL 64.185A-186B. What he changes is his gender.

[16] *Orthographiam. Orthographa* is the word applied to the "truth of Jupiter" which the Fates must study and actualize: Mart. Cap. 1.65, ed. Dick 30.7. *Orthographia Veneris* means the expressed will of Venus.

[17] *Analogia* and *anastrophe*. The basic notion in *analogia* is resemblance. Its application differs somewhat in grammar and rhetoric: Varro, *De lingua latina* 101.74; Charisius, *Ars grammatica* 1.17, ed. Keil 1.116.30; Diomedes, *Ars grammatica* 2, ed. Keil 1.456.5; Probus, *Instituta art.*, ed. Keil 4.47.22; Quintilian 1.5.13; 1.5.34. *Anastrophe* is a change in the regular order of words: Donatus, *Ars gram.* 3.6, ed. Keil 4.401.9; Quintilian 8.6.65.

[18] *Syneresi-themesim. Synaeresis* is the contraction of two syllables into one, e.g., *Batavi* for *Batavii*, Juv. 8.51; Priscian, *Instit.* 17.21, ed. Keil 2.590.6. *Tmesis* is the separation of a compound word by an intervening word or words, e.g. *antequam venit, patrem vidit* (before he came he saw his father) is written *ante patrem vidit quam venit*: Donatus, *Ars gram.* 3.6, ed. Keil 4.401.14.

the fair figure of Venus by ugliness, that he discolours the colour of beauty by the meretricious dye of desire, that he deflowers the flower of pulchritude by having it bloom into vice.

Why did I deify with a godlike beauty the face of Tyndareus' daughter[19] who forced the use of her beauty to decline to the abuse of harlotry when, sullying the covenant of her marriage-bed, she formed a disgraceful alliance with Paris. Pasiphae, too, driven by the furies of an over-venereous Venus, under the appearance of a heifer entered a bestial marriage with an animal by a trick and making her point by a disgraceful fallacy, forced the dazed bull to draw a false inference.[20] Myrrha,[21] also, goaded by the sting of the myrrh-scented Cyprian,[22] in her love for her father corrupted a

[19] Helen of Troy.

[20] Minos, King of Crete, begged Poseidon to send him a bull from the sea as a sign that he should be ruler. He promised to sacrifice the bull to Poseidon. The bull came but was so magnificent that Minos kept him. Poseidon, or Aphrodite, caused his wife, Pasiphae, to fall in love with the bull. Daedalus constructed a covering for her in the shape of a wooden heifer. By this she tricked the bull into having relations with her. The outcome of this union was the Minotaur, half man, half bull: Ovid, *Met.* 9.738-744; Hyginus 40.1

[21] Myrrha, through no fault of her own, fell in love with her father, Cinyras. She fought against her unnatural feelings and even tried to commit suicide but was prevented by her old nurse. The latter realised that Myrrha must have her father or die. When Cinyras' wife, Cenchreis, was absent, the nurse arranged for Myrrha to go to the bed of her father who was drunk. The visits were repeated. Finally Myrrha's identity was discovered, but not before she had become pregnant. She fled and wandered around for nine months. She prayed for deliverance and was turned into the myrrh tree. Later Adonis was born from the tree: Ovid, *Met.* 10.298-518.

[22] Venus.

daughter's affection and played a mother's role with her father. Medea,[23] turning stepmother to her natural son, destroyed a beautiful little product of Venus to produce a work that brought Venus no glory. Narcissus,[24] when his shadow faked a second Narcissus, was reflected in a reflection, believed himself to be a second self, and was involved in the destruction arising from himself loving himself. Many other youths, too, clothed by my favour in grace and beauty, intoxicated with thirst for money, converted Venus' hammers to the functions of anvils. This great multitude of men monsters are scattered hither and thither over the whole expanse of earth and from contact with their spell, chastity itself is bewitched. Of those men who subscribe to Venus' procedures in grammar, some closely embrace those of masculine gender only, others, those of feminine gender, others, those of common, or epicene gender. Some, indeed, as though belonging to the heteroclite[25] class, show variations in deviation by reclining with those of female gender in Winter and those of masculine gender in Summer. There are some, who in the disputations in Venus' school of logic, in their conclusions reach a law of interchangeability of subject and predicate. There are those who take the part of the subject and cannot function as predicate. There are some who function as predicates only but have no desire to have the subject term

[23] Medea was abandoned by her husband Jason. As part of her revenge she killed her two sons by him. Alan seems to think that she had only one son by Jason: Ovid, *Met.* 7.394-403.

[24] See I n. 14.

[25] Heteroclite nouns are those that in their case-endings show forms from more than one declension, e.g., *domus*: Priscian, *Instit.* 8, ed. Keil 2.357.11. Reference is to homophiles who are bisexual.

duly submit to them.[26] Others, disdaining to enter Venus' hall, practice a deplorable game in the vestibule of her house.[27]

Against all these, edicts lodge their complaints, laws take up arms and with the sword of retribution seek to avenge the injury done them. Do not be surprised, then, that I go beyond limits in my use of this strange and profane language when impious men dare to revel in wicked manner. In my indignation I belch forth such words so that men of restraint may revere the mark of modesty and that men without restraint may be kept away from trafficking in the brothels of immodesty. The knowledge of evil is advantageous as a preventive measure to punish the guilty, who are branded with the mark of shame, and to forearm the unaffected with the armour of precaution.

Now the file of my answer has smoothed the troublesome point of your question. For this reason, then, did I leave the secret abode of the kingdom in the heavens above and come down to this transitory and sinking world so that I might

[26] This section is not easy to explain in detail. The meaning is tolerably clear. He is classifying homophiles as either active or passive. In normal relations the man was regarded as the active partner, the woman as the passive. For Alan man is represented by the subject of sentence or the major of a syllogism, woman by the predicate of a sentence or the minor of a syllogism. The simplest explanation would be that Alan is maintaining that some by perverted logic reach the conclusion that the subject and predicate of a sentence are interchangeable. However as the major and minor of a syllogism are themselves a sentence, I suspect that Alan may be dealing in intricate and untranslatable punning on *suppositum*, which can mean the subject of a sentence or the minor of a syllogism, not forgetting the possibility of a double entendre from its etymological signification.

[27] Reference seems to be to auto-eroticism.

lodge with you, as my intimate and confidant, my plaintive lament for the accursed excesses of man, and might decide, in
consultation with you, what kind of penalty should answer
such an array of crimes so that a conformable punishment,
meting out like for like, might repay in kind the biting pain inflicted by the above-mentioned misdeeds.

Then I said:

O mediatrix in all things, did I not fear that my host of
questions might raise disgust in your kind nature, I would ex-
pose the haze of another doubt of mine to the light of your
discernment.

Then she replied:

Nay, impart to my ears all your questions, not only those of
more recent growth but also those made old with the mildew
of great age, so that the pressure from your doubts may be
relieved by the secure certainty of my answers.

Then I said:

I wonder why, when you consider the statements of the
poets, you load the stings of the above attacks against the con-
tagions of the human race alone, although we read that the
gods, too, have limped around the same circle of aberration.
For Jupiter, translating the Phrygian youth[28] to the realms

---

[28] Ganymede, a Phrygian youth, was beloved by Jupiter and taken
up to heaven to be his cupbearer and beloved. He became the constellation Aquarius: Ovid, *Met.* 10.154-161; Hildebert, *Carmen* 68, ed. A. B.
Scott, *Hildebertus, Carmina minora* (Leipzig 1969) 38; Bern. Silv.
1.3.451. Alan's terminology is from grammar. It is impossible to render
it in idiomatic English.

above, transferred there a proportionate love for him on his transference. The one he had made his wine-master by day he made his subject in bed by night. Bacchus and Apollo, likewise, coheirs of their father's wantonness, by inversion turned boys into women,[29] not on orders from the divine power but by a trick of irreligious Venus.

Then she, giving her naturally severe countenance a grimacing expression said:

Are you in your interrogations[30] clothing with the garmet of inquiry a question which is not worthy to lay claim to the appearance of a doubt? Are you trying to give credence to the poets' shadowy figments which the efforts of the poetic art have painted? Do not a reappraisal from more profound discernment and a more advanced treatment by philosophy erase what has been learned in the childhood cradles of poetic teaching? Do you not know how the poets present falsehood, naked and without the protection of a covering, to their audience so that, by a certain sweetness of honeyed pleasure,

[29] Reference is to Apollo's love for Hyacinthus and Cyparissus: Ovid, *Met.* 10.106, 162; Hyginus 271.1. Bacchus forced his followers to dress in female garb: Hyginus 131.2. Cf. Euripides, *Bacch.* 820-836. Alan reacted strongly against a man's adopting women's clothes. Cf. *Anticl.* 9.265-269, Sheridan 211.

[30] Nature's answer is thoroughly Platonic. In *Rep.* 3.387D-390B Plato emphasizes that accounts in Homer of defects of gods or heroes are neither true nor useful. The principal danger arising from them is that they furnish man with an excuse for his own misconduct. He labours this point. Such poetry is all the more dangerous because its beauty appeals to, even bewitches, us. Plato knows that an attack on Homer is an attack on all Greek poetry. It may be noted that in *Anticl.* 1.142 Alan says that Virgil's Muse "shades many a lie." The rejection of Virgil would involve the rejection of all Latin poetry.

they may, so to speak, intoxicate the bewitched ears of their hearers? Or, how they cover falsehood with a kind of imitation of probability so that, by a presentation of precedents, they may seal the minds of men with a stamp from the anvil of shameful tolerance?[31] Or, how the poetic lyre gives a false note on the outer bark of the composition but within tells the listeners a secret of deeper significance so that when the outer shell of falsehood has been discarded the reader finds the sweeter kernel of truth hidden within?[32]

However, at times poets combine accounts of historical events and entertaining fables in a kind of elegant overlay so that, from an effective combination of diverse elements in their narrative, a more elegant picture may emerge.[33] However, when the poets rave about a plurality of gods and the gods themselves are said to have passed beyond the discipline of Venus,[34] in these passages the shade of falsehood begins to appear. In this respect the poet is not found to differ from the class that shares his characteristics. For since the dreams of Epicurus[35] are now put to sleep, the insanity of

[31] "If the great ones do this, why should not I?" This, for instance, is the line of reasoning that occurred to Byblis when she tried to find some justification for her love for her brother: Ovid, *Met.* 9.497-508.

[32] For example, it is not true that there was an Aeneas or a Dido. It is true that dalliance with a woman can militate against a man's success in fulfilling his greatest obligations.

[33] Probably refers to such works as the *De bello civili* of Lucan.

[34] Terminology is from Juvenal 1.15 where Juvenal is stating that he is qualified to write Satire. The matter is from Plato, *Rep.* 390B-C. Plato is criticising the representation of Zeus as unable to control, or even defer, his sex urges.

[35] Epicurus (ca. 341-ca 270 BC) founded his school of philosophy in Athens around 307 BC. Misunderstanding of his teaching, particularly

Manichaeus[36] healed, the subtleties of Aristotle made clear, the lies of Arrhius[37] belied, reason proves the unique unity of God, the universe proclaims it, faith believes it, Scripture bears witness to it. No stain forces its way to Him, no baneful vice makes an assault on Him, no impulse of temptation is associated with Him. He is the bright light that never fades, the life that never tires or dies, the fountain that ever flows, the seed-plot supplying the seed of life, the principal principle of wisdom, the original origin of good. Because then, many men, as we know from the testimony of the poets, have misused, by a literal interpretation, the terms applied to Venus, this account of theirs which falsely states that there is a plurality of gods or that these gods have wantoned in the playgrounds of Venus, comes to the evening and sunset that await extreme falsehood.[38] Over these statements I draw the cloud of silence, the ones preceding them I unfold to the light of truthful narrative.

Hereupon I said:

Mother, I now realise that my questioning smacks of deep, shameful ignorance. However, if one poor little question should dare to present itself before you for your attention,

---

on pleasure, led to misrepresentations and attacks both by pagan and Christian writers.

[36] Manes would be a more correct form of his name. His teaching was a developed form of gnosticism.

[37] Frequently written Arius. He was an heresiarch, condemned at the Council of Nicea in 325. His teaching dealt with the Person of Christ.

[38] Venus was given several titles — the Cyprian, the Cytherean, the Erycinan, the Dionaean, etc. It is not easy to see how such terms could lead to polytheism.

which is the surety for my humble worth, I would like to ask you something by way of lament rather than direct question.

Hereupon she said:

Have I not long since handed you a free rein to ask questions without check or barrier on my part?

Then I said:

I wonder why some parts of your tunic, which should approximate the interweave of a marriage, suffer a separation at that part in their connection where the picture's phantasy produces the image of man.

Then she said:

From what you have already sampled you can deduce what is the symbolic signification of the representation of the parenthesis-like rent.[39] For since, as we have said before, many men arm themselves with vices to injure their own mother and establish between her and them the chaos of ultimate dissension, in their violence they lay violent hands on me, tear my clothes in shreds to have pieces for themselves and, as far as in them lies, compel me, whom they should clothe in honour and reverence, to be stripped of my clothes and to go like a harlot to a brothel. This is the hidden meaning symbolised by this rent — that the vesture of my modesty suf-

[39] The simile of the rent garment goes back to Boethius *De cons. phil.*, Pr. 1 (Stewart-Rand 130ff.). Violent hands had torn off and carried away parts of Philosophy's robe. The violent hands referred to philosophical sects. Here the rents indicate the assaults made on Nature by man. Cf. *Anticl.* 1.313, Sheridan 58.

fers the insults of being torn off by injuries and insults from man alone.

Then I said:

The billows of my doubts, now quieted by the calm of your answers, grant my mind a respite from their onrush. But if it should please your goodwill, I would be deeply interested in trying to discern what unreasonable reason, what indiscreet discretion, what indirect direction forced man's little spark of reason to become so inactive that, intoxicated by a deadly draught of sensuality, he not only became an apostate from your laws, but even made unlawful assaults on them.

Then she said:

If you wish to know the original seeds of this plague, fan to higher flame the little fire of your reason, renew with greater eagerness your desire for knowledge. Let acuteness of mind dislodge dulness, let constancy in attention check the turbulent flow of your thoughts. As I am to begin from roots quite deep and wish to arrange the sequence of my narrative in a style above average, I first of all refuse to explain my theme on the plain of plain words or to vulgarise the vulgar with vulgar neologisms, but choose to gild things immodest with the golden trappings of modest words and to clothe them with the varied colours of graceful diction. The result will be that the dross of the above-mentioned vices will be beautified with golden phrases and the stench of vice will be balsam-scented with the perfume of honey-sweet words, lest the great dunghill stench should spread too far on the breezes that carry it and should induce in many a vomiting from sickening indignation. Nevertheless, as we experienced above, since the language of our discourse should show a kinship with the matters about which we speak,[40] there should be at times an uncouthness of style to conform to the ugliness of the subject-matter. In the following disquisition, however, it is my intention to contribute a mantle of fair-sounding words to the above-mentioned monsters of vice to prevent a poor quality of diction from offending the ears of readers or anything foul finding a place on a maiden's lips.

Then I said:

Already the hunger of my intellect, the keenness of my ardent nature, the ardor of a mind afire, the constancy of my confirmed attention call out for what you promise.

Then she said:

When God willed to call forth the fabric of the palace of the Universe from the "ideal" bridal bed within which it had been preconceived and to give expression to the idea of its creation, an idea which He had conceived from eternity, by giving it real existence by, so to speak, a material word,[41] as the choice architect of the universe, as the golden constructor of a golden construction, the skilled artisan of an amazing work of art, as the operative producer of an admirable work, He constructed the marvellous form of the kingdom of the world by the command of His deciding will alone, not by the operative aid of

[40] Cf. Alan of Lille, *Theologicae regulae* 34, PL 210.637D. Horace insists that diction must be in keeping with the character of the speaker and the matter under discussion: *Ars poetica* 87-119. Cf. Longinus, *On the Sublime* 19; Boethius, *De cons. phil.* 3 Prose 12.111 (Stewart-Rand 292).

[41] *Timaeus* 27C-29D. Cf. *Anticl.* 5.289, Sheridan 147.

any external factor, not by the help of pre-existing matter, not at the insistent urgings of any need. Accordingly God assigned various species of things to the palace of the Universe and these, though separated by the strife between differing classes, He regulated by agreement from law and order; He imposed laws on them, He bound them by sanctions. Thus with an exchange of kisses, arising from a certain mutual affinity, He leagued together things hostile to one another by generic opposition, things whose position had placed them on opposite sides, and He changed the strife of contrariety into the peace of friendship.[42] When all things, then, were harmonised by the fine chain of an invisible connection, in a peaceable union plurality made its way back to unity, diversity to identity, discord to concord.

When the artisan of the universe had clothed all things in the outward aspect befitting their natures and had wed them to one another in the relationship of lawful marriage, it was His will that by a mutually related circle of birth and death, transitory things should be given stability by instability, endlessness by endings, eternity by temporariness and that the series of things should ever be knit by successive renewals of birth.[43] He decreed that by the lawful path of derivation by propagation, like things, sealed with the stamp of manifest resemblance, should be produced from like.

---

[42] The harmony of the elements. Fire's flame goes upward; if it spread laterally, it would destroy earth. Water naturally gathers in wells and lakes or flows in rivers; otherwise earth would be submerged and fire extinguished. Cf. *Anticl.* 1.190-196, 203-206; 5.311-324; Sheridan 53, 54, 147-148.

[43] Cf. Bern. Silv. 1.2.57-60.

Accordingly he appointed me as his substitute, his vice-regent, the mistress of his mint, to put the stamp on the different classes of things so that I should mould the images of things, each on its own anvil, not allow the product to deviate from the form proper to its anvil but that, by my diligence in work, the face of the copy should spring from the countenance of the exemplar and not be defrauded of any of its natural gifts. I obeyed the commander's orders in my work and I, to use a metaphor, striking various coins of things according to the mould of the exemplar and producing copies of my original by fashioning like out of like, gave to my imprints the appearance of the things imaged. However, under the mysterious power of God, I carried out the administration of this office in such a way that the right hand of the supreme authority should direct my hand in its work, for my writing-reed would instantly go off course if it were not guided by the finger of the superintendent on high. But because without the supporting skill of a sub-delegated artisan, I could not put the finishing touches on so many species of things and because I decided to spend my time in the delightful palace of the ethereal region, where the contending winds do not destroy the peace of unadulterated calm, where no nightfall with its clouds buries ether's never-tiring light of day, where no distructive storm rages, where there is no threat from the thunder's mad rage, I stationed Venus, learned in the artisan's skill, on the outskirts of the Universe to be the subdelegate in charge of my work that she, under my will and command, with the active aid of Hymenaeus, her spouse, and Desire, her son, might exert herself in the reproduction of the varied animal-life of earth and, fitting her artisan's hammer to its anvil according to rule, might tirelessly maintain an unbroken linkage in the chain of the human race lest it be severed by the hands of the Fates and suffer damage by being broken apart.[44]

Since a mention of Desire was made at this stage of the narrative, I added to the above account, by way of a short insert in my own words, a question along the following lines.

Ha Ha. If I were not afraid of trespassing on your kindness by an unjustified interruption of your discourse and by chasing you with questions, I would express a wish to come to understand, by a descriptive picture[45] from you, the nature of Desire, whom you have touched on in a brief reference in your discourse. Although many authors have given an outline, concealed in symbols, of his enigmatic nature, yet they have left us nothing that we can follow with certainty. A story based on experience goes that his power and influence over the human race are so great that no one, even though sealed with the seal of nobility, or clothed in the graces of wisdom with its prerogatives, or protected with the armour of fortitude, or gowned with the robes of beauty, or adorned with other honours and favours, can exempt himself from the universal dominion of Desire.

[44] We have here a fatal flaw from an artistic point of view. Alan's heroine, Nature, decides to abandon the work that God had given her to do. No sufficient reason is given. Nature simply wished to live in more pleasant surroundings. Here she says that Venus would work under her "will and command." As the tale progresses, we are to discover that after her preliminary instructions to Venus, Nature takes no further interest. Thus far she has been a noble and tragic figure. We can no longer look on her in this way. The flaw is compounded by the fact that Nature, who in the rest of the *De planctu* is all but omniscient, here makes a fatal error in judgement. She chooses an incompetent deputy.

[45] For a picture in words, see Cicero, *Tusc. disp.* 5.5.14; 5.39.114.

Then she, with a restrained movement of her head and in words that showed that a rebuke was coming, said:

I believe that you are a soldier drawing pay in the army of Desire and are associated with him by some kind of brotherhood arising from deep and close friendship. For you are eagerly trying to trace out his inextricable labyrinth when you should rather be directing your attention of mind more closely to the account enriched by the wealth of my ideas. However, since I sympathise with your human frailty, I consider myself bound to eliminate, as far as my modest power allows, the darkness of your ignorance before the course of my narrative goes on to what follows next in order. Moreover, I am bound by a vow and promise to answer your questions. Either by describing with reliable descriptions or defining with regular definitions, I will demonstrate the indemonstrable, extricate the inextricable, although it is not bound in submission to any nature, does not abide an investigation by reason and thus cannot be stamped with the stamp of any one description.

Let the following, then, be set forth as a delimiting of the unlimited, let this emerge as an explanation of a nature that is inexplicable, let this be regarded as knowledge of the unknown, let this be brought forward as a doctrine on the unknowable; let it, however, be refined by the sublimity of the writer's pen.

IX

Metre 5

Love[1] is peace joined to hatred, loyalty to treachery, hope to fear and madness blended with reason. It is sweet shipwreck, light burden, pleasing Charybdis,[2] sound debility, insatiate hunger, hungry satiety, thirst when filled with water, deceptive pleasure, happy sadness, joy full of sorrow, delightful misfortune, unfortunate delight, sweetness bitter to its own taste. Its odour is savoury, its savour is insipid. It is a pleasing storm, a lightsome night, a lightless day, a living death, a dying life, a pleasant misery, pardonable sin, sinful pardon, sportive punishment, pious misdeed, nay, sweet crime, changeable pastime, unchangeable mockery, weak strength, stationary movable, mover of the stationary, irra-

[1] Metre is elegiac. It is worth noting that *cupido* is equated with *amor*. The predominant note of physical desire in the classical use of *amor* must be in Alan's mind.

[2] Charybdis was a whirlpool in a narrow sea-channel. Opposite it was Scylla, a sea monster in Homer, but later a dangerous rock. It required expert seamanship to navigate the channel. As early as Thucydides (ca. 457-ca. 400 BC) there was a tradition identifying the channel with the Straits of Messina: *Hist.* 4.24. Virgil has a description of Scylla and Charybdis: *Aen.* 3.320 and Paul the Deacon (ca. 720-ca. 800 AD) gives an account of the phenomena: *Hist. Lang.* 1.6. There is nothing in the Straits of Messina even faintly resembling the things in these descriptions.

tional reason, foolish wisdom, gloomy success, tearful laughter, tiring rest, pleasant hell, gloomy paradise, delightful prison, spring-like Winter, wintry Spring, misfortune. It is a hideous worm of the mind which the one in royal purple feels and which does not pass by the simple cloak of the beggar. Does not Desire, performing many miracles, to use antiphrasis,[3] change the shapes of all mankind. Though monk and adulterer are opposite terms, he forces both of these to exist together in the same subject. When his fury rages, Scylla[4] lays aside her fury and Nero[5] begins to be the good Aeneas,[6] Paris' sword flashes, Tydeus[7] grows soft with love, Nestor[8] becomes a youth, Melicerta[9] becomes an old man. Thersites[10]

[3] Antiphrasis is the use of a word in a sense opposite to its literal meaning. *Miracula* means wonderful things, i.e. good things.

[4] See note 2 supra. Alan obviously thought of Scylla as a sea monster.

[5] Roman emperor (54-68 AD). The murders and maladministration of the first six years of his reign made him a byword for extravagance and cruelty.

[6] Hero of Virgil's *Aeneid*. Son of Anchises and Aphrodite, he was commissioned to found Rome.

[7] Father of Diomedes and friend and fellow soldier of Polynices. He was a small but powerful and valiant man. His fierce battle rage at the siege of Thebes is mentioned by Aeschylus, *Seven Against Thebes* 377ff.

[8] Ovid, *Met.* 12.187-188, has Nestor saying "I lived for two centuries, now I am living in my third." Ovid must have misunderstood the more than "two generations" (= 60 years) mentioned in *Iliad* 1.250.

[9] Son of Athamas and Ino. His mother fled with him as a little boy in her arms to avoid the attacks of his mad father. She threw herself into the sea and through Venus' intercession Melicerta was turned into the sea-god Palaemon, and Ino into Leucothoë: Ovid, *Met.* 4.512-542.

[10] The first man in Western literature to attack the Establishment when he railed at Agamemnon. He was ugly and foul-mouthed: *Iliad* 2.212ff.

begs Paris for his beauty and Davus[11] begs the beauty of Adonis,[12] who is totally transformed into Davus. The wealthy Croesus[13] is in need; Codrus,[14] the beggar, abounds in wealth. Bavius[15] produces poems, Maro's[16] muse grows dull; Ennius[17] makes speeches and Marcus[18] is silent. Ulysses[19] becomes foolish, Ajax[20] in his madness grows wise. The one who formerly won the victory by dealing with the tricks of Antaeus,[21] though he subdues all other monsters, is overcome

[11] Stock name for a slave in Comedies of Plautus and Terence.

[12] Son of Cinyras and Myrrha. See viii, note 21. He was killed by a boar. The anemone sprang from his blood: Ovid, *Met.* 10.524ff., 708ff., 735.

[13] Last king of Lydia. His name became synonymous with wealth. Ovid, *Tristia* 3.7.42; Bern. Silv. 1.3.41.

[14] Codrus, an unknown poet: Virgil, *Ecl.* 5.11; 7.22; Juvenal 1.2; 3.203-209 (where his poverty is mentioned).

[15] A wretched poetaster: Virgil, *Ecl.* 3.90.

[16] Virgil.

[17] Ennius (239-169 BC) was a Latin poet. Only fragments of his voluminous works remain. Horace had a low estimate of his poetry: *Ars poetica* 259-262.

[18] Cicero.

[19] King of Ithaca, a Greek hero at the siege of Troy. He was known as a master of intrigue and stratagem and a very persuasive speaker: *Iliad* 3.200ff.

[20] The gigantic, courageous, stable "bulwark of the Greeks" in the Trojan war. In *Od.* 11.543ff. his death is attributed to the arms of Achilles having been given to Odysseus rather than to him. Later sources, the best known of which is the *Ajax* of Sophocles, state that the loss of the arms drove him to madness and suicide.

[21] Antaeus was a Libyan giant who compelled all comers to wrestle with him, overcame them and killed them. The tricks probably refer to the fact that Antaeus, a son of Poseidon and Earth, could regain his strength by falling on the ground. He was slain by Hercules: Pindar, *Isthm.* 4.56ff.; Plato, *Theaet.* 169B; Apollod. 2.115; Ovid, *Met.* 9.183.

by this one. If this madness sickens a woman's mind, she rushes into any and every crime and on her own initiative, too. Anticipating the hand of fate, a daughter treacherously slays a father, a sister slays a brother, or a wife, a husband. Thus by aphairesis[22] she wrongly shortens her husband's body when with stealthy sword she cuts off his head. The mother herself is forced to forget the name of mother and, while she is giving birth, is laying snares for her offspring. A son is astonished to encounter a stepmother in his mother and to find treachery where there should be loyalty, plots where there should be affection. Thus in Medea[23] two names battle on equal terms when she desires to be mother and stepmother at the same time. When Byblis[24] became too attached to Caunus, she could not be a sister or conduct herself as one. In the same way, too, Myrrha[25] submitting herself too far to her father became a parent by her sire and a mother by her father. But why offer further instruction? Every lover is forced to become an item at Desire's auction and pays his dues to him. He carries his warfare to all. His rule exempts practically no one. He lays everything low with the fury of his lightning stroke. Against him goodness, wisdom, grace of beauty, floods of riches, height of nobility will be of no avail. Deceit, trickery, fear, rage, madness, treachery, violence, delusion, gloom, find a hospitable home in his realms. Here reasonable procedure is

[22] Shortening a word by dropping a letter or syllable at the beginning, e.g., *temnere* for *contemnere*.

[23] See vııı, note 23.

[24] Byblis, daughter of Miletus, fell in love with her twin brother, Caunus. She was turned into a fountain. Ovid, *Met.* 9.454-665.

[25] See vııı, note 21.

to be without reason,[26] moderation means lack of moderation, trustworthiness is not to be trustworthy. He offers what
is sweet but adds what is bitter. He injects poison and brings
what is noble to an evil end. He attracts by seducing, mocks
with smiles, stings as he applies his salve, infects as he shows
affection, hates as he loves. You can by yourself, however,
restrain this madness, if you but flee; no more powerful an-
tidote is available. If you wish to avoid Venus, avoid her
places and times. Both place and time add fuel to her fire. If
you follow, she keeps up the pursuit. By your flight she is put
to flight. If you give ground, she gives ground. If you flee, she
flees.[27]

---

[26] Cf. description of Fortune in *Anticl.* 8.17ff., Sheridan 189.
[27] Cf. *Anticl.* 7.114; 9.248, Sheridan 176, 210-211.

X

Prose 5

Now from this artistic exposition of my teaching, the theory of the workings of Desire begins to become clear to you. The practical side you will be able to procure from the book of experience. You must not be surprised that in the foregoing description of Desire I have interjected some items of censure despite the fact that he is connected with me by a certain bond of true consanguinity. It is not the blind blight of spiteful detraction or the heat of flaming hatred seeking an outlet or the tyrant of envy raging without that leads me to use these stings of invective[1] and accusation but my desire not to give the impression of choking by silence[2] the clear statements coming from the very lips of truth. I bring no charge of dishonourable conduct against the basic nature of Desire, if it restrains itself with the bridle of moderation, checks itself with the reins of temperance, avoids over-stepping the assigned bounds of its natural ambit or allowing its ardour to boil forth in excessive passion, but only if its tiny flame[3] turns

[1] Cf. *Anticl.* Prose Prologue, Sheridan 42.

[2] Gilbert of Poitiers, *Expositio in Boecii libros de Trinitate* 7, ed. N. M. Häring, *The Commentaries on Boethius by Gilbert of Poitiers* (Toronto 1966) 54.38. Cf. *Anticl.* 7.128-129, Sheridan 177.

[3] Cf. Boeth. *De Trin.* 1 (Stewart-Rand 2); *Anticl.* Prose Prologue, Sheridan 40.

into a conflagration, if its little fountain grows into a torrent, if its luxurious growth calls for the pruning-hook to shorten it, if its excessive swelling needs treatment to heal it. For every excess interferes with the progress that comes from the temperateness of the mean and distention from unhealthy surfeit swells and causes what we may call ulcers of vice.[4] The above historic discourse, that has wandered off in jests and jokes, is offered as a dish fit for your naïvete. Now let the mode of narration, that has digressed a little into the trivial, crude pieces suited to your undeveloped literary ability, return to the prearranged sequence of the prescribed discourse. As I informed you when touching on the matter before, I selected Venus to be in charge of the work of propagation of earth's living things so that she might in producing things mould various materials and submit them for examination. I, in the varied formation of their nature, would add to her works the final, refining touch. To insure that the reliability of the instruments should preclude confused and defective workmanship, I assigned her two approved hammers[5] with which to nullify the snares of the Fates[6] and also make a variety of things ready for existence. I also set aside outstanding workshops with anvils in which to do this work, giving instructions that she should apply these same hammers to these same an-

---

[4] Pliny 20.8.16; 25; Isid., *Etym.* has the form *apostoma*.

[5] One hammer for human life, another for the rest of creation. Alan had man in mind almost exclusively and the hammer symbolises the male sex, perhaps even the male genitalia while the anvil refers to the female sex or female genitalia.

[6] The Fates bring man to inevitable death. They show no interest in birth. Nature's work is to prevent the Fates from exterminating the human race.

vils and faithfully devote herself to the production of things and not allow the hammers to stray away from their anvils in any form of deviation. I had also bestowed on her an unusually powerful writing-pen for her work so that she might trace the classes of things, according to the rules of my orthography, on suitable pages which called for writing by this same pen and which through my kind gift she had in her possession, so that she might not suffer the same pen to wander in the smallest degree from the path of proper delineation into the byways of pseudography.[7]

But since she was bound by the appointed embraces of generative coition to bring together in contraposition differing parts of the different sexes so as to effect the propagation of things, with imperial precepts from my magisterial teaching I taught her, as if she were a pupil needing instruction, which procedures in the art of Grammar she should adopt in the artistic combinations of her constructions and which she should reject as irregular and unredeemed by any excusing figure,[8] so as to insure that she should use in her connections the regular constructions of the art of Grammar and that the nobility of her artistic work should not suffer impairment from any ignorance of art on her part.

Since the plan of Nature gave special recognition, as the evidence of Grammar confirms, to two genders,[9] to wit, the

[7] Nature had an effective and reliable blueprint. If this were followed without any change whatsoever, the continuation of the race would be guaranteed. She gave a special pen and special paper to Venus to copy down this blueprint. Cf. Mart. Cap. 1.65, ed. Dick 30.8.

[8] The Romans were suspicious of Figures of Speech and felt that only a thin line separated a Figure and a solecism: Quint. 1.5.5.

[9] Alan is thinking only of human beings.

masculine and feminine (although some men, deprived of a sign of sex, could, in my opinion, be classified as of neuter gender), I charged the Cyprian, with secret warnings and mighty, thunderous threats, that she should, as reason demanded, concentrate exclusively in her connections on the natural union of masculine and feminine gender.

Since, by the demands of the conditions necessary for reproduction, the masculine joins the feminine to itself, if an irregular combination of members of the same sex should come into common practice, so that appurtenances of the same sex should be mutually connected, that combination would never be able to gain acceptance from me either as a means of procreation[10] or as an aid to conception. For if the masculine gender, by a certain violence of unreasonable reason, should call for a gender entirely similar to itself, this bond and union will not be able to defend the flaw as any kind of graceful figure but will bear the stain of an outlandish and unpardonable solecism.[11]

Moreover,[12] my command instructed the Cyprian that in

[10] *Evocatio* is the reading best supported. The meaning "to call into, to bring into, existence" is well attested: Virgil, *Geor.* 1.18; Varro, *De re rustica* 2.2.14; Columella 3.12.1; Pliny 16.50.114; Fulgentius, *Mitologiarum* 1.8, ed. R. Helm (Leipzig 1898) 21.11.

[11] A strained metaphor from grammar. The meaning is: confusion of gender can never be justified on the grounds of being a figure of speech. It is always a flaw.

[12] This passage is an almost incredible mélange of words whose ordinary, metaphorical, technical and etymological signification must be kept in mind simultaneously. *Suppositio* means "placing underneath" (etymology) and calls *suppositum* "a noun" (technical sense) to mind. *Appositio* means "placing" one thing "along another" (etymology), an "adjective" (technical). Adjective symbolises man, noun symbolises

her unions she should observe the regular procedure in matters of subjacent and superjacent and should assign the role of
subjacent to the part characteristic of the female sex and
should place that part that is a specific mark of the male sex in
the prestigious position of superjacent in such a way that the
superjacent cannot go down to take the place of the subjacent
nor the subjacent pass over to the demesne of the superjacent.
Since each requires the other, the superjacent with the
characteristic of an adjective is attracted by the law of urgent
need to the subjacent which appropriates the special
characteristics of a noun.

In addition to this I gave instructions that the conjugations
of Dione's daughter should restrict themselves entirely to the
forward march of the transitive[13] and should not admit the
stationary intransitive or the circuitous reflexive or the recurring passive, and that she should not, by an excessive extension
of permission to go to and fro, tolerate a situation where the
active type, by appropriating an additional meaning, goes
over to the passive or the passive, laying aside its proper
character, returns to the active[14] or where a verb with a passive

---

woman. Background idea concerns the implications of position in
coitus. No translation can deal adequately with the passage.

[13] The active element in sexual relationship is the man, the woman's
role is passive. Man is represented by the subject of a sentence, woman
by the object. Only the transitive verb, which expresses the direct action
of subject on object can symbolise the sex relationship. With intransitive verbs there is no direct object. The action in reflexive and passive
verbs is referred back to the subject. Cf. *Carmina burana* 95.17, ed. A.
Hilka and O. Schumann (Heidelberg 1930) 2.123.

[14] The roles of man and woman cannot be interchanged.

ending retains an active meaning and adopts the rules of deponents.[15]

It is no wonder, then, that very many far-reaching constructions, labelled with the sign of the discipline of Grammar, suffer rejection from the home of Venus' art while she admits to the embraces of intimate friendship with her these constructions which obey her preceptive rules, stays with the curse of eternal exclusion those which try to storm her laws by insults and contradictions most eloquently expressed. For statements with the authority of philosophy admit that many of the most far-reaching constructions are common to several disciplines while some others have no permission to go beyond the abodes of their own discipline.[16] However, I knew that Venus would enter the conflict and contest in argument against the clever sallies of the Fates and lest by some subterfuge and deceit, she might have to suffer, at the hand of Atropos, the cunningly devised restrictions of the conclusion,[17] I gave her instruction in this discipline to enable her to work out her own form of argument according to these rules of the discipline of argumentation and taught her how to discover the lurking places of fraud and fallacy in her opponents' arguments, so that she might with a greater sense of security carry on her contest in argument against the snares of the opponents and

[15] A deponent verb is passive (a woman) in form, but active (a man) in meaning.

[16] Grammar, Dialectic and Rhetoric were regarded as closely related disciplines and certain terms are common to more than one of them. Other terms belong exclusively to one discipline.

[17] *Conclusio* in Dialectic refers to the final term of a syllogism. In Rhetoric it refers to the peroration of a speech. These two are closely related. It is quite possible that Alan had its military meaning, "a blockade," in mind also.

with comparable counter-arguments rebut the arguments of her adversaries.[18]

I also charged her to have the form of her syllogism woven from a fitting arrangement of three propositions but yet willing to accept an abridgement to two terms and be free from subjection to any Aristotelian figure.[19] This, however, was to be done in such a way that in each set of propositions, the major, an extreme, performs the role of predicate and the minor holds itself bound by the laws of subject. In the first proposition, however, the predicate is not to inhere in the subject by any manner of real inherence but just by way of external contact as when a term is predicated of a term.[20] As regards the second proposition, the major is to have a more pronounced connection with the minor by the adoption of mutual and reciprocal kisses. Finally in the conclusion the carnal connection of subject and predicate is to be solemnised by

[18] *Instantia* is the contrary of a proposition: Boethius, *Prior anal. Arist. inter.* 26, PL 64.710A-D. See Section II, n. 14.

[19] The Aristotelian syllogism has three terms — a major, a minor and a conclusion. This is the method of reasoning proper to Dialectic. The mode of proof in Rhetoric is by the enthymeme, which Aristotle defines as "a rhetorical syllogism": *Rhet.* 1356^{b}C. The true syllogism has three terms: "man is mortal; John is a man; therefore John is mortal." The enthymeme has two terms: "John is a man," "therefore he is mortal." Nature claims that she instructed Venus in argumentation suitable for either dialectic or rhetoric.

[20] Cf. Arist., *Anal. post.* 1.8.75^{b}24ff. and *Cat.* 1.2, 1^{a}16ff.; Boethius, *In Cat. Arist.* 1, PL 64.182B-C; St. Thomas Aquinas, *De ente et essentia* 2, ed. M.-D. Roland-Gosselin (Paris 1948) 11ff. The meaning is: the predicate (woman) is not to be an inherent part of the subject (man). Manhood and womanhood can make contact but they are mutually exclusive.

the true bond of very close intercourse.[21] The following was also part of my advice — that the terms in Venus' arrangement should not, by claiming the rights of analogy in speech, interchange their respective positions by any baleful process of retrogradation by conversion.[22] To prevent the Fallacy of the Consequent,[23] the product of regarding as identical things that are only alike, from interfering with Venus' activity, I even identified the terms with individual signs so that she could, by a personal glance of unimpeded perception, clearly recognise which terms the low-grade subject, which the top-grade predicate called for in keeping with the rightful demands of the condition of each, lest an illogical combination of terms should not observe the demands of their relative

[21] We have now passed on to Dialectic. In the syllogism, the Major = Predicate = man: the Minor = the Subject = woman: conclusion = carnal relations.

[22] Conversion in Logic refers to inverting a proposition so that the predicate becomes the subject. "All men are animals" by conversion becomes "some animals are men." *Retrogradatio*, though not a technical term in logic, has the same meaning — the predicate term "goes back" to take the place of the subject. What he is emphasising is that man cannot change place with woman. I rather suspect double entendre in both *conversionis* and *retrogradatione*.

[23] This fallacy consists in deducing the truth of the Antecedent from the truth of the Consequent. An example may make this clear. The following is a valid syllogism: "if it has rained, the streets are wet; it has rained; therefore the streets are wet." The following is invalid: "if it has rained, the streets are wet; the streets are wet; therefore it has rained." Other factors could account for the wetness of the streets. One could say: "if it has rained, the streets are wet; the streets are wet; therefore, it is likely that it has rained." In the fallacy likelihood is confused with certainty. In homosexuality things that are alike (man and woman) are treated as if they were identical.

conditions and a general disability, marked by boorish absurdities, should arise.[24]

Just as I decided to excommunicate from the schools of Venus certain practices of Grammar and Dialectic as inroads of the most ill-disposed enemy, so too I banned from the Cyprian's workshop the use of words by the rhetors in metonymy[25] which mother Rhetoric clasps to her ample bosom and breathes great beauty on her orations, lest, if she embark on too harsh a trope and transfer the predicate from its loudly protesting subject to something else, cleverness would turn into a blemish, refinement into boorishness, a figure of speech into a defect and excessive embellishment into disfigurement. When Venus' renown had been established by these remarkable tokens of splendour, Earth was given over to her as her habitat and native land. With her tools to aid her in piecing together the successive stages in the reproduction of the human race, she began, with more than ordinary skill, to bind together what was cut asunder by the hands of the Fates, as with toil and sweat she continued the mending process with her fine needle. Thus for some time she discharged with a most ready diligence what was due to me

[24] There are many resemblances between men and women but the differences are clearly marked. Failure to recognise those differences leads to unnatural and absurd results.

[25] Metonymy is the substitution of one name for another with which it has some connection. The Grammarians all use practically identical examples — use of *Ceres* (goddess of wheat) for bread, *Liber* (god of wine) for wine: Charisius *Ars grammatica* 4, ed. Keil 1.273.10-21; Diomedes, *Ars grammatica* 2, ed. Keil 1.458.13-30; Donatus, *Ars gram.* 3.6, ed. Keil 4.400.7-14. Alan's point is not too clear. Possibly he means substitution of some word like *amans* or *coniunx* (which can refer to man or woman) for *mulier* or *uxor*.

from her tributary post. However, since a mind, that from birth has been disgusted by the cloying effect of sameness, grows indignant and the impact of daily toil destroys the desire to continue a task to the end, the frequent repetition of one and the same work bedeviled and disgusted the Cytherean and the effect of continuous toil removed the inclination to work. Accordingly, desiring to live the soft life of barren ease rather than be harassed by fruitful labour, disliking the strain of her task with its continuous work, enervated by thoughts of slothfulness and excessive ease, she began to wanton with childish indiscretion. For, whenever sluggishness bivouacs with any man, all military valour is cashiered by him and a barren ease is wont to become pregnant and fecund with an evil progeny. A deluging flood of drink, too, foams[26] into excessive lusts and unrestrained ingestion of food belches forth a vomit proportionate to the excess.

Venus, goaded by these deadly furies into turning against her husband, Hymenaeus, and defiling the chaste marriage-couch by the blight of adultery, began to live in fornication and concubinage with Antigenius.[27] Trapped by the deadly suggestions arising from her own adultery, she barbarously turned a noble work into a craft,[28] a work governed by rule into something ruleless, a work of refinement into something

[26] For *despumare* see Jerome, *Ep.* 69.9, CSEL 54.696.12ff.; Pachomius, *Ep.* 7, ed. Dom A. Boon, *Pachomiana latina* (Louvain 1932) 95.25.

[27] *Antigenius*, not *Antigamus*, is the reading supported by the best manuscripts. I can find no use of the word before Alan. It means "opposed to Genius." For Genius see Introd., pp. 59-62.

[28] The Greeks regarded handicrafts as low and vulgar: Arist., *Polit.* 3.1278ᵃ23; 4.1291ᵃ1; 7.13.28ᵇ39; 8.1337ᵇ9; *Eth. Nic.* 4.1123ᵃ20.

boorish, and studiously corrupting my precept, she dispossessed the hammers of fellowship with their anvils and sentenced them to counterfeit anvils. These natural anvils could be seen bewailing the loss of their own hammers and begging for them with tears. The one, who with the shield of defence, used to confront the sword of Atropos as it moved down all things, was now joined to it in a mutual pact of confirmed reconciliation, permitted the Fate's sickle to range too widely over the human harvest and did not counterbalance the loss by causing life to begin afresh from new seed. On the contrary, destroying herself with the connections of Grammar, perverting herself with the conversions of Dialectic, discolouring herself with the colours[29] of Rhetoric, she kept turning her art into a figure and the figure into a defect. While she was maintaining her alluring concubinage on a permanent basis by her excessive fornications with her adulterer, she begat a child from him and gained a bastard instead of a son. Since he took no pleasure in the charms of love, refused to relax in the delights of sport, the result was that he was, by antiphrasis, so to speak, called Sport[30], a word derived from sportiveness, and usage has stamped him with the name. Two sons were given, then, to Dione's daughter, different by discrepancy of

[29] Colour is frequently applied to diction: Cicero *De or.* 3.25.75; 3.52.199; Quint. 12.10.71; Hor. *Ars poetica* 236; Mart. Cap. 5.471, ed. Dick 235.23-24.

[30] *Jocus*, personified as a god, appears early in Latin literature. In Plautus, *Bacch.* 1.2.116 he is in company with *dis damnossimis*. In Hor., *Od.* 1.2.34 he is associated with *cupido*. Porphyrion, on Hor. *Od.* 1.33.10-12, interprets Horace as equating Love and cruel Joke, ed. F. Havthal, *Acronis et Porphyrionis commentarii in Q. Horatium Flaccum* (Amsterdam 1966) 1.127-128. In Prudentius, *Psych.* 336, he is associated with triflers.

origin, dissimilar by law of birth, unlike in their moral reputation, different by diversity of skill. Hymenaeus is closely related to me by the bond of brotherhood from the same mother and a lineage of outstanding merit gives him an exalted position. He begat from Venus a son, Desire. On the other hand the buffoonish Antigenius, sprung from an ignoble line, in rakish fashion fathered, in adultery with Venus, a bastard son, Sport. The former's birth finds its defence in a solemnised marriage, the commonness of a commonly-known concubinage arraigns the latter's descent. In the former there shines the urbanity of his father's courteousness; the boorishness of his father's provincialism denigrates the latter. The former dwells by the silvery fountains, bright with their besilvered sheens; the latter tirelessly haunts places cursed with unending drought. The latter pitches his tent in flat wastelands; the former finds his happiness in sylvan glades. The latter forever spends the entire night in his tents; the former spends day and night without interruption in the open air. The former wounds the one he chases with spears of gold; the latter pierces what he strikes with javelins of iron. The former makes his guests merry with nectar that is not gone sour; the latter ruins his guests with a bitter potion of absinthe.

Now my speech has inscribed on the tablet of your mind an account of how the ruinous destruction of idleness took hold of forceful Venus, how a deluging flood of drink produced the fires of love, how the elephantine leprosy of lust, arising from gorging of food, ruined many.

Behold, in wretchedness and lamentation, I have sung my song of complaint about mankind languishing from Venus' piercing fever. Now let us tune our harp for a plaintful discourse in elegiac verse about others whom an unwholesome tribe of different vices disturbs. For many, who steal past and avoid the whirlpool mouths of voracious Charybdis, suffer a miserable shipwreck from an unexpected peril in the depths of malicious Scylla.[31] Many, too, while they escape from ruinous encounters with fast-flowing torrents, stick fast in the greedy slime of a sluggish pool. Others, guided by caution, avoid the precipices of the over-hanging mountain but are bruised on the level plain by a self-caused fall.

Hold fast under the key of your retentive memory what I shall discuss and shake off the drowsy torpor from your vigilant mind so that, moved with me by a mother-like heart, you may feel pity and compassion for men in danger of shipwreck and, armed with the shield of forewarning, may go forth to combat the monstrous army of vices and may, if any herb from an evil seed should dare to sprout in the garden of your own mind, remove it by a timely use of the cutting hook.

Then I said:

For some time now my mind has been cheered by what I have gained from your teaching and I lend a most ready ear to your corrections.

Then she said:

[31] See IX, note 2.

XI

Metre 6

Alas, what headlong fall has virtue suffered[1] that it struggles under the dominion of vice? Virtue of every kind is in exile, the reins of madness are being loosed for vice. The day of justice fades; scarcely a shadow of its shade remains to survive it; bereft of light, immersed in night, it bewails the death of the star that brought it honour.[2] While the lightning-flash of crime blasts the earth, the night of fraud darkens the star of fidelity and no stars of virtue redeem the Stygian darkness of that night. The evening of fidelity lies heavy on the world, the nocturnal chaos of fraud is everywhere. Fidelity fades in the face of fraud; fraud, too, deceives fraud by fraud and thus trickery puts pressure on trickery. In the realm of customary behaviour, accepted practices are lacking in morality. Laws lack legal force; rights lose their right of tenure. All justice is

[1] Metre is Aesclepiad Minor Catalectic. See G. Raynaud de Lage, *Alain de Lille, Poète* 104, note 233; 153. For first line see Boeth. *De. cons. phil.* 1.M.2.1 (Stewart-Rand 134). Cicero describes *virtus* as "nothing other than Nature completed in itself and brought to perfection": *De leg.* 1.8.25.

[2] Astraea, goddess of justice, was the last of the celestials to leave earth on account of man's wickedness. She is said to have been changed into the constellation Libra or Virgo. If Alan opted for Libra, he may have the faintness of the constellation in mind. None of its stars is above the third magnitude: Ovid, *Met.* 1.149-150.

administered without justice and law flourishes without legality. The world is in a state of decline: already the golden ages of the world are in decay.[3] Poverty clothes a world of iron, the same world that noble gold once clothed. Fraud no longer seeks the cloak of pretence nor does the noisome stench of crime seek for itself the fragrant balsam of virtue so as to supply a cloak for its evil smell. Thus does the nettle hide its impoverishment of beauty with roses, the seaweed with hyacinth, dross with silver, archil with purple so as to make up for the defects in appearance of what lies within. Crime, however, doffs all its trappings and does not give itself the colours of justice. It openly defines itself as crime. Fraud itself becomes the external expression of its frenzy.[4]

What remains safe when treachery arms even mothers against their offspring? When brotherly love is afflicted with fraud and the right hand lies to its sister? The obligation arising from righteousness, to respect upright men, is considered a thing of reproach; the law of piety is impiety; to have a sense of shame is now a shame in every eye. Without shame a man, no longer manlike, puts aside the practices of man. Degenerate, then, he adopts the degenerate way of an irrational animal. Thus he unmans himself and deserves to be unmanned by himself.

[3] Ovid, *Met.* 1.1-150.
[4] Men once tried to give fair names to the actions that proceeded from the fraud in their hearts. They no longer try to hide the true motivation for their deeds.

XII

Prose 6

In reply I said:

Since rational observation tends to lose its way in this open ground of generalities and specialisation within defined limits is the friend of the intellect, I would wish you to unwind the vices which you wind in what I may call a small clew of generic statements and show the several shades of differentiation in each species.

Then she said:

Since it would not be fitting that your reasonable and deserving request should be robbed of the reward of fulfilment, it is right to mark for you each and every vice, one by one, with its individual marks. Since an account has been given of how the whole world is in danger in the all but universal conflagration caused by Venus on earth, it now remains to tell how the same world is being shipwrecked in a world-wide deluge of gluttony, as gluttony is, so to speak, a preamble to acts of lust and a kind of antecedent to the consequent venery.[1]

---

[1] Alan has been concentrating on homosexuality. He now wishes to pass on to other vices. He first deals with gluttony. In *De arte praed.* 4, PL 210.119A-121B, he points out that gluttony is a daughter of idolatry

Note well that some of the daughters of Idolatry[2] of old,
which was once thoroughly uprooted, are at the present moment trying to restore their mother's dominion and, by certain
conjuring incantations, to raise her from the dead for a new
life. These daughters, playing the role of strumpets, with faces
made white to give a false impression of pleasure,[3] attract
their lovers and seduce them by their wiles. With gloomy joy,
tender cruelty, hostile friendship, they, like the Sirens,[4] deadly
sweet as far as their faces go, feature a delightful melody but
lure their lovers to the shipwreck of idolatry. One of these, to
coin a word, may, in keeping with her characteristics, be
called Bacchilatria.[5] She, robbing her lover of his little spark
of reason, exposes him to the darkness of brutish sensuality
and harlot-fashion, so intoxicates her lover that he is com-

---

and refers to St. Paul's statement about those "whose God is their
belly" (Philipp. 4.19). He emphasises the connection between gluttony
and lust and advises us to "consult Nature; she will tell you what ought
to be the law of life." To sum up: gluttony is the daughter of idolatry; it
leads to lust and is contrary to Nature. Here we have the basis for what
follows.

[2] Broadly speaking, Idolatry means making anything but God the
end of our activities. In Alan contempt for Nature, the mouthpiece of
God, would constitute Idolatry.

[3] This refers to the pleasure that their faces promise their devotees.

[4] The Sirens were sea songstresses, referred to in Homer, *Od.* 12.39,
184. Their beautiful singing lured sailors to rocks and shipwreck.
Homer gives no account of their appearance. Alan's references to their
faces may be based on the story that they were half-maidens, half-birds
or that they were the partly metamorphosed daughters of Acheloüs, retaining their presumably beautiful features. Ovid, *Met.* 5.552-563;
14.87-88.

[5] *De arte praed.* 4, PL 210.120c. *Latria* refers to the supreme worship
given to God alone. Bacchus was God of Wine.

pelled to pursue Bacchus with undue insistence and to such an extent, indeed, that, as a toper chained to Bacchus by the bond of excessive love, he is believed to offer him the sovereign honour of divine worship. As a result the Bacchilatrate very often cannot bear to have Bacchus separated from him by an intervening space, just as if he were the relics of his favourite saint, and does not allow his god to tarry long in storage in casks apart from him but, to have the divine assistance of this same god more closely united to him, he confines Bacchus in the jar of his belly. However, since it often happens that the little repository of the stomach cannot for long entertain so great a divine guest, the same god disappears disgustingly in air either by the North Pole of the eastern gate or the South Pole of the region towards the west.[6] Very often, too, the worshipper of Bacchus constructs a guest room for him in fancy goblets,[7] rich in value from their price material, so that his divinity may sparkle more divinely in a golden vessel. Thus with his brightness he competes with the lustre of the heavens, with his green hue contends with the green of the emerald, with the excellence of his taste transcends most other tastes and he so stimulates the children of his drinking bouts by his affected divine qualities that they join in honouring Bacchus as though he were a secret, ineffable deity, with ineffable

[6] Alan is saying that flatus caused by excess of wine must "come up" or "go down." North gives the idea of "up," e.g. "up North"; South gives the idea of "down," e.g. "down South." The Latin word for the East is *Oriens*, "rising," i.e. the quarter where the sun "comes up." The word for the West is *Occidens*, "setting," i.e. where the sun "goes down." Alan telescopes the images in a strange fashion.

[7] *Capsulis. Capsula* literally means a small box. Metaphorically it is used to describe anything that is the height of fashion: Seneca, *Ep.* 115.2.

love. They, too, swallow Bacchus down to the dregs so that nothing of this divinity may remain undrunk and thus they force their god to make an undignified descent into the Tartarean depths of their bellies. Thus, as they descend to the most common kind of drinking, they ascend to the highest degree of drunkenness.[8]

This plague is the enemy not only of the low and common herd but also forces prelates to bend their proud necks to it. The pleasures which Nature's favour pours over Bacchus are not enough for these prelates; rather, indeed, they employ the suction-process of a broad whirlpool[9] and gulp down with the greedy throat of a Charybdis[10] a Bacchus, now rejoicing in marriage with the rose, now breathing a bouquet of another flower, now claiming certain privileges for himself because of his association with the hyssop, now enriched with extrinsic endowments from other sources. They carry this so far that they experience shipwreck where there is no sea, tears where there is no grief, listlessness where there is no illness, the sleep of drunkenness where there is no drowsiness. When they have been struck by the force of a drinking bout and are devoting their attention to chanting the psalms, they break the sequence by excessive separation of the verses, as they interpolate an unseasonable north-wind due to intoxication.[11]

Not only the above-mentioned desire for drink but also a wolfish greed for food allure large numbers. Their disordinate

---

[8] *Superlativum gradum.* The terminology is from comparison of adjectives.

[9] See Paul the Deacon, *Hist. Lang.* 1.6.

[10] See IX, note 2.

[11] This refers to belching during public recitation of the Office by clerics who have over-indulged in wine.

desires and vulgar thoughts lead to dreams of sumptuous banquets. Since they pay far more than is due to the collector[12]
who calls daily for food, he is bound to return the surplus to
the debtor. Whatever these people possess they deposit as
treasure in the safe of their stomach. Although rust with its
corrosive teeth does not bite into this deposit nor the trickery
of the fox-like thief pilfer it,[13] it disappears, nevertheless, in a
more shameful way and by the more shameful thievery of the
heat that burns it up. These men provoke their maws to vomit
up their coins, their coffers to throw up their marks in nausea,
so as to be in a position to offer tokens of a more pronounced
respect to the collector for their stomachs. They endow their
stomachs internally with the riches of food, externally they
are placed in a position of naked, sheer and unrelieved poverty.

This pestilence does not restrict itself to the lowly, common
crowd but extends itself more widely to prelates. With the
varied martyrdoms of fire, they torture salmon, pike and
other fish distinguished by a comparable excellence. Profan-
ing the rite of baptism, they baptise them at the sacred font of
pepper so that baptised with such a baptism, they may obtain

---

[12] What follows is a long-drawn-out metaphor based on a mixture of
terms taken from banking and paying debts. The following may
simplify it:

arca	=	safe (strong-box)	=	stomach
commissum	=	deposit	=	food
exactor	=	collector	=	hunger of stomach
debtor	=	debtor	=	rational man
creditor	=	creditor	=	stomach
decoquere	=	to go bankrupt	=	to burn up
superhabundans	=	overpayment	=	overweight

[13] Cf. Matthew 6.19

diverse graces of taste. On the same table the land animal is submerged beneath a flood of pepper,[14] the fish swims in pepper, the fowl is held fast in the same sticky substance. When so many kinds of animals are imprisoned in the gaol of one belly, the water animal is surprised that the species proper to earth and air are buried with him in the same sepulchre.[15] If they were given permission to leave, the door would scarcely be sufficient in size for their outward passage.

The above-mentioned pests construct a bridge over which the brothel of lust is reached. These are the preliminary steps by which one enters the practice of robbery. These beget disease and sow the seeds of poverty. These nurse discord, are the sisters of insanity, the mothers of intemperance, the huntresses of impurity. Through these the human race exceeds the bounds of modesty, disregards the restraints of temperance, breaks the seal of chastity, ignores the beauty of my gifts. Although my bounty spreads so many dishes in front of men, pours them so many cups, they, nevertheless, showing no gratitude for my favours, abuse what is lawful in a very unlawful way, give a loose rein to their gluttony, when they exceed limits in eating, produce the lines of drinking to infin-

[14] Pepper was expensive and a delicacy. Horace, *Ep.* 2.1.270 mentions it with frankincense; Juvenal 14.293 shows that merchants regarded it as a precious cargo. For pepper as a delicacy, see Jerome, *Ep.* 52.12, CSEL 54.435.9.

[15] Land and water animals were shown separately on Nature's robe in section II. Cf. Bern. Silv. 1.3.415ff. where fish have their own *regnum*, "kingdom." The Code of Canon Law, Canon 1251.2, states that meat and fish may be taken at the principal meal on a day of Fast. This shows there was once a general or local law or custom which forbade this.

ity. They beguile the palate with the sharp taste of salted foods so that they may drink often and deeply, but more often still are forced to feel the pangs of thirst.

There is also another daughter of Idolatry; if a proper name is to retain some relationship in expression with what it denotes, it is logical to call her by the suitable name of Nummulatria.[16] This is Avarice[17] through whom money is deified in men's minds and a right to divine veneration is openly granted to cash. It is due to her that when cash speaks, the trumpet of Tullius'[18] eloquence grows hoarse; when cash takes the field, the lightning of Hector's[19] warfare ceases; when cash fights, the strength of Hercules[20] is subdued. If one is armed with money, as with a silver breastplate, he does not give a straw for the attack of Tullius' eloquence, for the lightning assault of Hector, for the power of Hercules' strength, for the clever wiles of chameleon-like Ulysses.[21] So hot has the hunger for possessions grown that the subtlety of Dialectic is stilled, the role of deliberative Rhetoric is in a decline. When an abundance of cash winds up its speech, Tullius right away

[16] Worship of Cash.

[17] In *De arte praed.* 6, PL 210.123B, Alan speaks of avarice as a type of idolatry and refers to Paul's statement that "avarice is the service of idols" (Col. 3:5). He also has Nature declaim against it to the effect that, since men come into the world and leave it without posessions, riches cannot be natural for them: PL 210.123D, 124A.

[18] Cicero, Rome's greatest orator.

[19] Eldest son of the Trojan King, Priam, and bravest of the Trojan warriors.

[20] For Hercules' feats of strength, see Ovid, *Met.* 9.182-199. Cf. Bern. Silv. 1.3.44.

[21] See IX, note 19.

sells the mould for his eloquence, Lucretia[22] exchanges the
jewels of her chastity for their price in gold; Penelope,[23] offering her chastity for hire, lays her modesty aside for a price;
Hippolytus,[24] too, if he should hear the whispered prayers of
money, would not adopt a step-mother's attitude towards a
step-mother's prayers. For if money whispers in the judge's
ear, the lyre of Orpheus,[25] the song of Amphion,[26] the muse of
Vergil[27] would be stifled by its voice. Yet the rich man, shipwrecked in the depths of his riches, is tortured by the forces of
dropsical thirst.

Although the poor man cannot actually indulge in real
avarice, he nevertheless keeps in his heart the archetype of
miserliness. For shame! Loads of metal bestow offices proportionate to the metal's weight. Now not Caesar but cash is
everything.[28] Like an interagent it works its way through each
and every office from the most restricted to the most extensive. Now cash is our patriarch; it enthrones some at the top

[22] Wife of Tarquinius Collatinus. Sextus, son of Tarquinius Super-
bus, forced her to submit to him. She reported the matter to her husband and then committed suicide. The incident led to the expulsion of
the Tarquin King from Rome and the foundation of the Republic: Livy
1.58.

[23] Penelope was the faithful wife of Ulysses. Though beset by
suitors, she refused to marry during the twenty years that Ulysses was
absent.

[24] See I, note 16.

[25] A Theban singer and musician who could charm even animals and
inanimate objects: cf. *Anticl.* 2.351; 3.403, Sheridan 82, 110.

[26] He was given a magical lyre by Hermes. With it he drew stones
after him and used them to wall Thebes: cf. *Anticl.* 3.407, Sheridan 110.

[27] Author of the *Aeneid*, the greatest work in Latin literature.

[28] Cf. Lucan 3.108.

as archbishops; it raises others to the height of honour as bishops; it fits these into the office of archdeacon; it adjusts others to the commonplace work of other ranks. Why say more? Cash conquers, cash rules, cash gives orders to all.[29] What does it profit one, if, with precise Ptolemy's[30] chariot he reach a knowledge of the motions described in elusive Astronomy, investigate what the stars predict and scrutinise the spontaneous wanderings of the planets? If with Euclid[31] he examine the inner secrets of the obscurities of Geometry, descend by intellect to the depths of the sea, reach the heights of heaven by measurements made by intellect? If with the Milesian[32] he discover the friendly harmonies of relationships in Music? If, by the power of multiplication, he review with

[29] Adapted from *Christus vincit, Christus regnat, Christus imperat.* This is first found in earlier Carolingian Laudes (783-787): E. Kantorwicz, *Laudes regiae* (California 1946) 22. Cf. H. Walther, *Carmina medii posterioris latina* 1, *Initia carminum* (Göttingen 1959) 139, no. 2789.

[30] Ptolemy's *Almagest* was the recognised authority on astronomy until the late Middle Ages, cf. *Anticl.* 1. 137-139, Sheridan 49-50. C. Ptolemy. *Almagest*, Ed. by Johan Heiberg, (Leipzig, 1898, 1903). For the introduction and importance of Ptolemy's works, see C. H. Haskins, *Studies in the History of Medieval Science* (Harvard 1924) 103-112.

[31] His name became synonymous with geometry, although he wrote on other subjects, e.g. astronomy and music. Cf. *Anticl.* 3.522-533, Sheridan 115-116.

[32] Timotheus, a dithyrambic poet of Miletus, claimed in his *Persae* that he had revolutionised Music: fr. 20, ed. O. Page, *Poetae melici graeci* (Oxford 1962) 2.413. Alan's claim that he discovered the ratios in Music seems to have little to support it. That honour goes to Pythagoras.

Pythagoras[33] the troops of numbers? If with Tullius[34] he set a speech aglitter with the stars of his style in Rhetoric? If with Aristotle he separate true from false with the two-edged sword of Dialectic? If with Zeno[35] he dress falsehood with a sophistic cloak of probability? If with Donatus[36] he join words in fitting rhythms. This happens because in our day wisdom is rewarded with no pay for her produce, no favouring breeze of fame raises her on high, while money buys titles to offices and the glory of public recognition.

Nevertheless wisdom[37] alone, a noble possession, surpasses all other goods. Though scattered she remains concentrated,

[33] Pythagoras is said to have discovered the numerical ratios determining the principal intervals of the musical scale and to have gone on from there to interpret the world as a whole through numbers, the systematic study of which he originated. Martianus Capella represented the soul of Pythagoras as dealing with "heavenly numbers": 2.213, ed. Dick 78.19.

[34] Cicero.

[35] Zeno of Elea was a defender of the monism of Parmenides. He sought to show that the arguments of its opponents led to contradictory conclusions, e.g. that any group of many things must be limited and unlimited in number, like and unlike, at rest and in motion. This is probably what Alan has in mind here. In the *Anticl.* he praises him highly and would seem to agree with Aristotle's statement that Zeno was the founder of dialectic: Plato, *Parm.* 128c, 125e, 130a; Arist., *Fragment* 54, V. Rose, *Aristotelis opera* (Berlin 1870) 5.1484; *Anticl.* 3.129-133, Sheridan 96.; H. Diels, *Die Fragmente der Vorsokratiker* (Berlin 1951) 1.247-258.

[36] Donatus' *Ars maior* was the primer in Grammar in the Middle Ages, and a fairly close translation of it was the basic grammar in many European countries until comparatively recent times: *Anticl.* 2.488-494, Sheridan 89-90.

[37] *Anticl.* 1.397-413; 7.228-244; Sheridan 61, 180-181.

when expended she returns, when shared with one and all, she experiences an increase.[38] Through her the noble treasure of knowledge is born in the secret depths of the mind, the fruits of interior delight are secured. She is the sun through which daylight shines on the mind's darkness, the eye of the heart, delightful paradise of the spirit. By the influence of a deific transformation she changes the earthly into the heavenly, the perishable into the immortal, man into God. She is the one remedy for your exile, the only solace in human misfortune, the one and only morning star to end man's night, the specific redemption for your misery. No darkness in the heavens confuses her keen vision, no thickness of earth blocks her operation, no water's depth dims her vision.

Accordingly, although she grows weak from being held too cheaply in the many who live like animals in brutish sensuality, she does not, however, cheat out of her gift of fame, that is proclaimed afar, those who have restored the little spark of reason to its original fire. For although prudence may reject the praise and plaudits of fanciful flattery, yet since the glorious characteristic of true fame is this — that it despises those who enslave themselves to it and seeks out those who despise it, a man by fleeing fame attains the fame he would lose by pursuit of it.

Thus, if you should see that with some people money rules, prudence lies prostrate, riches perform their military service, wisdom is in exile, yet with a victor's spirit trample on and subdue the inert mass of wealth and, with the affectionate love of your heart, pursue prudence, so that you may be able

[38] *Anticl.* 2.334-335, Sheridan 80.

to turn an unobstructed gaze on the inner resting place of the mother of wisdom.

Then I said:

I would wish that you give rein to reproof and attack the sons of Avarice with even deeper feeling.

Then she, turning her narrative in the direction of the most bitter and incisive invective, said:

XIII

Metre 7

When the accursed greed for gold[1] pierces the heart of man, the hungry human mind can feel no fear. It weakens the bonds of friendship, begets hatred, gives rise to anger, sows the seeds of war, fosters contentions, reknots the severed line of battle, unties the knots of covenants, stirs up children against their fathers,[2] mothers against their offspring, causes brother to ignore the peaceful intent[3] of brother. This one madness harmfully disunites all whom unity of blood makes one.

When the eagerness of the mind for gain causes a dropsy in the stomach, the heart grows thirsty by drinking, a second Tantalus[4] is parched amid these waters and the size of one's

[1] Metre is Dactylic Hexameter. For curse of gold, see Virgil, *Aen.* 3.57.

[2] Cf. Ovid, *Met.* 1.144-150.

[3] *Togas.* The *toga* was the outer garment of the Romans in time of peace. See Ralph of Longchamp, *In Anticlaudianum Alani commentum*, ed. Sulowski 196; Cicero, *In Pisonem* 30.73.

[4] Tantalus, son of Zeus and Pluto, and possibly a symbol of the union of the sky-father with the earth-mother, was the extremely wealthy king of the fertile kingdom of Sipylos. He stole and ate the food of the Gods and thus became immortal. For his crime he was set in water up to his chin, with fruit-laden trees above him. He is eternally tortured by hunger and thirst. When he tries to drink or reach for the fruit, the

estate adds strength to his thirst. With stomach full, he feels hunger; full of drink, he feels thirst; with goods aplenty, he yearns for more. One man desires to possess everything and by this very desire is made a beggar: on the surface he is rich, deep down he remains poor. The unhappy man has nothing since he thinks that he has nothing. While he tries in his longings to counterbalance his poverty by riches, a host of enemies make their way into the guest-chamber of his heart and into the ramparts of his greedy mind, and with a great uproar they disturb the entire citadel of the human breast. For fear besets his mind, desire in like fashion throws it off balance and impoverishes the entire city of the mind. Thus a double whirlwind of worry agitates the miser. While he fears things really to be feared, his mind itself often dreams up new fears, conceives new dreads and by his fear of loss he suffers the pain of loss, in his dread of losses he suffers the pains of misfortune. Thus his terrified dreams show him various mishaps. His dread brings news of a wife's infidelities, a robber's trickery, an enemy's attack: in his imagination he sees swords threatening his throat and the dread lightning of the mighty ones.[5] Now he calls to mind the devastation of fire, now he imagines the ocean's rage and through fear alone he stands shipwrecked. The rich man's mind, while he lays his cash to rest in a coffer, plays at philosophy with cash and the buried cash is dead and gone as far as practical advantages to the miser go. The coffer, not he, has possession of it and makes good its claim to complete use of it. To serve his coffers a varied menu

---

water disappears or the wind blows the fruit away: Hom., *Od.* 11.583; Plato, *Prot.* 3.5c; Ovid, *Met.* 4.458-459; 6.173-174; 10.41-42; Hyg., *Fab.* 82.1.

[5] The Gods.

of coins, the rich man imposes fasts on his own stomach. The stomach quakes in fear of avarice, is astonished that its due revenue[6] is being denied it and calls on the coffer for aid, but the coffer turns a deaf ear to the stomach. There is food to be viewed and the dear eye alone revels in silver but the stomach is forced to be philosophic and suffer fasts with a prayer not soon to be answered.[7] Not tears, not honied prayers,[8] not the very poverty itself of a man can succeed by its pleas in deterring the rich man from devouring the poor man by his interest rates, as he reduces the bulk of the unhappy man's little purse.[9]

He laughs at the tears of the poor, he feeds on the toil of the unhappy and makes punishment his own relaxation. Grief is waiting for one, laughter for the other; merriment for one, mourning for the other. One groans, the other laughs; this one grieves, that one has done with grief. Every feeling of the rich miser is let go to make place for the love of money. For the mind has no desire to help it turn its gaze elsewhere. The rich man does not possess his riches but is possessed by them; he is not the possessor of money, money possesses him and the soul of the miser lies buried in his coins. These are the gods he worships, these are the idols he enriches with the honour of divine worship, and money bestows divine authority. Thus man's reason, trodden under foot by greed, becomes a slave to flesh and is forced to wait upon it as its handmaid. Thus the eye of the heart, darkened by the fog of the flesh,

[6] See XII, note 12.

[7] Statius, *Theb.* 1.323. Cf. *spem longam* of Hor., *Od.* 1.4.15; *Ars poetica* 172.

[8] *Anticl.* 2.79, Sheridan 69.

[9] *De arte praed.* 6, PL 210.124D.

grows weak and suffering an eclipse, becomes isolated and inactive. Thus the shadow of the flesh debasingly cloaks the radiance of a human sense and the glory of the mind becomes exceedingly inglorious.

This discourse does not disparage riches or the rich but rather seeks to sink its teeth into vice. I do not condemn property, riches or the practices of the rich, provided that the mind, with reason as mistress, is in command, brings this wealth into subjection to itself and treads upon it — in a word, provided that reason, the noble charioteer, shall direct the use of riches. Even if the rich man scattered all his wealth, if he poured out gifts, if he longed for fame and if he tried to win favour by gifts, yet unless good judgement is the originator, guide and charioteer of these gifts, there will be no fruit from them, since gifts, unless made with propriety and discretion, do not earn praise but rather buy it. In return for a gift there is often tendered a hypocritical accolade, a deceptive pretence of fame, a false aping of praise, a shadowy honour, the shade of favour.[10]

[10] *Anticl.* 7.351-363, Sheridan 184-185.

XIV

Prose 7

There now, you know how the clinging bird-lime of avarice deprives the wings of the human mind of their freedom of movement. Now we must consider how the pompous conceit of haughty arrogance develops into a tumour in men's minds and from contact with this deadly disease very many are corrupted when they haughtily rise above themselves and fall down in ruins[1] below themselves — decreasing by trying to increase, hurling themselves down by trying to push themselves up, losing by trying to gain. The religiously maintained ostentation of these men's diction, or their taciturnity that begets suspicion, or some individualised actions, or the adoption of unusual gestures, or the excessive adornment of the body is an index to the pride of mind within.[2]

Others, too, whom the lowliness of a slave's condition casts down, make impressive boasts of freedom. Others, indeed, although they live the life of the cheap slums of the scurrilous herd, distinguish themselves, as far as their talk goes, by claiming distinguished lineage. Others, while still wailing in

---

[1] *Anticl.* 4.311-321, Sheridan 129; *De arte praed.* 10, PL 210.132C-D.

[2] For much valuable information on the attitude towards pride in the Middle Ages, see W. Hempel, *Übermuot diu Alte: Der Superbia-Gedanke und seine Rolle in der Deutschen Literatur des Mittelalters* (Bonn 1970).

the cradles of the Art of Grammar[3] and being nursed at her breasts, affect the top-most height of Aristotelian subtlety. Others, while frozen stiff with a hare-like fear,[4] give the impression of the courage of a lion by their long-windedness. There are others who by an outward silence clearly declare what an inward haughtiness and disdain cover up within. For they disdain to share or participate in a mutual discourse with others who lie at a lower level of the moral scale, or are comparable to themselves by an equality of goodness, or are even superior to them by a loftier height of worthiness. Should anyone, using his right to ask a question, demand a word with these, the answer will be separated from the question by an interval of silence so long that one seems to bear no relationship to the other. Others, who delight in individualising their mode of action, try by every means to be individualistic in a crowd, separate in a class, to disagree amid universal agreement, to manifest diversity amid unity.[5] While others busy themselves with conversation, these give themselves up to silence. While others relax in merriment, these give the impression of being wrapped in serious considerations. While others are devoting themselves to a succession of business matters, these are taking their leisure and making merry. While the faces of others light up in some festive gaiety, the countenances of these betoken a storm, so to speak, of spiteful sternness. Others give a picture of the interior movements of their pride by adopting external mannerisms. These, as if they despised the things of earth,[6] with head thrown back look up to heaven,

---

[3] Cf. *Anticl.*, Prose Prologue, Bossuat 56, Sheridan 40.

[4] See II, note 126.

[5] *De arte praed* 10, PL 210.132D.

[6] *Anticl.* 7.131-134, Sheridan 177.

turn their eyes aside in hauteur, frequently raise their eyebrows, arrogantly thrust their chins forward, position their arms in bow-like fashion.[7] Their feet, too, skim over the ground just touching it with their toes.[8] Others over-feminise themselves with womanish adornments. With the help of a comb they assemble their hairs in a council so peaceful that a gentle breeze could not stir up a commotion between them.[9] Invoking the patronage of the scissors, they crop the ends of their bushy eyebrows, or they pluck out by the roots what is superfluous in this same forest of hair.[10] They set frequent ambushes with the razor for their sprouting beard with the result that it does not dare to show even a small growth. Their arms bemoan the close pressure of their tunics' sleeves. Their feet are confined in the prison of tight-fitting shoes.

Alas! What is the basis for this haughtiness, this pride in man? His birth is attended by pain, the penalty of toil lays waste his life, the greater penalty of inevitable death rounds off his punishment. His existence is the matter of a moment, his life is a shipwreck, his world is a place of exile. His life is gone or giving assurances of its going, for death is exerting its pressure or threatening it.

From Pride a daughter is born who by inheritance comes into possession of her mother's malice. She is Envy.[11] She

---

[7] This seems to refer to hands-on-hips stance: *Anticl.* 7.144, Sheridan 177.

[8] *Anticl.* 7.145-147, Sheridan 177.

[9] *Anticl.* 7.148-153, Sheridan 177-178. Alan uses the hackneyed adjective in *lenis aura*, "gentle breeze," although it is not suitable in the context.

[10] See II, note 4.

[11] In *De arte praed.* 8, PL 210.129c, Alan states that the envious man is making an attack on Nature.

ruins men's minds by the corrosive bite of her unending detraction.[12] Here is a worm[13] by whose gnawing the sound mind grows diseased and wastes away in corruption, the sincere mind rots away in decay, the peaceful mind melts away in distress. This is a guest who takes up unguest-like lodgings with her host and ruins her host's lodging-house.[14] This is a possession that possesses its possessor in the worst way. While she harasses others with her yapping detraction, by her gnawing within she disturbs more deeply still the soul of her possessor. This is Envy which lets the darts of her raging detraction lie idle in regard to those whom the vices of hell are sucking down, whom the plan of Nature excludes from bodily endowments, whom mad Fortune sends forth to poverty. But if anyone swims in a flood of riches with Croesus,[15] scatters his wealth abroad with Titus,[16] thunders in vehemence with Turnus,[17] contends in beauty with Narcissus,[18] casts Hercules[19] into the shade in strength, is intoxicated by Pegasean nectar[20] with Homer, stands face to face in philosophy with

[12] Alan emphasises the harm that envy does to the mind of the envious man. *De arte praed.* 8, PL 210.128c.

[13] *De arte praed.* 8, PL 210.129A-B.

[14] Envy ruins the one who entertains her.

[15] See IX, note 13.

[16] Roman Emperor (79-81). He had a reputation for liberality, though most of it consisted in a rather free use of public funds (Suet., *Titus* 7). Cf. Bern. Silv. 1.3.43; *Anticl.* 1.147, Sheridan 50.

[17] King of the Rutulians. The *Aeneid* 7-12 describes his fight against Aeneas. Cf. Bern. Silv. 1.3.43; *Anticl.* 1.148, Sheridan 50.

[18] For Narcissus, see III, note 5.

[19] See XII, note 20.

[20] Pegasus, the winged steed, by a blow of his hoof caused Hippocrene, the fountain of the Muses, to open on Mt. Helicon: Ovid, *Met.* 5.258-268.

Plato,[21] is stamped as a mirror of chastity with Hippolytus,[22] on this one she uses up her entire store of detraction. For she puts the stamp of courage on the rashness of madness; she twists wisdom either into the cunning of fraud or verbosity and bombast. Through her process of detraction even chastity degenerates into gilded hypocrisy. This corruption from detraction causes many to decay, for while they try to rub away the splendour of another's reputation, they experience the first impairments of their own goodness. In their judgement, another's prosperity is their adversity, another's adversity is their prosperity. These are saddened by the compliments paid to others and rejoice in the sadness of others. These measure their own riches by the poverty of others, their own proverty by the riches of others.[23] They try to becloud the calm, clear fame of others with the clouds of detraction or to hide it just by maintaining silence. These either cause the pure unadulterated goodness of another to spoil, or wed the leaven of falsity to truth. Alas! What monster is more monstrous than Envy? What destruction is more destructive? What fault is more culpable? What punishment is more painful? This is the abyss of blind error, the hell of man's mind, an incitement to dispute, a spur to brawls. What are the operations of envy but the enemies of man's peace, the henchmen in the work of plundering the mind, the ever wakeful enemies of a troubled

[21] Cf. Bern. Silv. 1.3.51; *Anticl.* 1.134; 2.345, Sheridan 49, 81.

[22] See I, note 16.

[23] This might, on the face of it, seem a rational approach to riches and poverty. However, Alan is referring to the millionaire who regards himself as poor, if someone in his milieu has slightly greater possessions, and to the beggar who is rich in his own eyes, if he has a little more than his neighbours.

soul, the sleepless watchers of another's happiness? What advantage is it to a man that fortune shows its approbation by bright, untroubled prosperity, that his body is gay with the beauty of purple, that even his mind is aglow with the brightness of wisdom, since robbery at the hands of spiteful Envy despoils the riches of the mind, turns the bright calm of prosperity from fortune into clouds of adversity, changes the gold of honour into the dross of baseness and inglorious envy takes away the glory of wisdom?

However, if one should wish to outlaw from the treasure of his mind the rust of jealousy, the moth of envy, let him by sympathy find his own pain in another's pain, by a united rejoicing let him make another's joy his own, let him reckon another's resources as his own wealth, let him bewail another's poverty as his own.[24] If you should see that the glory of another's goodness is being celebrated in solemn rites, do not by any detraction turn a feast-day of praise into a ferial[25] but by the noonday light of your testimony, let the lamp of the other's goodness be brought before all and shine more gloriously. If you should see that any are indulging in yelps of detraction against other's titles to renown, withdraw from the pack of yelping dogs, or by interposing a warning, dull their tongues, wipe out their yelping, crush their gnawing teeth, bite off the bites of detraction.

Flattery adds her portion of malignity to the foregoing collection of vices. Stricken by the plague of this disease are the henchmen of princes, the palace dogs, the artisans of flattery,

[24] Cf. *Anticl.* 7.339-343, Sheridan 184.

[25] A *Ferial* is a day on which there is no celebration of a Mystery of Religion or of a Saint: when such are solemnised, it is called a Feast Day.

the forgers of praise, the moulders of falsehood. These are the ones who, with the loud-sounding trumpet of praise, play for the ears of the rich; who belch forth to the world honeycombs of mellifluous flattery; who, to get gifts by cheating,[26] anoint the heads of the rich with the oil of flattery; who put cushions of praise under the heads of prelates; who either flick imaginary dust from these prelates' cloaks or, captiously remove the down from a downless garment. With the suffrages of a beggar's praise, these men redeem acts of the rich which indignant fame has favoured with a spit. These make praise a possession of gifts, favours of presents, the noising abroad of a flattering reputation the possession of a fee. If the rich man's gifts flash forth in a prodigious flood, the flatterer pours his whole self forth in prodigal praise. If, however, the rich man's gift smacks of the torpor of a wintry avarice, the flatterer, grows miserly in praise and commendation, grows cold in the performance of his duty. However, if an expression to describe the gift seems to call for the drums of praise, the poet of flattery grows swollen in a bombastic style of eulogy. If, however, a poor gift begs aid for fame, he robs the account of worth by a more lowly style. But when the loftiness of the gift is to condition the peroration, the flatterer, from the treasure house of his heart, belches forth hypocritical praise, unsubstantiated reports, minor perjuries. For if the one for whom the gift is speaking were laid low by a tempest of baseness so great that scarcely the broken pieces of the natural gifts were to be seen in him, the compositions of the flatterer will dream up a claim to excellence for him. They will lyingly state that the dwarfish, narrow confines of his beggarly spirit are palaces of great-souledness. They will raise the

[26] Hor., *Ars poetica* 238.

lowly lurking-places of his sluggish avarice to heights beyond prodigality. With the title of the nobility of a Caesar they lyingly bestow majesty on his low plebeian origin.[27]

What more? If a large host of vices should pitch camp on the demesne of a man who has not one virtue to mitigate his vices, provided that cash steps forward as interagent, the flatterer, who has praise for hire, palliates the obvious vices by a light outer covering of commendation. On the contrary, if the noon light of every grace should shine in joy on a man's face, if his language should sparkle with the silvery gems of eloquence, if the chamber of his mind should glow with the ornaments of virtue, yet, if the artisan of flattery does not look forward to the favour of a gift, he tries hard to mingle clouds of disgusting vices with the light of a goodness so great.

What, then, is the ointment of flattery but cheating for gifts? What is the act of commendation but a deception of prelates? What is the smile of praise but a mockery of the same prelates? For since speech is wont to be the faithful interpreter of thought, words the faithful pictures of the soul, the countenance an indication of the will, the tongue the spokesman of the mind, flatterers separate, by a wide distance and divergence, the countenance from the will, the words from the soul, the tongue from the mind, the speech from the thought. For externally they smile on many as they whitewash them with praise, while internally they laugh at them in mockery. Externally they praise very many with convincing applause, while internally they cheat them with a derision that gives the lie to the applause. Externally they applaud with a

---

[27] This means that they devise an impressive family-tree for him, or perhaps, that they apply the epithet *augustus* to him.

countenance of virgin innocence, internally they are stinging with the scorpion's sting. Externally they rain down showers of honied flattery, internally they are heaving with storms of detraction.

Then I, checking the unbroken course of the narration, said:

I would have you strengthen the little town of my mind by the rational ramparts of your instruction against the furious armies of these vices.

Then she said:

XV

Metre 8

To prevent Scylla[1] with her greedy whirlpool from plung-
ing you into the deep night of lust, apply the restraint of
moderation to your palate. Pay a more modest tribute to your
stomach. Let your gullet moderate its taste for the liquid of
Lyaeus, the cups of Bacchus.[2] Drink sparingly that your lips
may be thought to kiss, so to speak, the cups of Bacchus. Let
water break Lyaeus' pride and an abundance of it temper Bacchus' rage. Let Thetis[3] offer herself in marriage to Lyaeus and
let her, once married to him, restrain her husband's tyrannical
sway. Let a meal of food, that is ordinary, plain and rarely
taken, grind down the proud complaining flesh, so that the
tyrant, ever arrogantly reigning in that flesh, may exercise a
more moderated pressure on you. Thus tenacious Cupid will
take a rest. Let the reins on Cupid within you be tightened and
the sting of the flesh[4] will grow faint and dull: the flesh will
thus become the handmaiden of the spirit. Add bolts to the
door of your sight to keep your eyes in check, lest your eager

[1] Metre is Alcaic. For Scylla see IX, note 2.

[2] *Lyaeus* means "the Deliverer from Care." It is an epithet applied
to Bacchus, God of wine: Ovid, *Met.* 4.11; Cf. Virg., *Aen.* 3.354.

[3] Sea-nymph, mother of Achilles. Here she is a personification of
water.

[4] 2 Corinthians 12:7.

eye hunt abroad[5] with too little shame and bring back to your mind a report of game.

If the desire of possessions intoxicates some, let them compel money to quit their minds. Let ambition feel the mind's triumph over it. Let greed be overcome and its neck put beneath the yoke. Let not money itself tarry in closed purses and indulge in a sluggard's sleep,[6] devoting itself to no one: rather let it rise from its bed to be the guardian of right and to be of use to the rich man. If the opportunity offers, if the occasion demands it, let the mass of buried treasure arise, let the purses completely disgorge their cash. Let every gift be a soldier in the army of the right. If you wish to trample on pride's neck, on the winds of vanity, on the powers[7] that destroy the spirit, consider the burden of being born destined to die, the toils of life, death that cuts you off at the end.[8]

[5] *Anticl.* 7.156, Sheridan 178.

[6] *Anticl.* 1.43-46; 7.378-396, Sheridan 46, 185-186.

[7] *Fulmina.* This literally means lightning. It can hardly mean that here, as it is the object of *calcare*, "to trample on." However, it can mean any destructive force. Ovid, *Met.* 10.550; Cicero, *Tusc.* 2.27.66; Juv. 8.92.

[8] *Apocopam.* Apocope is the shortening of a word by dropping a letter or syllable at its end, e.g., *magi* for *magis, do* for *domum*: Charisius, *Ars gram.* 4, ed. Keil 1.278.21; Diomedes, *Ars Gram.* 2, ed. Keil 1.441.31; Donatus, *Ars Gram.* 3.4, ed. Keil 4.396.12, gives *Achilli* for *Achillis* and *pote* for *potest* as examples. Cf. *Anticl.* 3.20, Sheridan 91. Alan frequently insists on the brevity of human life: see *Poem on Transitory and Mortal Nature of Man*: PL 210.579A-580C.

XVI

Prose 8

While Nature's speech was proceeding along this path of specialised instruction, behold, a man was there and presented himself to our view in a miraculously sudden appearance and without any standard ahead of him to claim our attention. As he seemed subject to the laws of no age, he was now blooming in the Spring of youth, now a countenance of maturer years proclaimed his seriousness, now his face gave the impression of being ploughed by the furrows of old age.[1] Just as face followed face in many a change of age, so, too, at one time a rather restricted size lowered his unfixed stature towards the ground; at another time the scales of a balanced mean reduced his deficit in stature; at another time stretching to a bold height, he vied in size with the abnormal tallness of giants.[2] On his face there showed no signs of feminine softness; rather the authority of manly dignity alone held sway there. His face was neither drenched with the rain of tears nor calm with playful laughter but, resting modestly away from either extreme, was inclined more to tears.

[1] For classical antiquity the ideal man would possess the vitality and energy of youth and the maturity and judgement of age. For fuller treatment see Sheridan, *Anticl.* 30-31.

[2] Cf. Boeth., *De cons. phil.*, Pr. 1.8ff (Stewart-Rand 132); *Anticl.* 1.298-302, Sheridan 57.

His hair had secured a truce to snarling[3] and bespoke the energetic work of a mechanical comb. By the first offering of a modest dressing,[4] his hair lay in orderly fashion to prevent it from appearing to degenerate into feminine softness by the vagaries of devious arrangements.[5] To prevent a cloudlet of hair from burying his expanse of forehead, the ends of his hair had felt the scissors' bite.

His face, as manly dignity demanded, was missing in no grace of beauty. His chin was now sprouting its first down, now it was fringed with a longer growth, now it seemed to run riot in a fleece of luxuriant beard, now it had its excess of beard corrected by the hard razor.

Rings, adorned with star-clusters of precious stones, made his hands sparkle with unusual brightness and resemble the rising sun. You would imagine that his clothes at one moment were inferior, the product of common workmanship on rather coarse material, at another moment that they were showing their pride in a highly skilled weave of finer material. On these clothes tales, told in pictures, showed, as in a dream, the circumstances connected with marriage. The black paint of age, however, had almost forced the images in the pictures to fade out. Yet the picture's message kept insisting that there had been woven there the faithfulness proceeding from the sacrament of matrimony, the peaceful unity of married life, the inseparable bond of marriage, the indissoluble union of the wedded parties. For in the book of the picture there could be read in faint outline what solemn joy gives approval to marriage at its beginning, what sweet melody

---

[3] Cf. *Anticl.* 1.273, Sheridan 56.

[4] There may be an echo here of the offering up of hairs at the beginning of a sacrifice: Virgil, *Aen.* 6.246.

[5] *Anticl.* 7.148-149, Sheridan 177.

gives a festive, religious tone to the nuptials, what special gathering of guests shows their approbation of the marriage, what general joy rounds off the Cytherean's ceremonies.

A large company of skilled musicians, in ordered array,[6] adorned[7] the above-mentioned man's path of approach. These skilled men, however, reflecting in themselves their master's sadness, had imposed silence on their instruments. Thus these instruments, whose role the numbness of silence muted, seemed disposed to moan. When proximity of place, then, had brought the man into the vicinity of Nature, she, indicating him by name and first of all offering him a kiss, poured forth her greetings. From the signification of his name and other revelatory circumstances, I realised that the one who had arrived was Hymenaeus.[8] Nature, placing him on her right, bestowed on him the honour of her right hand.

While a certain joyful conversation was being held between Nature and Hymenaeus, behold, a maiden, attractive to all by her dawn-like beauty, was seen, like the sudden actualisation of an unexpected event, eagerly directing her course into our presence. There shone forth in this maiden's beauty the sacred care of a craftsmanship so great that in no detail had the finger of refining Nature slipped. This maiden's face did not beg the

---

[6] *Decuriare* has a meaning "to put in order," "to call to task": Ducange, s.v.

[7] *Decusabat.* See II, note 3.

[8] God of marriage. Martianus Capella says that he is the Cyprian's (Venus') chief concern. His presence and song give the ceremony divine sanction; his absence bodes evil for the marriage (1.1 ed. Dick 1.13). Cf. Ovid, *Met.* 4.758; 6.429; 9.762-765. A specimen of his song is to be found in Mar. Cap. 9.902-903, ed. Dick 477.14-479.2.: See Raynaud de Lage, *Alain de Lille, poète* 115.

hypocritical aid of any adventitious colouring:[9] rather the right hand of super-powerful Nature, by a miracle of grafting, had planted on her face roses vying with lilies. Her eyes, guarded by simple modesty, did not wanton in any impudent forays. Her lips, retaining their natural vitality, were neither drained by osculation nor did they give the impression of having experienced the fore-play of Venus' kisses. You would think that her face, dissolving in tears, was suffering shipwreck beneath their flood. Her wreath, made from lilies joined together in a marriage of cross-pattern weaving, flattered her head with its ornaments. The sheen of her swan-like hair, disdaining to worship the brightness of lilies, boasted a different whiteness.[10]

Her garments with their snow-white colour would have checked with more valid arguments the whiteness of the things mentioned above, but for the fact that the pictures on them, representing objects of various colours, caused the whiteness of the garments to go unnoticed. For there could be seen woven on these garments an account, contrived in the form of a picture, of how the chastity of Hippolytus,[11] fortified by a wall of constancy, persisted in resisting the lascivious advances of his stepmother. There Daphne,[12] to prevent the bolts and locks of her

[9] Cf. *Anticl.* 1.279-280, Sheridan 57.

[10] *Contradictoriam.* This word could come from Logic. The propositions "All A is B" and "Some A is Not B" are contradictories. It may be derived from *contradictio* in Rhetoric, meaning that one whiteness challenges the other. The sentences that follow give some indication that Alan had Rhetoric in mind.

[11] See I, note 16.

[12] Daphne was Apollo's first love. Apollo insulted Cupid and he in revenge pierced him with the dart of love for Daphne and pierced her with a dart that made her flee his love. Apollo pursued her. She appealed to Peneus, her father and a river-god, and was turned into the

virginity from being broken, by flight put to flight Phoebus with his enticements. There Lucretia[13] rids herself of the effects of the loss of her violated chastity by a saving death. There in the mirror-like picture I could see the mirror of Penelope's[14] chastity.

To compress in the course of a brief narrative the picture's long, elusive story — the picture's studied representation cheated none of Chastity's daughters out of the support of its approbation. By the excellence of its gold, her seal, which was stellate with a multitude of jasper-clusters, shone day-bright on the above-mentioned maiden's right hand. A turtle-dove, perched on her left hand, adjusted the harp of its voice to dire cries in the form of an elegiac ode. A band of young girls, none of whom gave the impression of having sported in Venus' arena, who had come to be a comfort in her journey and to render her obedient service, followed close at her heels. When Nature saw her close and near in place to her, she went to meet her with stately tread and revealed her attitude of mind for all to see by an introductory greeting, by a prefatory kiss, by a marital-like embrace. As the name of the above-mentioned maiden had become clear from the introductory greeting, I realised that Chastity had come and was amongst us.

While Nature was expressing her approbation in her joyous conversation with Chastity, behold, a matron, regulating her progress with disciplined step, was seen directing her course

---

laurel which became Apollo's tree. Ovid describes Apollo's fascination with the various visible beauties of Daphne and adds "what lay hidden he deemed more beautiful still." Alan was to use this remark again and again in his description of beautiful maidens: Ovid, *Met.* 1.452-567.

[13] See xii, note 22.

[14] See xii, note 23.

straight towards us. Her stature kept within the limits of the mean. Her age verged towards the noon hour of life but the noon of life proved no obstacle to any aspect of the beauty of dawn. However, the hoar-frost of old age was beginning to besprinkle her hair with its whiteness. This maiden did not allow her hair to play wantonly by flowing in disorder over her expanse of shoulder but restricted its vagaries by the restraint of a ribbon.

Her garments seemed neither to pride themselves on nobility of material nor to bewail the detriment arising from meanness in this respect. Observing the canons of the mean, not shortened by excessive cutting and curtailment, they did not go abroad from the surface of the earth, nor did they cloak the face of the earth with superfluous parts, but tasted it with the touch of a light kiss. For a belt, controlling the drop of the tunic, called its undue length to order. A necklace, keeping guard in the forecourt of her bosom, prevented a hand from entering there. On the garments a picture taught, by the realism of its lines, what should be excised from man's words, what limitation should be on his acts, what observance of the mean there should be in his dress, what calm dignity in his carriage, what restraint on his mouth in food, what restrictions on his throat in drink. The above-mentioned maiden, flanked by a few attendants, Nature received with an approbation shown by her hastening to meet her, and she showed the depth of her love by the addition of many a kiss and by the favourable sign of a personalised greeting. The express reference to her by her proper names expressed the fact of the welcome arrival of Temperance.

While Nature, in performance of the office of friendly greeting, was introducing Temperance, behold, a woman, such that the actual daylight, aided by the splendour of her loveliness, boasted a calmer, brighter beauty of mien, was seen hastening her quickened course and directing her steps straight towards us. Her natural height, despising beggarly human stature, normally exceeded the norm.[15] Her head did not demean itself by inclining towards the ground nor did it cause her face to turn downwards but, with neck erect, turning her gaze on high, she commissions her eyes to travel to loftier things.[16] Nature had fashioned this woman's beauty with so many smoothings of her file that she could admire in her the diligence of her workmanship.

There glowed on her head a diadem that did not make up for poor workmanship by excellence of material nor counterbalance cheap material by excellence of workmanship, but showed a unique superiority in both and was free from the corrosion of any destructive characteristic. Her golden hair, more flame-coloured than pleasing fire, seemed to resent having to supply a base for the golden diadem. This hair was neither cut short by the use of scissors nor had it its locks gathered in troops of plaits, but running riot in divergent sallies, went beyond the limits of her shouders and seemed to incline graciously towards the impoverished earth. One would think that her arms, unimpaired by the defect of shortness and swinging in extensive length, did not bend back on themselves but were directed towards things in front of her. Her hands, not curved in any bow-like tightness but

[15] Her height, though above average, had nothing disproportionate or bizarre about it. Cf. description of Charlemagne's physique in Einhard, *Vita Karoli magni* 22, ed. H. W. Garrod and R. B. Mowat (Oxford 1915).

[16] The theory was that in order to see there must be a ray from the eye, light outside and a material object in the path of the ray: William of Conches, *Philosophia* 4.26, PL 172.96; Thierry of Chartres, *Tractatus de sex dierum operibus* 11-13, ed. N. M. Häring, *Commentaries on Boethius by Thierry of Chartres and his School* 560. 43-67.

unfolded and stretched wide open, devoted themselves to the office of bounteous giving.[17]

Her gaments secured their material from gold and silk threads united by the kiss of an interweave: so that the fine precision of the workmanship might not fall below the nobility of the material, the garments showed their joy in the eminent characteristics of a craftsmanship so great that one would think that not a corporeal hand but one truly from heaven above had toiled over the work. On these garments a picture, unreal but credible by reason of the sophistic delusion inherent in painting,[18] damned with the disgrace of anathema men who are afflicted with the notorious crime of Avarice. On the other hand, the sons of Generosity, given a title to widespread fame, gained the favour of a blessing. When the above-mentioned woman, flanked by just three attendants, was pressing forward with hurried steps, behold, Nature, welcoming her approach by going to meet her in solemn fashion, interrupted her kisses with words of greeting and cut short her greetings with kisses. As the distinction of her particular beauty, the simplicity of her distinctive dress, the individuality of her bearing, the name clearly pronounced in the greeting announced the arrival of Generosity, I dispelled the cloud of doubt from my belief in her coming.

While Nature was fulfilling the duty of a first greeting and of a friendly, demonstrative reception for Generosity, behold, a young girl, lingering in slow and lagging steps, calm in the tranquility of her dove-like face, lowly in her restricted, modest

[17] The maiden is Generosity. Her outstretched arms and hands indicate giving to others, not grasping for herself. The terminology is taken from transitive and reflexive verbs. The transitive verb points towards an object, the reflexive is directed back to the subject.

[18] See п, note 18.

height, was encouraging herself to turn her controlled, snail-like steps towards us. Her grace and beauty, however, came to the defence of her lowly stature. For they had not been acquired by the contrived trickeries of man's artistry but flowed full from the living fount of Nature and had breathed the adornments of loveliness on her whole body. Her hair had been shortened by a cutting with the scissors so extensive that its apocope[19] had turned from a figure into a defect. One would think that the strands of her hair, straying in a kind of devious crisscrossing and tangled in an intricate snarl, were indulging in mutual litigation.[20] Her head, sunk low in a deep bow, was humbly inclined towards the earth.

Her garments, with the native hue of their material uncorrupted by adulteration from an applied colour, found a counterbalance for the quasi-rustic commonness of their material in the aid of artistic workmanship. There, inscribed in invented stories, could be read how in the catalogue of virtues Humility shines forth with the standard of distinction, while Pride, suspended by the brand of excommunication from the sacred synod of virtues, is condemned to the exile of ultimate banishment.

On her coming, Nature went to meet her with strenuous haste and sweetening the feast of her greeting with the sauce of kisses, showed a countenance betokening a love in the very marrow of her bones. From the specific terms directed towards this person, the fact of Humility's arrival became shining clear to me.

While Hymenaeus and the above-mentioned maidens patterned their faces on the expression of internal mourning that showed on Nature's face and were struggling to bring forth the

---

[19] *Apocope*: see xII, note 8.
[20] Cf. *Anticl.* 1.273, Sheridan 56, note 50.

forms of internal grief in images of external weeping, behold,
Nature, anticipating their words with her own says:

O sole lights for man's darkness, morning stars of a world
going down, planks[21] specially devised for the shipwrecked,
outstanding harbours for those tossed on the waves of the
world, by my mature and deep-rooted knowledge I know
what is the reason for your visit, what occasions your coming
here, what causes your lamentation, what gives rise to your
grief. Men, the only species formed with the quality of
humanity, becoming depraved within by the vileness of bestial
inconstancy, men, whom I regret having clothed with the
cloak of humanity, are trying to dispossess you of your
patrimony of a home in the world by totally usurping control
on earth and forcing you to return to your home in heaven.[22]
Since my interests are at stake when the partition wall between
is in fiery flames,[23] sympathising with your suffering and con-
doling with you in your grief, in your groans I encounter my
own and find my own loss in your misfortune. Accordingly,
ignoring no pertinent fact and finding the proper motivation
in myself, in so far as I can extend the arm of my power, I will
smite men with a punishment commensurate with their
crimes. However, since I cannot pass the limits of my strength
and it is not in my power to eradicate completely the poison of

[21] *Tabulae. Tabulae* was the word used for pieces of wreckage on
which those shipwrecked made their way ashore.

[22] In the Golden Age, the Virtues and many gods lived on earth.
Man's conduct forced them to abandon their home on Earth: Ovid,
Met. 1.125-150. Their return to Earth is described in *Anticl.* 9.391-393,
Sheridan 216.

[23] Horace, *Ep.* 1.18.84; *Anticl.* 6.314, Sheridan 166; Bernard, *Ep.*
342, PL 182.547A.

this pestilence, I will attain what is allowed my power and will burn with the brand of anathema men who are ensnared in the tangle of the vices that I have mentioned. It is fitting, however, to consult Genius[24] who serves me in a priestly office. With the support and assistance of my judiciary power, with the favour and aid of your assent, let him, with the pastoral staff of excommunication, remove them from the catalogue of the things of Nature, from the confines of my jurisdiction. Hymenaeus will discharge the office of ambassador to him in the most approved manner: in Hymenaeus the shining stars of eloquence show their light; with him is stored the equipage for a plan of scrutiny.

Then those standing by took time off from their tears and complaints and lowering their heads in a profound bow, returned profuse thanks to bounteous Nature. Hymenaeus, in Nature's presence and before her eyes, humbled himself on bended knee and professed obedience to the terms of the mission to be entrusted to him. Then Nature, with the aid of a reed-pen, inscribed on a sheet of paper an official[25] formula[26] of the following kind:

Nature, by the grace of God, vicar-governess of the city of earth: to Genius, her other self, greetings and wishes that in all things he may be befriended by the delights of fair fortune.

Since like, with disdain for unlike, rejoices in a bond of

[24] For Genius, see Introduction pp. 59-62.

[25] *Epistularis.* The *epistulares* were state secretaries. *Cod. Theod.* 6.30.7; *Cod. Just.* 7.62.32.

[26] *Carminis.* There was a very ancient practice of composing religious formulas in Saturnian verse. From this *carmen* came to mean a religious formula: Livy 10.38.10; Pliny 28.3.12.

relationship with like, finding myself your alter ego by the likeness of Nature that is reflected in you as in a mirror, I am bound to you in a knot of heartfelt love, both succeeding in your success and in like manner failing in your failure. Love, then, should be a circle so that you, responding with a return of love, should make our fortunes interchangeable. The evidence of crime committed, evidence that all but shouts aloud, tells you at length of the shipwreck of the human race. For you see how men dishonour the dignity of their original nature by succumbing to bestial allurements, and abandoning a nature with the privilege of humanity, cross over to join the beasts by degeneration in their morals, as they follow their own inclinations in the pursuit of Venus, suffer shipwreck in whirlpools of gluttony, burn with the hot vapour of greed, fly on the counterfeit wings of pride, give themselves over to the bites of envy, gild others with the hypocrisy of flattery. No one brings medicinal remedies to bear on these diseases of vice. No one restrains the torrent of crime by placing a barrier of defence in front of it. There is no reliable harbourage to check the waves of these misdeeds. The Virtues, entirely unable to withstand the great pressure of the hostile conflict, have fled to us as to a sanctuary of defence that takes the place of a remedy. Since, then, our interests are being damaged by a common attack, sweetening you with prayers, laying injunctions on you by virtue of your obligation of obedience, mingling admonitions with orders and orders with admonitions, I urge that, laying aside every specious excuse, you make haste to come to us so that you, with the ready help of myself and my maidens, may remove the sons of abomination from participation in the sacred rites of our church and may, with due solemnity of office, strike them with the punitive rod of excommunication.

After this she handed over to be given to the emissary the letter stamped with the mark of her seal on which expert craftsmanship had moulded the name and image of Nature. Then Hymenaeus, with dignity and joy in his countenance, wound up the affair with an expression of gratitude and, as a beginning for the assigned mission, roused his companions from their sluggish sleep, giving orders that those in charge of the musical instruments should stir them up from their sleep of silence and summon them to the strains of a harmonious melody. Then the musicians, tuning their instruments with what one might call proems, proceeded to reproduce in oft-changing strains the sound that has uniformity amid multiformity, similarity amid dissimilarity.

XVII

Metre 9

Now the trumpet,[1] hailing war, blared forth with dread sound,[2] telling of the preliminary skirmishes, the kin of war, and indicating like din with like blare. The horn inflicted its scarless wound[3] on the air. This instrument's wandering sound and unregulated tone know not how to obey the melody of instrumental music and, scorning to countenance art and music, admire measures without restraint. The pleasing sound of the cither brings notes more sirenic[4] and alluring then the former; it offers the ear feasts of honey-sweet sound and by its variations introduces varying configurations of tones.[5] Now it brings tears

---

[1] The metre is Dactylic Hexameter. The *tuba* was normally the war-trumpet. It was straight as opposed to the *cornu*, "the horn," which was curved; Ovid, *Met.* 1.98. It was used in religious celebrations: Ovid, *Fast.* 1.716; Virgil, *Aen.* 5.113; Varro, *L.L.* 6.14; Statius, *Silvae* 3.1.139; Mart. Cap. 9.226, ed. Dick 492.9.

[2] Cf. Ennius, quoted in Priscian, *Instit.* 8, 104, ed. Keil 2.450.7.

[3] Cf. *Anticl.* 4.130, Sheridan 122.

[4] *Sirenans.* See *Sirenes*, XII, note 4. For *cithara* see Mart. Cap. 9.926ff., ed. Dick 493.6ff.

[5] *Cantus, colorans.* Martianus Capella uses *cantus* for any musical composition, oral or instrumental: 5.425; 9.926, ed. Dick 210.9; 498.8. *Colores* is a term frequently used in Rhetoric. Its application to Music is due to the Greek use of *chromatikos* (adjective from *chroma*, "colour"). Between black and white there are various colours. *Colores*

by its notes as it counterfeits grief, now represents in its sound the pretence of feigned laughter. The lyre,[6] which nightingale-like ever sounds in charming song, as it sweetly soothes, reads the introduction to a story that brings sleep to our eyes and lays to rest the worryings of a harassed mind. The pipes,[7] which keep watch by night like an alert sentry, nay, with its music offsets the loss of sleep for those who keep guard, falls pleasingly on the ears and by it stony hardness of heart is made wax-soft, the rigidity of the unyielding mind is forced to grow tender and rid itself of its inflexibility. The drums,[8] coming in with their muted boom, slowed this stream of music and the swiftness of its keen song. They are not, however, robbed of every honour of song, should one but strike them with practised beat, stir them up with a stroke and tone them down by a friendly touch of the hand. The organs, well provided with a deep current of air, that is being forced out, belched in a sweet sound.[9] The equal inequality

---

is used for variations and *colorans* for varying: Mart. Cap. 9.962, ed. Dick 502. 16-503.1.

[6] Martianus Capella (9.926) states that many Greek cities recited their laws publicly to the notes of the lyre. Soothing and civilising effect of non-martial music is frequently mentioned: Boeth., *De musica* 1.1 ed. Friedlein 184; Macrobius, *Comm.* 2.3.7, ed. J. Willis 105.5ff.; Cassiodorus, *De art. et discip. lib. litt.* 6, PL 70.1212A-B.

[7] The power of the pipes, even on animals, is attested by Pliny 8.50.114. This is repeated (probably copied) by Solinus 19.11, ed. Mommsen 94.12; Mart. Cap. 9.927, ed. Dick 493.11.

[8] The terminology indicates that the reference is based on Martianus Capella 2.133, ed. Dick 58.11.

[9] The term *ructabant* seems poorly chosen. The organ is very frequently mentioned in the OT. Its role was to accompany song: Gen. 4:21; 1 Par. 16:42; 2 Par. 7:6; Judith 15:15; Job 30:31. For later development see *Larousse Encyclopedia of Music* (London 1971) 55-57.

of the music of these instruments, their concordant discord, their disunited agreement, their united disagreement of tones are joined and divided, divided and joined. With lowly sound and beggarly note, the cymbals[10] resounded. Their clangor never completely wins us over when we listen and they scarce deserve to get a hearing from man. No sound was greater, better or softer than that one in which the sweet music of the pentachord[11] all by itself put the other music mentioned above in the shade. The ordinary people, vying in song, adored even the traces of its music. As the psaltery[12] contended in rivalry of sound with the harp, its pleasing notes, seasoned from the honeycomb and honey-sweet in taste, rang out bringing its dear little gift of song. The sistra,[13] that call for the touch of a maiden's right hand, the voice of a female Mars and prophetess of war, sang of the wonders of a voice yet unheard of.

[10] This instrument, too, is frequently mentioned in OT as an accompaniment for song and occasionally its noisiness is noted: 1 Par. 13:19. See Cassiodorus, *Expositio in psalterium*. Psalm. 150:5, PL 70.1053B.

[11] The only account we have of this is in Martianus Capella 9.962-963, ed. Dick 513.10-514.11.

[12] There are many references to this in OT and it was obviously meant to accompany song: 1 Par. 25:1; 2 Par. 9:11; Psalms 48:5; 150.3. Quintilian considered the psaltery of his day as degenerate: 1.30.31.

[13] The *sistrum* was a rattle used by the Egyptians in celebrating the rites of Isis: Ovid, *Met.* 9.693, 778, 784; 1 Sam. 18:6. The Romans sarcastically referred to it as "Cleopatra's war-trumpet": Virgil, *Aen.* 8.696; Lucan 10.63; Mart. Cap. 2.170, ed. Dick 70.7.

XVIII

Prose 9

Accordingly, while Hymenaeus was attending to the duties of his mystic[1] legation, Nature, composing an elegiac oration[2] to complain of her miserable plight, reviewed the wrongs done by those through whose crimes of violence the honour of her native state had suffered serious injury and extensive damage. Amongst these there was one above all the rest whom she plied in a more calculated manner with the goads of reproof. More than the others he had with undue disrespect made it his concern to censure and dishonour Nature.[3] Although Fortune flattered him with the favour of noble lineage, Prudence showed her friendship by her office, nay, by offices, Magnanimity raised him aloft, Generosity made him learned, yet, because the whole suffers from the tartness arising from a small leaven,[4] the setting sun of one virtue brought a deep cloud over the dawn of the others and the eclipse of one component of uprightness forced

---

[1] Martianus Capella 2.133, ed. Dick 58.14.

[2] In Latin prose-works we often find sentences ending in a succession of words that form part of a line of some recognised metre. Elegiac endings are not too common. Cicero, according to Martianus Capella has at least one such in *oderat ille bonos*: 5.517, ed. Dick 255.12.

[3] For *decuriatam*, see xvi, note 6.

[4] Osee 7.4; Matthew 13:33; Luke 13:20; 1 Cor. 5:6.

the stars of all his other components to die in an eclipse-like waning.

When Generosity saw that these reproaches were directed at her foster-child,[5] she did not dare to shade his vices with a cloak of defence, but with a deep bow of her head she took refuge in the relief of tears. Nature, assessing the significance of the bowed head and tears shed, said:

O Maiden, by whose outstanding architectonic skill, the mind of man is destined to be a palace of virtues: through this mind man attains the rewards of favouring grace, through it the long-dead days of the Golden Age come again to life, through it men bind themselves together by the bond of heart-felt love; you, whom eternal Being generated, bringing you forth from the eternal kiss of his Noys[6] and granted me an uterine sister, not only does the bond of blood-relationship by birth join you to me but in addition the nexus of chaste love links us together. Thus good and balanced judgement does not suffer your will to deviate from the perfect balance[7] of my will. Such unity of accord, rather, such unity of oneness, leagues our minds in unfailing peace, with the result that not only is that coexistent unification clothed in an image of unity but rather, with the ghost of unification laid, it seeks to approximate identity of being. Consequently no man's injurious conduct rages against one of us without spreading its fierce attack to the other, no one's evil seduction plays the stepmother to one of us without playing it to the other too. Therefore, whoever labours to dishonour the dignity of my title by the

---

[5] Prodigality is a distorted offshoot of Generosity.

[6] See vɪɪ, note 2.

[7] *Examen.* This means the tongue of a balance.

raucous blasphemy of unchaste actions tries to detract from your honour by the vehemence of injurious harassment. The one who misuses the gifts of Nature by an excessive flood of prodigality strips himself of Fortune's benefits by the excessive losses arising from his squandering and while a harlot-like relationship with Prodigality lyingly advertises itself as a tribute of respect to Generosity, the torrent of riches flows away leaving an arid waste of poverty, the bright star of wisdom goes off its course to set in folly, the steadfastness of magnanimity weakens into the bravado of rashness. I am, then, so to speak, worn out wondering why you cannot restrain a flood of tears at the prospect of the condemnation of one who tried, in a manner more destructive than all others, to bring about our destruction.

Then Generosity, removing the flood of tears from the region of her face by the expedient of wiping it, raised aloft her bowed head and said:

O first principle of all things born, O special preserver of all things, O queen of the earthly regions, O faithful vicar of heaven's prince, you, who under the authority of the eternal commander corrupt your faithful administration with no leaven; you, whom the entire universe is bound to obey by the demands of original justice: a golden chain of love links me with you as the manifest equality of close kinship requires. He, then, who in putting his nature up for sale by his abominable losses assails you with the affront of an extraordinary rebellion, revolts against me with the insolence of an equally shattering attack. Although he may be deceived by a belief[8] in shades and phantoms and think that he is bearing

---

[8] *Credulitas.* Later in this sentence we have *suspenditus.* This seems

arms under the flag of my interests, and men, deceived by a staged display of prodigality, may scent traces of Generosity in him, yet he is suspended from the benefit of friendly relationship with us by banishment to a far-off place. However, since it is our practice to show compassion for, and sympathy with, the detours of wayward error, I cannot help being moved by the baleful deviation of his foolish will.

While this alternating conversation in dramatic form was taking place between these maidens, behold, to the joyful, applauding sound of the musical instruments, Genius came into view in a shining new apparition.

His height, kept within fitting limits by the rule of the mean, neither had a complaint to make about shortening by contraction nor was he saddened by superfluous elongation.[9] His head, covered with hair hoar-frosted by greyness, bore minor signs of winter-like old age. However, his face, smooth with the regularity of youth, had not been furrowed by the plough of age.[10] His garments, with workmanship suiting material, suffered from no defect in the former or the latter and seemed now to be aflame with purple, now to have the brightness of the hyacinth, now to be afire with scarlet, now to have the clear white of linen. On these garments images of objects, lasting but a moment, faded so quickly that they eluded the pursuit of our minds. In his right hand he held a pen, close kin of the fragile papyrus, which never

---

like an echo of Ovid, *Met.* 15.101, where the poet says that Pythagoras taught that in the early ages the credulity (*credulitas*) of the fish did not hang (*suspenderat*) him on the hook.

[9] Aphairesis is the dropping of a letter or syllable at the beginning of a word, e.g., *temnere* for *contemnere*. Prothesis (prosthesis) is the prefixing of a letter or syllable to a word, e.g., *gnatus* for *natus*.

[10] Young — old appearance, see xvi, note 1.

rested from its task of enfacement. In his left hand he held the pelt of a dead animal, shorn clear of its fur of hair by the razor's bite. On this, with the help of the obedient pen, he endowed with the life of their species images of things that kept changing from the shadowy outline of a picture to the realism of their actual being.

As these were laid to rest in the annihilation of death, he called others to life in a new birth and beginning.[11] There Helen,[12] a demi-goddess in beauty, could, by reason of her impressive beauty, be styled "The Beauty." There the thunderbolt of impetuosity held sway in Turnus,[13] strength in Hercules.[14] There a giant's stature rose high in Capaneus,[15] the cleverness of the fox was active in Ulysses.[16] There Cato[17] was intoxicated with the golden nectar of modest sobriety; Plato glowed with the shining star of genius. There Cicero's peacock with its bestarred tail exulted. There Aristotle ensconces his ideas in the coverts of enigmatic expressions.

After this solemn process of enfacement, his left hand, as if it were helping a weary sister, came to the aid of his right which had grown tired from the toil of continuous painting and the left

[11] This symbolises the birth-death cycle so often emphasised by Nature.

[12] See I, note 12.

[13] See XIV, note 17.

[14] See XII, note 20.

[15] One of the "Seven against Thebes." He was killed by lightning sent by Jupiter: Ovid, *Met.* 9.404.

[16] See IX, note 19.

[17] Cato is probably Cato, the Censor (234-149 BC). He was an upholder of Roman tradition, opponent of Greek influence and stern moralist. The *Catonis Disticha*, once attributed to him, belongs to a much later date.

took over the work of portrayal while the right took possession of the tablets and held them.[18] The left hand, limpingly withdrawing from the field of orthography to pseudography, produced in a half-completed picture outlines of things or rather the shadowy ghosts of outlines. There Thersites,[19] dressed in his disgraceful rags, impeached the expertness of one more skilled in strategy. There Paris[20] was being broken down by the wantonness of the lewd Cyprian.[21] There Sinon[22] was arming himself with subterfuges for a sinuous speech. There the verses of Ennius,[23] destitute of elegance of idea, crossed the bounds of metrical practice in unrestrained license. There Pacuvius,[24] unskilled in arranging the sequence of his narrative, places the beginning of his discourse at a stage that points backwards.

While Genius was seriously devoting his attention to these ingenious paintings, Truth, like a father's reverential daughter, stood by in obedient service. She was not born of Aphrodite's[25] promiscuous itch but was entirely the offspring of the generative kiss of Nature and her son[26] at the time when the eternal Idea

[18] Cf. *Anticl.* 8.50-52, Sheridan 190.

[19] See IX, note 10.

[20] His abduction of Helen led to the Trojan war.

[21] Venus.

[22] A pretended defector from the Greek cause at Troy. His false tale about the purpose of the wooden horse induced the Trojans to bring it into the city. This caused the fall of Troy: Virgil, *Aen.* 2.57-194.

[23] See IX, note 17.

[24] Pacuvius was a nephew of Ennius. He was a tragic poet. He is praised by Cicero (*Brutus* 64.229; *De fin.* 1.2.4; *Orator* 11.36) and commended in more restrained fashion by Quintilian 10.1.97.

[25] The Greek counterpart of Venus. In fact Venus, as we know her, is almost entirely a Romanisation of Aphrodite.

[26] Genius. See Introduction pp. 59-62.

greeted Hyle as she begged for the mirror of forms[27] and imprinted a vicarious kiss on her through the medium and intervention of Image. On her face could be read the divinity of heavenly
beauty which disdains our mortal nature. Her garments, pro-
claiming the work of the right hand of a heavenly craftsman,
alight with a never-failing glow of red, could not be wiped out by
the moths of age. These garments had been joined to the
maiden's body by a bond so close that no separation by
removal[28] could every make them Separatists[29] from the
maiden's body. Other garments, like additions to nature and ap-
pendages to those previously mentioned, now offered a glimpse
to the viewer, now stole away from the eyes' pursuit. On the side
opposite Truth, enmity-causing Falsehood stood in strained
pose. Her face, darkened with the soot of ugliness, bespoke no
gifts given her by Nature; rather old age, subjecting her face to
the hollows of wrinkles, had gathered it all over into folds. It
was plain to see that her head was not clothed with a veil of hair
and it had no robe to cover its baldness:[30] rather, a countless
assemblage of rags, joined by a limitless conjunction of threads,
had woven a garment for her. This one, secretly lying in wait for
the picture of truth, disgraced by deformity whatever truth
graced by conformity.

[27] Bern. Silv. 1.1.32-34. Nature, Genius and Truth form a ternary,
i.e. a combination used to reflect and help understand the Trinity. For
other examples, see *Anticl.* 6.244, 254-261, Sheridan 164, note 28. See
Raynaud de Lage, *Alain de Lille, poète* 92.

[28] *Dieresis.* This is the separation of the two vowels of a diphthong so
that they are pronounced separately, e.g. *aula-i* for *aulae.*

[29] *Phariseas.* Pharisee comes from the Hebrew word *parush*, meaning "separated."

[30] See II, note 4.

Accordingly, Nature, giving freer rein to her steps, solemnly acknowledging the solemn meeting, offered Genius on his arrival kisses not corrupted by any poison of lawless Venus, but symbolic of the caresses of epicene attraction and even indicative of the harmony of mystic love.

When the mutual greetings, finished and completed, had been brought to an end, Genius, with a demanding gesture of his hand, enjoined silence; after this he coined from the mint of his voice a speech along the following lines:

> O Nature, it is not without the divine breath of interior inspiration that there has come from your balanced judgement this imperial edict, to the effect that all who strive to make our laws obsolete by misuse and desuetude, by not keeping holiday on our solemn days of rest, should be struck with the sword of anathema.[31]

> Since this legitimately promulgated law is not at variance with the law of justice and your studied and balanced judgement agrees with the results of my own judicious inquiry, I am eager to reinforce with all haste the directions issued by you. For, although my mind, straitened by man's disgusting vices, travels down to the hell of gloom and knows not the paradise of joy, yet the seedlings of delightful joy are sending me their fragrance because I see that you join in my sighs of longing for due punishment. Nor is it surprising that I find a melody and harmony in the agreement and union of our wills since the

---

[31] A series of puns on *feriae*, "days of rest," *feriantes*, "keeping holiday," and *feriantur* from *ferire*, "to strike." Anathema, when used to translate the Hebrew *cherem*, means one doomed to death on religious grounds. Successively it came to mean a person or thing accursed, a curse, excommunication: Num. 21:2-3; 1 Macc. 5:5; Rom. 9:3; 1 Cor. 12:3; 16:22; Gal. 1:8-9.

conceptive exemplar of one idea brought us to birth and existence, since our status as administrators of one office brings us into accord, since it is no hypocritical love that joins us by a superficial bond of attachment but, rather, it is a pure and modest love that dwells in the deeper recesses of the soul.

While Genius was reining in the running commentary of his speech in the above short-cut of words and removing to some extent the darkness of gloom by what might be called the rising dawn of his outburst, Nature, mindful of his honour and dignity, returned him due thanks.

Then Genius, laying aside his everyday robes and adorning himself more fittingly in his priestly dress with its distinguished ornaments, called forth from the deep recesses of his mind the prearranged formula of excommunication and proceeded with a speech along the following lines:

By the authority of the super-essential Usia[32] and his eternal Idea, with assent of the heavenly army, with the combined aid and help of Nature and the other recognised virtues, let everyone who blocks the lawful path of Venus, or courts the shipwreck of gluttony or the nightmares of drunkenness, or indulges the fire of thirsty avarice, or scales the shadowy heights of insolent arrogance, or submits to the death of the heart in envy, or makes a companion of the hypocritical love of flattery — let every such be separated from the kiss of heavenly love as his ingratitude deserves and merits, let him be demoted from Nature's favour, let him be set apart from the harmonious council of the things of Nature.

Let him who makes an irregular exception to the rule of

---

[32] *Usia*, from Greek *ousia*, here means "Being": Plato, *Tim.* 29c.

Venus be deprived of the seal of Venus. Let him who buries himself in the abyss of gluttony be punished by a shameful impoverishment. Let him who benumbs himself in the Lethe-flood[33] of drunkenness be harassed by the fires of perpetual thirst. Let him who has a burning thirst for gain be assailed by the wants of unceasing poverty.

Let him who has raised himself to the top of the precipice of avarice and belches forth his wind of exaltation come down in ruination to the valley of humiliation and dejection. Let him who in envy gnaws the riches of another's happiness with the worm of detraction be the first to discover that he is his own enemy. Let him who hunts for paltry gifts from the rich by his hypocritical flattery be cheated by a reward of deceptive worth.

When Genius had brought his speech to an end in this anathema of expulsion,[34] the attendant maidens, applauding his imprecation with ready words of approbation, lent strength to his edict. The wax candles, that burned in the maiden's hands with a noonday light and in a certain way spurned extinguishment by being lowered to earth, seemed to sink in slumber.

Accordingly, when the mirror with these images and visions was withdrawn, I awoke from my dream and ecstasy and the previous vision of the mystic apparition left me.

[33] Lethe was the river of forgetfulness in Hades.

[34] *Exterminium*. This means expulsion from one's territory. It is also used in Scripture with the meaning of destruction: Judith 4:10; Wisdom 18:3; 1 Macc. 7:7. If it has this meaning here, the translation would be "in fateful anathemas."

Bibliography

A. ALAN OF LILLE

Anticlaudianus
——. PL 210.488-574.
——. In *The Anglo-Latin Satirical Poets and Epigrammatists of the Twelfth Century*, ed. Thomas Wright, 2:268-426. Roll Series, 59. London: Longman and Trübner, 1872.
——. *Anticlaudianus. Texte critique, avec une introduction et des tables.* Ed. Robert Bossaut. Paris: J. Vrin, 1955.
——. *Alanus ab Insulis. Der Anticlaudian.* In *Aus der Schule von Chartres*, ed. Wilhelm Rath, vol. 2. Stuttgart: Mellinger, 1966.
——. *Anticlaudianus.* Translation and commentary by James J. Sheridan. Toronto: Pontifical Institute of Mediaeval Studies, 1973.
——. In "The 'Anticlaudianus' of Alain de Lille; Prologue, Argument and Nine Books Translated with an Introduction and Notes," by William H. Cornog. University of Pennsylvania, Ph.D. thesis, 1935.
De arte praedicatoria
——. PL 210.111-198.
De fide catholica contra haereticos
——. PL 210.307-430.
De planctu naturae
——. PL 210.431A-482C.

——. *Liber de planctu naturae.* In *The Anglo-Latin Satirical Poets and Epigrammatists of the Twelfth Century*, ed. Thomas Wright, 2:429-522. Roll Series, 59. London: Longman and Trübner, 1872.

——. Ed Nikolaus M. Häring. *Studi Medievali*, terza serie, 19.2, (1978): 797-879

——. *The Complaint of Nature.* Trans. Douglas Maxwell Moffat. Yale Studies in English, 36. New York: H. Holt, 1908.

De sex alis cherubim

——. PL 210.270-280.

De virtutibus et de vitiis et de donis Spiritus Sancti

——. "Le Traité d'Alain de Lille sur les vertus, les vices et les dons du Saint-Esprit." Ed. Odon Lottin. *Mediaeval Studies*, 12 (1950): 20-56.

——. "Le Traité d'Alain de Lille sur les vertus, les vices et les dons du Saint-Esprit." Ed. Odon Lottin. In *Psychologie et morale aux xiie et xiiie siècles*, 6:45-92. Gembloux: Duculot, 1960.

Elucidatio in Cantica canticorum

——. PL 210.51-110.

Epistola Magistri Alani quod non est celebrandum bis in die

——. In *Alain de Lille, textes inédits*, ed. Marie-Thérèse d'Alverney, pp. 290-294. Paris: J. Vrin, 1965.

Expositio cuiusdam super orationem Dominicam

——. "A Commentary on the Our Father by Alan of Lille." Ed. Nikolaus M. Häring. *Analecta Cisterciensia*, 31 (1975): 149-177.

Expositio Prosae de angelis

——. In *Alain de Lille, textes inédits*, ed. Marie-Thérèse d'Alverney, pp. 185-217. Paris: J. Vrin, 1965.

Expositio super symbolum

——. "A Commentary on the Creed of the Mass by Alan of Lille." Ed. Nikolaus M. Häring. *Analecta Cisterciensia*, 30 (1974): 281-303.

Hierarchia
——. In *Alain de Lille, textes inédits*, ed. Marie-Thérèse d'Alverney, pp. 223-235. Paris: J. Vrin, 1965.
Liber in distinctionibus dictionum theologicalium (= *Distinctiones*)
——. PL 210.686-1012.
Liber parabolarum (= *Parables*)
——. PL 210.582-594.
Liber poenitentialis
——. PL 210.279-304.
——. Ed. Jean Longère. 2 vols. Analecta Mediaevalia Namurcensia, 17-18. Louvain: Nauwelaerts, 1965.
——. "Alain de Lille Liber Poenitentialis. Les Traditions moyenne et courte." Ed. Jean Longère. *Archives*, 32 (1965): 169-242.
Rhythmus de incarnatione Christi
——. PL 210.577A-580A.
Rhythmus de natura hominis fluxa et caduca
——. PL 210.579A-580C.
Sermones
——. PL 210.198-228.
——. In *Alain de Lille, textes inédits*, ed. Marie-Thérèse d'Alverney, pp. 241-306. Paris: J. Vrin, 1965.
——. "Alain de Lille docteur de l'Assomption." Ed. Palémon Glorieux. *Mélanges de science religieuse*, 8 (1951): 16-18.
——. In *Notices et extraits de quelques manuscrits latins de la Bibliothèque Nationale*, ed. Barthélemy Hauréau, 6:194-196. Paris: Klincksieck, 1893.
——. ——. *Sermo de sphera intelligibili*. In *Alain de Lille, textes inédits*, ed. Marie-Thérèse d'Alverny, pp. 297-306. Paris: J. Vrin, 1965.
——. ——. "Un Sermon d'Alain sur la misère de l'homme," Ed. Marie-Thérèse d'Alverny. In *The Classical Tradition*.

Literary and Historical Studies in Honour of Harry Caplan, ed. Luitpold Wallach, pp. 515-535. Ithaca: Cornell University Press, 1966.

——. ——. "Variations sur un thème de Virgile dans un sermon d'Alain de Lille." Ed. Marie-Thérèse d'Alverney. In *Mélanges d'archéologie et d'histoire offerts à André Piganiol*, ed. Raymond Chevallier, pp. 1517-1528. Paris: SEVPEN, 1966.

——. ——. "Eine unbekannte Predigtsammlung des Alanus von Lille in Münchener Handschriften." Ed. L. Hödl. *Zeitschrift für Katolische Theologie*, 80 (1958): 516-527.

Summa Quoniam homines

——. "La Somme Quoniam homines d'Alain de Lille." Ed. Palémon Glorieux. *Archives*, 20 (1953): 113-359.

Super symbolum apostolorum

——. "A Commentary on the Apostles' Creed by Alan of Lille (O. Cist.)." Ed. Nikolaus M. Häring. *Analecta Cisterciensia*, 30 (1974): 7-45.

Super symbolum Quicumque

——. "A Poem by Alan of Lille on the Pseudo-Athanasian Creed." Ed. Nikolaus M. Häring. *Revue d'histoire des textes*, 4 (1974): 226-238.

Theologicae Regulae (= *Regulae*)

——. PL 210.622-684.

Tractatus Magistri Alani

——. "Deux questions sur la foi inspirées d'Alain de Lille." Ed. Guy Raynaud de Lage. *Archives*, 14 (1943): 323-336.

Tractatus Magistri Alani de virtutibus et vitiis

——. "Über die Verknüpfung des Poetischen mit dem Theologischen bei Alanus de Insulis." Ed. Johann Huizinga. In *Mededeelingen der Koninkl. Akademie van Wetenchappen, Afdeeling Letterkunde 34B*, pp. 95-110. Amsterdam: Noord-Hollandsche, 1932.

——. "Le Traité d'Alain de Lille sur les vertus, les vices et les dons du Saint-Esprit." Ed. Odon Lottin. *Mediaeval Studies* 12 (1950): 20-56.

——. "Le Traité d'Alain de Lille sur les vertus, les vices et les dons du Saint-Esprit." Ed. Odon Lottin, in his *Psychologie et morale aux xii* *et xiii* *siècles*, 6:28-36. Gembloux: Duculot, 1960.

Vix nodosum

——. "The Poem *Vix Nodosum* by Alan of Lille." Ed. Nikolaus M. Häring. *Medioevo. Rivista di storia della filosofia medievale*, 3 (1978): 165-185.

DUBIOUS WORKS

Declarare fidem

——. "Two Theological Poems Probably Composed by Alan of Lille." Ed. Nikolaus M. Häring. *Analecta Cisterciensia*, 32 (1976): 238-246.

Omne datum optimum

——. "Two Theological Poems Probably Composed by Alan of Lille." Ed. Nikolaus M. Häring. *Analecta Cisterciensia*, 32 (1976): 247-250.

Quinque digressiones

——. In *Alain de Lille, textes inédits*, ed. Marie-Thérèse d'Alverny, pp. 313-317. Paris: J. Vrin, 1965.

Summa de sacramentis: Totus homo

——. Ed. Humbertus Betti. Spicilegium Pontificii Athenaei Antoniani, 7. Rome: Pontificium Athenaeum Antonianum, 1955.

B. PRIMARY SOURCES

Aeschylus. *Choephoroi. Seven Against Thebes.*
Alberic of Trois-Fontaines. *Chronica.* MGH, SS 23.631-950.

Alcuin. *De virtutibus et vitiis.* PL 101.614C-638D.

Ambrose. *Hexaemeron.* Ed. Carolus Schenkl. CSEL 32 (1897): 1-261.

——. *Hexaemeron.* PL 14.133-288.

Andrewe, Laurence. [Extracts from] "The noble lyfe and natures of man, Of bestes serpentys fowles and fisshes y be moste knowen." In *The Babees Book,* ed. Frederick J. Furnivall, pp. 229-239. EETS OS, 32. London, Trübner 1868; reprinted, New York, Greenwood 1969.

Anonymous. "Isidorus Versificatus: Ein Anonymes." Ed. Christian Hünemörder. *Vivarium,* 13 (1975): 103-118.

Anonymous. *Liber XXIV philosophorum.* Ed. Clemens Baeumker. *Beiträge,* 25 (1927): 194-214.

Anonymous. *Vita sancti Deicoli.* In *Acta sanctorum,* ed. Johannes Bollandus, Januarii tomus secundus, pp. 563-574 (= 18 Jan.). Paris: Palmé, n.d.

Apollodorus. *The Library.* Ed. James George Frazer. London: W. Heinemann; New York: G. P. Putnam's Sons, 1921.

Apuleius. *De deo Socratis.* In *Opera omnia,* ed. Gustav Friedrich Hildebrand, 2:111-160. Leipzig: C. Cnoblochius, 1842.

Apuleius Barbarus. *The Herbal of Apuleius Barbarus.* Ed. Robert J. Gunther. Oxford: Printed for the Roxburghe Club, at the University Press, 1925.

Aristotle. *Analytica posteriora; Categoriae; Ethica Nicomachea; Historia animalium; Metaphysica; Politica; Rhetorica.*

——. *Fragmenta.* In *Aristotelis opera,* ed. Valentinus Rose, 5:1464-1583. Berlin: Typis Georgii Reimiri, 1870.

Arnobius. *Adversus nationes libri vii.* Ed. Auguste Reifferscheid. CSEL 4 (1875).

[Asclepius]. In *Corpus Hermeticum,* ed. Arthur Darby Nock and A. J. Festugiere, 2:295-404. Paris: Les Belles Lettres, 1945.

Augustine. *De civitate Dei libri xxii.* Ed. Emanuel Hoffman. 2 vols. CSEL 40 (1898, 1900).

Aulus Gellius. *Noctes Atticae.* Ed. P. K. Marshall. 2 vols. Oxford: Clarendon Press, 1968.

Ausonius. *Epigrammata.* PL 19.825-838.

——. *Mosella.* (= *Idyllium X.*) PL 19.887-895.

——. ——. Ed. Carolus Schenkl. MGH, Auctorum Antiquissimorum, 5.2:81-97. Berlin: Weidmann, 1883.

——. *Opuscula. Epistulae.* Ed. Carolus Schenkl. MGH, Auctorum Antiquissimorum, 5.2. Berlin: Weidmann, 1883.

——. *Ausonius, with an English translation.* Ed. Hugh G. E. White. 2 vols. Cambridge, Mass.: Harvard University Press, 1949-1951.

Bernard, Saint. *Epistolae.* PL 182.67-662.

Bernardus Silvestris. *De mundi universitate libri duo sive megacosmus et microcosmus.* (= *Cosmographia.*) Ed. Carl Sigmund Barach and Johann Wrobel. Innsbruck: Wagner'-schen Universitaets-Buchhandlung, 1876; reprint: Frankfurt a. M.: Minerva, 1964.

——. *The Cosmographia of Bernardus Silvestris.* Trans. Winthrop Wetherbee. New York: Columbia University Press, 1973.

Boethius. *Commentaria in Porphyrium.* PL 64.71-158.

——. *De musica.* In *De institutione arithmetica libri duo. De institutione musica libri quinque,* ed. Gottfried Friedlein. Leipzig: Teubner, 1867; reprinted, Frankfurt a. M.: Minerva, 1966.

——. *De syllogismo categorico.* PL 64.791-832.

——. *De Trinitate.* In *The Theological Tractates: The Consolation of Philosophy,* ed. Hugh Fraser Stewart and E. K. Rand. Loeb texts. London and New York, 1926.

——. *In Categorias Aristotelis libri iv.* PL 64.159-293.

——. *In Topica Ciceronis commentaria.* PL 64.1039-1074.

——. *Interpretatio Elenchorum sophisticorum Aristotelis.* PL 64.1007-1040.

——. *Posteriorum analyticorum Aristotelis interpretatio.* PL 64.711-791.

——. *Priorum analyticorum Aristotelis interpretatio.* PL 64.639-712.

——. *The Theological Tractates: The Consolation of Philosophy.* Ed. Hugh F. Stewart and E. K. Rand. Loeb Texts. London and New York, 1926.

Bonaventure. *De sex alis seraphim.* In *S. Bonaventurae Opera omnia,* ed. Aloysius Laver, 8:131-151. Quaracchi: Collegium S. Bonaventurae, 1898.

Carmina burana. Ed. Alfons Hilka and Otto Schumann. Heidelberg: Winter, 1930.

Cato. *De re rustica.* Ed. William Davis Hooper and Harrison Boyd Ash. Loeb Texts. Cambridge, Mass.: Harvard University Press, 1936.

Cassiodorus. *De artibus et disciplinis liberalium litterarum.* PL 70.1150-1218.

——. *Expositio in Psalterium.* PL 70.9-1056.

Censorinus. *De die natali liber.* Ed. Otto Jahn. Hildesheim: G. Olms, 1965.

Charisius. *Artis grammaticae libri v.* In *Grammatici Latini,* ed. Heinrich Keil, 1:1-296. Leipzig: Teubner, 1850.

Cicero. *Brutus; De divinatione; De finibus; De legibus; De natura deorum; De oratore; In Pisonem; Orator; Pro Flacco; Pro Scauro; Tusculanae disputationes.*

——. *Timaeus.* In *M. Tullii Ciceronis opera quae supersunt omnia,* ed. J. G. Bauer and C. L. Kayser, 8:131-144. Leipzig: Tauchnitz, 1864.

Codex Justinianus. Ed. Paul Krüger. Berlin: Weidmann, 1877.

[Codex Theodosianus.] *The Theodosian Code and Novels and the Sirmondian Constitution.* Trans. Clyde Pharr. Princeton: Princeton University Press, 1952.

Columella. *De re rustica*. Ed. H. B. Ash, E. Forster, and E. Heffner. 3 vols. Loeb Texts. Cambridge, Mass.: Harvard University Press, 1941-1968.

Diomedes. *Artis grammaticae libri iii*. In *Grammatici Latini*, ed. Heinrich Keil, 1:300-529. Leipzig: Teubner, 1850.

Dionysius of Halicarnassus. *The Roman Antiquities of Dionysius of Halicarnassus*. Ed. Earnest Cary. 7 vols. Loeb Texts. Cambridge, Mass.: Harvard University Press, 1937-1950.

Donatus. *Ars grammatica*. In *Grammatici Latini*, ed. Heinrich Keil, 4:355-402. Leipzig, Teubner, 1864.

Einhard. *Einhard's Life of Charlemagne*. Ed. Heathcote W. Garrod and Robert B. Mowat. Oxford: Clarendon Press, 1915.

Euripides. *Bacchae; Hippolytus*.

Festus, Sextus Pompeius. *De verborum significatu quae supersunt cum Pauli epitome*. Ed. Wallace Martin Lindsay. Leipzig: Teubner, 1933.

Firmicius Maternus. *Consultationes Zaccaei et Apollonii*. Ed. Germanus Morin. Florilegium Patristicum, 39. Bonn: Hanstein, 1935.

Fulgentius. *Mitilogiarum libri tres*. In *Opera*, ed. Rudolph W. O. Helm, pp. 3-80. Leipzig: Teubner, 1898.

Gerard of Cremona. *Le Liber de Causis*. Ed. Adrien Pattin. Louvain: Uitgave van "Tijdschrift voor Filosofie," 1967.

——. *Die pseudo-aristotelische Schrift ueber das reine Gute bekannt unter dem Namen Liber de Causis*. Ed. Otto Bardenhewer. Freiburg im B.: Herder, 1882.

Gervais de Melkley. *Ars versificaria* [whence *Pyramus et Thisbe*]. Ed. Edmond Faral. In *Les Arts poétiques du xii* et du xiii* siècle, recherches et documents sur la technique littéraire du moyen âge*, pp. 331-335. Paris: Champion, 1924.

Gilbert of Poitiers. *Expositio in Boecii libros de Trinitate.* In *The Commentaries on Boethius by Gilbert of Poitiers,* ed. Nikolaus M. Häring. Toronto: Pontifical Institute of Mediaeval Studies, 1966.

——. "A Commentary on the Pseudo-Athanasian Creed." Ed. Nikolaus M. Häring. *Mediaeval Studies,* 27 (1965): 23-53.

Giraldus Cambrensis. *Topographia Hibernica.* In *Opera,* ed. James Francis Dimock, 5:3-138. Rolls Series, 21. London: Longman, 1867. 1867.

Guigo Cartusiensis. *Scala Claustralium.* PL 184.475-484.

Hero. *Automatopoetica.* In *Opera quae supersunt omnia,* ed. Wilhelm Schmidt, 1:338-453. Leipzig: Teubner, 1899.

Hilary. *De Trinitate.* PL 10.9-472.

Hildebertus. *Carmina minora.* Ed. A. Brian Scott. Leipzig: Teubner, 1969.

Homer. *Ilias; Odyssea.*

Horace. *Ars poetica; Carmina; Epodi.*

Hugh of Fouilloy. *De bestiis et aliis rebus.* PL 177.14-164.

Hyginus. *Fabulae.* Ed. Herbert J. Rose. Leiden: Sythoff, 1967.

Isidore of Seville. *De ecclesiasticis officiis.* PL 183.739-826.

——. *Etymologiarum sive originum libri xx.* Ed. Wallace Martin Lindsay. 2 vols. Oxford: Clarendon Press, 1911.

Isidorus Versificatus. See Anonymous: Isidorus Versificatus.

Jerome. *Epistulae.* Ed. Isidorus Hilberg. CSEL 54-56 (1910-1918).

——. *In Hieremiam prophetam libri sex.* Ed. Siegfried Reiter. CSEL 59 (1913).

John of Garland. *De triumphis ecclesiae libri octo.* Ed. Thomas Wright. London: Nicols, 1856.

John of Salisbury. *Joannis Saresberiensis episcopi Carnotensis Metalogicon.* Ed. Clement C. J. Webb. Oxford: Clarendon Press, 1929.

John Scotus, *Annotationes in Marcianum.* Ed. Cora Lutz. Cambridge, Mass.: Mediaeval Academy of America, 1939.

Juvenal. *Satirae.*

Liber xxiv philosophorum. See Anonymous: *Liber xxiv philosophorum.*

Livy. *Ab urbe condita libri.*

Longinus. *'Longinus' on the Sublime.* Ed. Donald Andrew Russell. Oxford: Clarendon Press, 1964.

Lucan. *De bello civili.*

Lucian. *The Dance* (= *De saltatione*). In *Lucian*, ed. Austin Morris Harmon, 5:210-289. Loeb Texts. Cambridge, Mass.: Harvard University Press, 1962.

Lucilius. In *The Greek Anthology.* Trans. William Paton. 5 vols. New York: Putnam's, 1918. (= *Anthologia Graeca.*)

Lucretius. *De rerum natura.*

Macrobius. *Commentarii in Somnium Scipionis.* Ed. John R. Willis. Leipzig: Teubner, 1963.

———. *Saturnalia.* Ed. John R. Willis. Leipzig: Teubner, 1963.

Marbod of Rennes. *Liber de gemmis.* PL 171.1738-1770.

Martianus Capella. *Libri de nuptiis Philologiae et Mercurii.* Ed. Adolphus Dick. Stuttgart: Teubner, 1925. Reprinted, with additions by Jean Préaux, 1969.

Matthew of Vendôme. *Ars versificatoria.* Ed. Edmond Faral. In *Les Arts poétiques du xii* et du xiii* siècle, recherches et documents sur la technique littéraire du moyen âge,* pp. 106-193. Paris: E. Champion, 1923.

Odericus Vitalis. *The Ecclesiastical History of Orderic Vitalis.* Ed. Marjorie Chibnall. Vols. 2-5. Oxford: Clarendon Press, 1969-1975.

Odo of Cluny. *De vita sancti Giraldi.* PL 133.639-704.

Otho of Sankt-Blasien. *Continuatio Sanblasiana.* Ed. Rogerus Wilmans. MGH *Scriptorum*, 20:302-337.

Otto of Freising. *Gesta Frederici I Imperatoris.* Ed. Rogerus Wilmans. MGH *Scriptorum*, 20:338-493.

Ovid. *Ars amatoria; Fasti; Heroides; Metamorphoses.*

Pachomius. *Pachomiana Latina: Texte latin de S. Jerome.* Ed. Amand Boon. Louvain: Bureaux de la Revue, 1932.

Paul the Deacon. *Historia Langobardorum.* Ed. Ludwig K. Bethmann and G. Waitz. In MGH *Scriptores Rerum Langobardicarum et Italicarum, Saec. V-IX,* pp. 12-187. Hannover, 1878.

Persius. *Satirae.*

Petrus Cantor. *Summa de sacramentis et animae consiliis.* Ed. Jean Albert Dugauquier. Analecta Mediaevalia Namurcensia, 7. Louvain: Nauwelaerts, 1957.

Petrus Divensis. *Gesta septem abbatum Beccensium.* PL 181.1709-1781.

Peter of Compostella. *De consolatione rationis libri duo.* Ed. Pedro Blanco Soto. *Beiträge* 8.4 (1912):1-151.

Peter of Poitiers. *Sententiae Petri Pictaviensis.* Ed. Philip S. Moore, Marthe Dulong, and Joseph N. Garvin. 2 vols. Notre Dame, Ind.: University of Notre Dame Press, 1943-1950.

Pindar. *Epinicia; Isthmian Odes; Nemean Odes.*

Plato. *Epinomis; Parmenides; Protagoras; Respublica; Theaetetus; Timaeus.*

Plautus. *Bacchides.*

Pliny. *Natural History.* Ed. Harris Rackham, W. H. S. Jones, and D. E. Eichholz. 10 vols. Loeb Texts. Cambridge, Mass.: Harvard University Press, 1947-1963.

Plotinus. *Opera.* Ed. Paul Henry and Henry R. Schwyzer. Paris and Brussels: Desclée de Brouwer, 1951-1973.

Porphyrion. *Acronis et Porphyrionis commentarii in Quintum Horatium Flaccum.* Ed. Ferdinandus Havthal. Amsterdam, 1966.

Priscian. *Institutionum grammaticarum libri xviii.* In *Grammatici Latini,* ed. Heinrich Keil, vols. 2-3. Leipzig: Teubner, 1855-1859.

Probus. *Instituta artium.* In *Grammatici Latini,* ed. Heinrich Keil, 4:47-192. Leipzig: Teubner, 1864.

Prudentius. *Liber cathemerinon.* Ed. Johan Bergman. CSEL 61 (1926): 3-76.

——. *Psychomachia.* CSEL 61 (1926): 167-211.

Ptolemy. *Almagest. Syntaxis mathematica.* Ed. John Heiberg. 2 vols. Leipzig: Teubner, 1898-1903.

——. *Tetrabiblos.* Ed. Frank E. Robbins. Loeb Texts. Cambridge, Mass.: Harvard University Press, 1940.

Quintilian. *The Institutio Oratoria of Quintilian.* Ed. Harold Edgeworth Butler. Loeb Texts. 4 vols. Cambridge, Mass.: Harvard University Press, reprinted 1933-1936.

Ralph of Longchamp. *In Anticlaudianum Alani commentum.* Ed. J. Sulowski. Breslau-Warsaw-Cracow-Danzig, 1972.

Rufinus of Aquileia. *Commentarius in symbolum apostolorum.* PL 21.335-386.

Seneca. *Epistulae; Phaedra.*

Sidonius Apollinaris. *Poems and Letters.* Ed. William Blair Anderson. Loeb Texts. Cambridge, Mass.: Harvard University Press, 1965.

Silius Italicus. *Punica.* Ed. John Wight Duff. Loeb Texts. Cambridge, Mass.: Harvard University Press, 1968.

Solinus. *Collectanea rerum memorabilium.* Ed. Theodor Mommsen. 2nd ed. Berlin: Weidmann, 1958.

Sophocles. *Ajax.*

Statius. *Silvae; Thebaid; Achilleid.* Ed. by John Henry Mozley. 2 vols. Loeb Texts. Cambridge, Mass.: Harvard University Press, 1961.

Stephen of Bourbon. *Tractatus de diversis materiis predicabilibus.* In *Anecdotes historiques, légendes et apologues tirés du recueil inédit d'Étienne de Bourbon, dominicain du xiii* siècle,* ed. Albert Lecoy de la March. Paris: Renouard, H. Loones, 1877.

Suetonius. *De vita Caesarum; Divus Titus; Tiberius.*

Tacitus. *Dialogus de oratoribus; Historiae.*

Testamentum Novum: Matthaeus; Lucas; Joannes; Acta
Apostolorum; Paulus ad Romanos, ad Corinthos 2, ad
Galatas, ad Philippenses, ad Colossenses; Jacobus; Petrus
1; Apocalypsis.

Testamentum Vetus: Genesis; Exodus; Leviticus; Numeri; 3
Regum; 2 Paralipomenon; Judith; Job; Psalmi; Sapientia;
Ecclesiasticus; Isaias; Jeremias; Baruch; Ezechiel; Daniel;
Osee; 1-2 Machabaeorum.

Theobaldus. *Physiologus.* Ed. P. T. Eden. Leiden: E. J. Brill,
1972.

Theodosiani libri xvi. Ed. Theodor Mommsen and Paul M.
Meyer. 2 vols. in 3. Berlin: Weidmann, 1905.

Thierry of Chartres. *Tractatus de sex dierum operibus.* Ed.
Nikolaus M. Häring. In *Commentaries on Boethius by
Thierry of Chartres and his School,* pp. 553-575. Toronto:
Pontifical Institute of Mediaeval Studies, 1966.

Thomas Aquinas. *Le "De ente et essentia" de S. Thomas
d'Aquin.* Ed. Marie-Dominique Roland-Gosselin. Paris,
1948.

Tibullus. *Carmina.*

Timotheus. *Persae.* In *Poetae Melici Graeci,* ed. Denys Lionel
Page, 2:399-418. Oxford: Clarendon Press, 1962.

Thucydides. *Historiae.*

Varro. *De lingua Latina.* Ed. Roland G. Kent. 2 vols. Cambridge, Mass.: Harvard University Press, 1951.

Vincent of Beauvais. *Speculum doctrinale.* Douai, 1644; reprinted, Graz: Akademische Druck, 1965.

Virgil. *Aeneis; Bucolica; Georgica.*

William of Conches. *Glosae super Platonem.* Ed. Edouard
Jeauneau. Paris: Vrin, 1965.

———. *Philosophia.* PL 172.39-102.

C. Secondary Sources

Alverney, Marie-Thérèse d'. "Alain de Lille et 'la Theologia'." In *L'Homme devant Dieu, mélanges offerts au Père Henri de Lubac*, 2:111-128. Paris: Aubier, 1964.

——. "Maitre Alain — Nova et Vetera." In *Entretiens sur la renaissance du 12e siècle*, ed. Maurice de Gandillac and Édouard Jeauneau, pp. 117-135. Paris: Mouton, 1968.

——. See also Alan of Lille: *Expositio Prosae de angelis; Hierarchia; Sermo de sphera intelligibili; Sermones;* (dubious works): *Quinque digressiones cogitationis.*

Analecta hymnica. See Dreves, Gudo Maria, et al.

Baker, Denise N. "The Priesthood of Genius: A Study of Medieval Tradition." *Speculum*, 51 (1976): 277-291.

Baumgartner, Matthias. *Die Philosophie des Alanus de Insulis im Zusammenhange mit den Anschauungen des 12. Jahrhunderts. Beiträge*, 2.4. Münster: Aschendorff, 1896.

Baxter, J., and C. Johnson, ed. *Medieval Latin Word-List.* Oxford: Oxford University Press, 1934.

Berger, David. "Gilbert Crispin, Alan of Lille and Jacob Ben Reuben: A Study in the Transmission of Medieval Polemic." *Speculum*, 49 (1974): 34-47.

Berthelot, Marcellin. *Collection des anciens alchimistes grecs.* Paris: Steinheil, 1887.

Betti, Humbertus. See Alan of Lille (dubious works): *Summa de sacramentis.*

Bossuat, Robert. See Alan of Lille: *Anticlaudianus.*

Brumble, H. D. "The Role of Genius in the 'De Planctu Naturae' of Alanus de Insulis." *Classica et Mediaevalia*, 31 (1970): 306-323.

Cappelli, Adriano. *Cronologia, chronografia e calendario perpetuo.* Milan: Hoepel, 1930.

Carmody, Francis. *Physiologus Latinus.* Paris: Droz, 1939.

Charlemont, C. *Series sanctorum et beatorum virorum sacri ordina Cisterciensium*. Paris, 1666.

Chaucer. *The Parliament of Fowls*.

Chenu, Marie-Dominique. "Un Essai de méthode théologique au xiie siècle." *Revue des sciences philosophiques et théologiques*, 24 (1935): 258-267.

——. "Grammaire et théologie aux xiie et xiiie siècles." *Archives*, 10 (1935/1936): 5-28.

——. *La Théologie au douzième siècle*. Études de philosophie médiévale, 45. Paris: Vrin, 1957.

Chevallier, Raymond. See Alan of Lille: *Sermones*.

Cilento, Vincenzo. *Alano di Lilla, poeta e teologo del seculo xii*. Naples: Libreria Scientifica editrice, 1958.

Codex iuris canonici. Pii x iussu digestus, Benedicti Papae xv auctoritate promulgatus. Rome: Vatican, 1919.

Collingwood, Robin George. *The Idea of Nature*. New York: Oxford, 1960.

Cornog, William. See Alan of Lille: *Anticlaudianus*.

Delhaye, Philippe. "Pour la 'fiche' Alain de Lille." *Mélanges de science religieuse*, 20 (1963): 39-51.

Diels, Hermann. *Die Fragmente der Vorsokratiker*. Berlin: Weidmann, 1941.

Dimier, M. Anselme. "Mourir a Clairvaux!" *Collectanea ordinis Cisterciensium reformatorum*, 17 (1955): 272-285.

Dreves, Guido Maria, and Clemens Blume. *Analecta hymnica medii aevi*. 55 vols. Leipzig: Reisland, 1886-1922; reprinted, New York: Johnson, 1961.

——. *Ein Jahrtausend lateinischer Hymnendichtung*. Leipzig: Reisland, 1909.

Du Cange, Charles du Fresne. *Glossarium ad scriptores mediae et infimae latinitatis*. 10 vols. in 11. Paris: Librairie des sciences et des arts, 1937-1938.

Duff, John Wight. *Roman Satire: Its Outlook on Social Life*. Berkeley: University of California Press, 1936.

Duhem, Pierre. *Le Système du monde.* 10 vols. Paris: Hermann, 1915-1959.

Dupuis, Albert. *Alain de Lille, Études de philosophie scolastique.* Lille: Danel, 1859.

Economou, George D. *The Goddess Natura in Medieval Literature.* Cambridge, Mass.: Harvard University Press, 1972.

Escoffier, J.-P. *Calendrier perpetuel développé sous forme de calendrier ordinaire.* Périgueux: Cassard Frères, 1880.

Furnivall, Frederick J. *The Babees Book.* EETS OS, 32. London: Trübner, 1868; reprinted, New York: Greenwood, 1969.

Gauthier, René-Antonin. *Magnanimité: l'idéal de la grandeur dans la philosophie païenne et dans la théologie chrétienne.* Bibliotheque Thomiste, 28. Paris: J. Vrin, 1951.

Glorieux, Palémon. "Alain de Lille, le moine et l'abbaye du Bec." *Recherches de théologie ancienne et médiévale,* 39 (1972): 51-62.

——. "Alan of Lille." In *New Catholic Encyclopedia,* 2:239-240. New York: McGraw-Hill, 1967.

——. "L'Auteur de la somme Quoniam homines." *Recherches de théologie ancienne et médiévale,* 17 (1950): 29-45.

Gonzalez-Haba, Maria. *La Obra De consolatione rationis de Petrus Compostellanus.* Munich: Bayerische Akademie der Wissenschaft, 1975.

Gredt, Joseph. *Elementa philosophiae Aristotelico-Thomisticae.* 2 vols. Freiburg im B.: Herder, 1929.

Green, Richard Hamilton. "Alan of Lille's Anticlaudianus, Ascensio mentis ad Deum." *Annuale mediaevale,* 8 (1967): 3-16.

Gregory, Tullio. *Anima mundi. La Filosofia di Guglielmo di Conches e la scuola di Chartres.* Florence: Sansone, 1955.

Grimm, Jakob, and Wilhelm Grimm. *Deutsches Wörterbuch.* Leipzig: Hirzel, 1877.

Häring, Nikolaus M. "A Latin Dialogue on the Doctrine of Gilbert of Poitiers." *Mediaeval Studies*, 15 (1953): 243-289. (= *Dialogus Ratii et Everardi*.)

———. "The Liberal Arts in the Sermons of Garnerius." *Mediaeval Studies*, 30 (1968): 47-77.

———. "Der Litteraturkatalog von Affligem." *Revue Bénédictine*, 80 (1970): 64-96. (= *Catalogus virorum illustrium*.)

———. "Chartres and Paris Revisited." In *Essays in Honour of Anton Charles Pegis*, ed. J. Reginald O'Donnell, pp. 268-329. Toronto: Pontifical Institute of Mediaeval Studies, 1974.

———. See also Alan of Lille: *De planctu naturae; Expositio cuiusdam super orationem Dominicam; Expositio super symbolum; Super symbolum apostolorum; Super symbolum Quicumque; Vix nodosum;* (dubious works): *Declarare fidem; Omne datum optimum.*

Haskins, Charles H. *Studies in the History of Medieval Science.* Cambridge, Mass.: Harvard University Press, 1924.

Hauréau, Barthélemy. *Histoire de la philosophie scolastique.* 2 vols. in 3. Paris: Durand et Pedone-Lauriel, 1872-1880.

———. "Mémoire sur la vie et quelques oeuvres d'Alain de Lille." *Mémoires de l'Academie des inscriptions et belles lettres*, 32 (1886): 1-27.

———. *Notices et extraits de quelques manuscrits latins de la Bibliothèque Nationale.* 6 vols. Paris: Klingksieck, 1890-1893.

———. See also Alan of Lille: *Sermones.*

Hempel, Wolfgang. *Übermuot diu Alte: Der Superbia-Gedanke und seine Rolle in der Deutschen Literatur des Mittelalters.* Bonn: Bouvier, 1970.

Hilka, Alfons, et al. See *Carmina burana.*

Hödl, Ludwig. *Die Geschichte der scholastischen Literatur und Theologie der Schlüsselgewalt. Beiträge* 38.4 (1960).

——. See also Alan of Lille: *Sermones.*

Holmes, Urban T. "Medieval Gem Stones." *Speculum,* 9 (1934): 195-304.

Huizinga, Johann. See Alan of Lille: *De virtutibus et vitiis.*

Jaeger, Werner. *Paideia: The Ideals of Greek Culture.* 3 vols. Oxford: Blackwell, 1943.

Javelet, R. "Image de Dieu et nature au xiiᵉ siècle." In *La Filosofia della natura nel medioevo: Atti del Terzo congresso internazionale di filosofia medioevale,* pp. 286-296. Milan: Vita e Pensiero, 1966.

Jeauneau, Edouard. " 'Nani gigantum humeris insidentes', Essai d'interpretation de Bernard de Chartres." *Vivarium,* 5 (1967): 79-99.

——. "Note sur l'École de Chartres." *Studi Medievali,* 3 ser, 5 (1964): 821-865.

Jolivet, Jean. *Arts du language et theologie chez Abelard.* Études de philosophie médiévale, 57. Paris: J. Vrin, 1969.

Kantorowicz, Ernst Hartwig. *Laudes regiae.* Berkeley and Los Angeles: University of California Press, 1946.

Lebeau, Marcel. "Decouverte du tombeau du bienheureux Alain de Lille. *Collectanea ordinis Cisterciensium reformatorum,* 23 (1961): 254-260.

Lefranc, Abel. *Oeuvres de François Rabelais.* Paris: Champion, 1913.

Lehmann, Paul. *Die Parodie im Mittelalter.* Stuttgart: Hiersemann, 1963.

Lesne, Emile. *Les Écoles de la fin du viiiᵉ siècle à la fin du xiiᵉ.* Histoire de la propriété ecclésiastique en France, 5. Lille: Facultés Catholiques, 1940.

Lexicon mediae et infimae latinitatis Polonorum. Wrocław-Kraków-Warszawa: Institutum Ossolinianum, 1953 —.

Longère, Jean. See Alan of Lille: *Liber poenitentialis*.

Lottin, Odon. "La Summa de sacramentis — Totus homo. Est-elle l'oeuvre d'Alain de Lille?" In his *Psychologie et morale aux xii͏ͤ et xiii͏ͤ siècles*, 6:107-117. Gembloux: Duculot, 1960.

Lutz, Cora. See John Scotus: *Annotationes*.

Mabillon, Jean. *Annales ordinis S. Benedicti*. 6 vols. Lucca: L. Venturini, 1739-1745.

Maccarone, Michele. *Lotharii cardinalis, De miseria humane conditionis*. Lucca: Thesaurus Mundi, 1955.

Manitius, M. *Geschichte der lateinischen Literatur des Mittelalters*. 3 vols. Munich: Beck, 1931.

Martène, Edmond, and Ursin Durand. *Veterum scriptorum et monumentorum . . . amplissima collectio*. 9 vols. Paris: Montalant, 1724-1733.

Moffat, Douglas. See Alan of Lille: *De planctu naturae*.

Moore, Philip. *The Works of Peter of Poitiers*. Washington: Catholic University of America, 1936.

Ochsenbein, Peter. *Studien zum Anticlaudianus des Alanus a Insulis*. Europäische Hochschulschriften. Bern and Frankfurt am M.: Lang, 1975.

Packard, Sidney Raymond. *Twelfth-Century Europe, An Interpretive Essay*. Amherst: University of Massachusetts Press, 1973.

Parent, J. M. "Un nouveau témoin de la théologie dionysienne au xii͏ͤ siècle." *Beiträge*, Suppl. 3.1 (1935) 288-309.

Pelster, F. "Der Heinrich von Gent zugeschriebene 'Catalogus virorum illustrium' und sein wirklicher Verfasser." *Historisches Jahrbuch*, 39 (1918-1919): 253-265.

Peltier, Henri. "Hugues de Fouilloy." *Revue du moyen âge latin*, 2 (1946): 25-44.

Rath, Wilhelm. See Alan of Lille: *Anticlaudianus*.

Raynaud de Lage, Guy. *Alain de Lille, poète du xii͏ͤ siècle*. Montreal: Institut d'Études Médiévales; Paris: J. Vrin, 1951.

——. See also Alan of Lille: *Tractatus Magistri Alani.*

Rouquette, J., and A. Villemagme. *Cartulaire de Maguelone.* Montpellier: L. Valat, 1912.

Russell, Jeffrey. "Interpretations of the Origins of Medieval Heresy." *Mediaeval Studies*, 25 (1963): 26-53.

Schneyer, Johannes B. "Alanus de Insulis." In *Repertorium der lateinischer Sermones des Mittelalters. Beiträge*, 43.1 (1961): 69-83.

Sheridan, James J. "The Seven Liberal Arts in Alan of Lille and Peter of Compostella." *Mediaeval Studies*, 35 (1973): 27-37.

——. See also Alan of Lille: *Anticlaudianus.*

Stallybrass, William Swan, ed., *Reynard the Fox, the Epic of the Beast by William Caxton.* New York: Dutton, [1924?].

Steinen, Wolfram von den. *Notker der Dichter und seine geistige Welt.* Bern: Francke, 1948.

Stock, Brian. *Myth and Science in the Twelfth Century.* Princeton: Princeton University Press, 1972.

Thouzellier, Christine. *Hérésie et hérétiques.* Rome: Edizioni di storia e letteratura, 1969.

Trout, J. M. "Alan the Missionary." *Citeaux*, 26 (1975): 146-154.

——. "The Monastic Vocation of Alan of Lille." *Analecta Cisterciensia*, 30 (1974): 46-53.

Vasoli, Cesare. *La Filosofia Medioevale.* Milan: Faltrinelli, 1961.

——. "Studi recenti su Alano di Lilla." *Bulletino dell'Instituto storico Italiano per il medio evo e archivio muratoriano*, 72 (1960): 35-89.

Visch, Carolus de. "Dissertatio de unico Alano Ripatorii abbate, Antissiodorensi episcopo, ac tandem monacho ordinis Cisterciensis, apud Cistercium anno 1203 mortuo." PL 210.9-26.

Walther, Hans. *Carmina medii posterioris latina*, 1: *Initia carminum*. Göttingen: Vandenhoeck, 1959.

Wetherbee, Winthrop. "The Function of Poetry in the 'De planctu naturae' of Alan of Lille." *Traditio*, 25 (1969): 87-125.

———. *Platonism and Poetry in the Twelfth Century*. Princeton: Princeton University Press, 1972.

White, Terence Hanbury. *The Book of Beasts, being a translation from a Latin Bestiary of the Twelfth Century*. London: Cape, 1954.

Wright, Thomas. See Alan of Lille: *Anticlaudianus; De planctu naturae*.

Index of Persons

Mythological characters are listed in the Subject Index.

Subject Index

Index of Biblical Citations

BIBLICAL CITATIONS